THE PERFECTIONISTS

RADICAL SOCIAL THOUGHT IN THE NORTH, 1815–1860

WILEY SOURCEBOOKS IN AMERICAN SOCIAL THOUGHT

Edited by *David D. Hall and Daniel Walker Howe*

THE PERFECTIONISTS

RADICAL SOCIAL THOUGHT IN THE NORTH, 1815–1860

Edited by
Laurence Veysey
Adlai E. Stevenson College
University of California, Santa Cruz

John Wiley & Sons, Inc.
New York • London • Sydney • Toronto

Copyright © 1973, by John Wiley & Sons, Inc.

Library of Congress Cataloging in Publication Data:

Veysey, Laurence R   comp.
  The perfectionists.

  (Sourcebooks in American social thought)
  Bibliography: p.
  1. United States—Social conditions.   2. Radicalism
—United States—History.   3. Social reformers—
United States.   I. Title.   II. Series.

HN64.V47   322.4′4′0974   73–4900
ISBN 0–471–90685–9
ISBN 0–471–90686–7 (pbk.)

Printed in the United States of America

10–9 8 7 6 5 4 3 2 1

CONTENTS

THE PERFECTIONISTS

RADICAL SOCIAL THOUGHT IN THE NORTH, 1815–1860

INTRODUCTION

The early nineteenth century is surely unique in one respect: with regard to no other period of American history have historians so persistently talked past each other. To an outsider beholding the scene from a distance, the spectacle is appalling. Moral reform crusades, the topic of the present anthology, have been attacked and defended over the years, but in a curious vacuum. Meanwhile, other scholars plunge into the mainstream political life of the epoch, Jacksonian and Whig, either to seek out the causes of the Civil War or to emerge with comments addressed to students of the party system. In still another corner, historians of religion push forward evangelical Christianity as the hallmark of the age. Finally, certain social historians write about the period as if a folksy version of daily life was its only important tendency. Too seldom is anything said that illuminates these decades as a whole.

We wonder how the various pieces relate to each other. One angle of approach is to turn again, but with the broadest possible lens, to the remarkable upthrust of radical social thought and activity that blossomed in America during the years between 1815 and 1860. A vast topic in its own right, it is also an important part of the larger puzzle. How does one account for such a sudden outbreak of fervor for religious, moral, and social transformation? Was it an extension of forces at work in the larger society, or a reaction against these rapid changes? Was it an understandable tactical response to the logic of events or an eccentric, highly emotional sideshow? Was belief in the possibility of the rapid attainment of a more perfect social order merely the most extreme version of a universal faith in progress, an optimism likely to be at its headiest during decades of continental expansion, or did it constitute an act of internal secession from mainstream politics and common sense, and therefore reflect an ominous new kind of social fragmentation?

The significance of this great reform movement is not confined to its own age. The radicalism of the 1960s brought a return to many of the same causes and lines of argument that first were voiced in that

1

earlier period. Furthermore, an underlying mood very strikingly repeated itself, involving rejection of established institutions and sources of authority. The vision of a drastically altered society, more freely unconventional and more just in its treatment of individuals, gained wide currency once again. In both instances the new social order was to be achieved through immediate, willful effort. Both periods witnessed the founding of many small communities dedicated to the immediate practice of a new way of living. Religious revivals, opposition to war, concern for women's rights, dress and diet reforms, the overcoming of inherited racial and sexual taboos—all these themes were present both in the radicalism of the pre-Civil War period and in the radicalism of the last fifteen years. The intervening period, which saw radicalism confined to certain political and trade union movements, begins to seem like a temporary interruption in a much longer rhythm of American perfectionist aspiration. At least, after reading the words gathered in this volume, it will be difficult to see the recent return to so many of these preoccupations as a mere coincidence. Closer inspection of these documents will reveal important differences between the radical tone then and now, but it will also confirm the existence of a long-lived radical tradition, or series of parallel traditions, that in most respects first emerged in the early nineteenth century.[1]

What is the meaning of this continuity? Some historians who are unfriendly to this version of social radicalism see in it a characteristically American attitude of hostility toward institutions, a distrust of political and bureaucratic action in favor of reliance on individual moral conversion to absolute "truths." These prejudices are seen to be implanted very deep in the American character, surfacing during seasons of crisis. From this point of view, the American style is "anti-institutional," and the American people are always pushing toward anarchy with a small "a," even if they reject with horror the concrete movement bearing that name. Unlike Europeans, Americans have rejected such stabilizing agencies as monarchies, established churches, and an extended family structure. Instead, especially in the nineteenth century, each individual was supposed to stand alone. Freedom meant the right of each person to seize the largest possible share of the material rewards available on a continent blessed with unparalleled abundance. Life was a race for economic success. The

[1]Elsewhere I have explored the question of novelty and continuity in the counterculture of the 1960s. See Laurence Veysey, *The Communal Experience* (New York: Harper and Row, 1973), Chapter 6.

few impediments surviving from a more paternalistic and hierarchical age in the eighteenth century were rapidly torn away. What a man made of himself, not his social origins, came to mean everything. Democracy signified equality of opportunity, the erasing of barriers to advancement. Children were taught from infancy to display a rugged independence of mind, even against their own parents.

Seen in this light, the constant danger was that there would no longer be anything to hold the society together. Laissez-faire theorists from Adam Smith forward blandly assumed that self-interest automatically coincided with collective interest. But to conservative observers, from Alexis de Tocqueville to the contemporary historians Stanley Elkins and Rowland Berthoff, the problem of order and long-term stability in a society is not so simple. Lacking the centripetal pull of revered fixed institutions and traditional obligations, a nation may fall apart easily. This is especially likely to happen when the institutional vacuum coincides with physical uprooting —dual in this case, involving an enormously quick flow of people toward the western frontier and a simultaneous incursion of foreign immigrants who diluted the common cultural memory. The wonder, therefore, is not that a civil war occurred, but that there were not five or ten such conflagrations, and that the nation survived the actual one intact.

It follows from this perspective that the pre-Civil War radicals were deeply dangerous to the national health. Working to inflame emotions, or at best to inspire men with a hundred conflicting false hopes about the possibilities of a perfect life on earth, these agitators catered to the worst tendencies in the American character. Americans already wrongly tended to believe that individual moral regeneration was an adequate substitute for realistic political bargaining. They were committed to a pursuit of happiness that was blithely asocial. Now these still more innocent prophets appeared in their midst, filling their minds with absurd illusions, for instance that slavery could be abolished through a general change of heart, or that utopia could be realized by separating oneself from neighborly restraints on an isolated plot of land. If America were to survive and become a great nation, what was needed was not these hollow fantasies, but an infusion of sobriety and discipline. The Metternichian model of life as a shrewd political game played for small goals would have been far more realistic and would have reduced the tendency toward chaotic disruption.

Such is the negative case concerning American radicalism in the early nineteenth century, and indeed in very recent years as well. Is it founded on an accurate diagnosis of American society and attitudes of mind? No one would deny that Americans, especially a hundred and more years ago, were intensely "individualistic" in the sense of being oriented toward economic success. Belief in the legitimacy of self-seeking on that level was very strong. And by every indication, children were assertive and unruly as compared with those in Europe. More ominously, there was a widespread tendency toward rioting, mob action, and vigilantism, sometimes tyrannically expressing majority sentiment on an issue, sometimes (as with the antiabolitionist mobs) reflecting the vested interests of powerful merchants. Yet American violence seldom had the flavor of political revolution. And when American violence is being stressed, it is often forgotten how many scenes of domestic turmoil Europe, including England, offered in this same period.

Was American society really devoid of institutions or of almost all universally accepted social norms? Was there no cement binding it together? To begin with, government certainly existed, and at many levels, providing a constant flurry of election excitement. The early nineteenth century was not an age of political apathy but of extraordinarily high participation (among white males, who were generally eligible to vote). The constitutions of the newly forming western states usually imitated those of the eastern seaboard, thus showing a conservative stability of form within the republican mold. And it was a great age of patriotism. Nationalistic ceremonials, such as the Fourth of July celebration, became standard as early as the 1820s. In most circles the Constitution was revered unquestioningly, along with the memory of the Founding Fathers. Here was perhaps an adequate substitute for monarchical fanfare. Religious institutions abounded also, and though they were going through important changes, they often proved relatively stable and long-lived. Exotic sects began forming, and denominational bickering grew after the 1830s, but an overwhelming share of Americans gave allegiance to a small number of churches, such as the Methodist and Baptist, that quickly became conventional, socially conservative forces in their communities—to the point of only tardily and halfheartedly joining the campaign against slavery, for example. The fact that many of these denominations did eventually split into northern and southern wings is perhaps mainly a comment on the depth of general sectional feeling by the mid-1840s. Beyond governments and churches, a host of voluntary organizations gave Americans an institutional life of a varied if unsophisticated kind. Some were dedicated to charitable work; others, such as the ubiquitous fraternal lodges, catered especially to the craving for pomp, ceremony, and ritual. As Americans traveled westward, they speedily reestablished this familiar network of institutions—which increasingly included elaborate school systems and colleges—wherever they went. Patriotism, political and church loyalties, fraternal ties—all these must modify our picture of mid-nineteenth-century America as no more than a collection of individual atomistic units.

Apart from these flourishing structures, American society in the early national period possessed a number of very widely shared cultural norms. Racial and ethnic prejudice, directed especially against people with dark skins, was one of the most universal. Refusal to admit the reality or legitimacy of social class was only somewhat less pervasive. Respect for private property was also extremely general. So was belief in sexual monogamy and male dominance. In a great variety of attitudes and customs, Americans of the day revealed the settled convictions, the conformist willingness to enforce them, in short, the considerable intolerance that, ironically enough, may well be the hallmark of a strong social order—provided that it does not slide over into jittery paranoia. Finally, the pursuit of economic self-interest in surroundings of abundance may indeed contribute to the collective strength of a society, as the right to build one's own stake becomes identified with the purposes of the culture itself. The success-oriented dream of Americans promoted patriotism more often than revolution, and in fact may have prevented the latter.

All these counterarguments suggest the danger was not that American society in the north and west would fall apart in the pre-Civil War decades, but rather that it might succeed only too well. From this viewpoint, the position of the radical advocates of reform becomes extremely different. Rather than exemplifying the centrifugal forces at work in a seamless, atomistic society, the radicals emerge as the germ carriers of a genuinely distinctive social vision, though one that to some degree fulfilled the promises of earlier revolutionary rhetoric. The reality of American life was decidedly "institutional," and slavery was the most conspicuous institution of all. Certain of the radicals were indeed "anti-institutional," but this was the symptom of their divorce from the money-grubbing, ploiticking, prejudice- and institution-serving mainstream of everyday American existence. And if the radicals substituted moral agitation for political involvement, they were in another sense building a pressure group that might ultimately force power-oriented leaders to listen to their appeals for humanitarianism and justice.

These, then, are the broad outlines of two entirely different ways of looking at this early period of American history, and of the place of radical social critics within it. All the readings brought together in this volume to illustrate the radicalism of the pre-Civil War generation may be interpreted from either of these two conflicting perspectives.

Is there any way to get beyond them both and reach a more direct understanding of the nature and meaning of the radical crusading spirit in those decades? At first sight the movement seems so diverse as to defy any sweeping generalizations about it. It comprehended men and women of viewpoints so varied as at times to seem mutually opposite—upholders of individualism, such as Henry David Thoreau and Stephen Pearl Andrews; upholders of socialism, such as Thomas Skidmore and Albert Brisbane; evangelical Christians, some of whom, for instance John Humphrey Noyes and Adin Ballou, founded utopian communities; humanitarians like Dorothea Dix and William Lloyd Garrison, who freely mixed religious appeals with rhetoric based on the secular notion of the modern conscience; outright anticlericals like Skidmore; and persons calling themselves Transcendentalists who remained religious but in an eclectic, non-Christian sense. Moreover, the religious views of leading crusaders for social reform often changed during the course of their lifetimes. It would seem difficult to construct a single label that would apply to all the members of such a variegated assemblage.

The arrangement of this anthology seeks to bring into the open these internal differences, so that they may be looked at clearly. Part One is devoted to men whose outlook centered in evangelical Christianity. This does not mean, of course, that they agreed with each other. But all of them continued to look to the Bible as the main source of their social vision. Three of the new Christian sects are represented in the readings—the Oneida Perfectionists, led by John Humphrey Noyes; the Mormons, whose prophet was Joseph Smith; and an obscure band of conservative Universalists, whose spokesman was Adin Ballou. Had space been available, several other important Christian groups characteristic of the "come-outer" spirit might have been included—in particular, the Shakers, who practiced communism and celibacy, and the Millerites, who gathered on hilltops to await the end of the world in 1843. Less clearly Christian were the spiritualists, who under Andrew Jackson Davis founded a temporarily utopian religion in the 1840s, based on alleged communication with the dead. Meanwhile, the anthology does include a very influential figure who did not break with the long-established Presbyterian church, Charles G. Finney, though Finney's views caused great controversy within his denomination.

Despite their many disagreements over concrete matters of divine revelation, these figures all retained an outlook steeped in the Christian religion. All, with the possible exception of Ballou, were more interested in saving individual souls than in the alleviation of suffering in the present life on earth. What at the same time distinguished these particular Christian believers from most earlier Christians, and from theological conservatives in their own day, was their assertion that the Kingdom of God, in one form or another, would literally be established on earth, indeed in the United States, at least partly through the willful effort of sanctified men and women in the very near future. Unlike earlier Christians, they were highly optimistic, seeing human nature as marked by a boundless capacity for achievement so long as it was "joined" (in Finney's term) to the true workings of the divine spirit. Thus, though the evangelicals who appear in the first part of this anthology may seem religious conservatives from our point of view, they had already broken with the mainstream of the Christian tradition from Paul and Augustine through Calvinism, which had insisted on man's natural depravity and on his powerlessness to change his fate. As the conservative Christians of the time were well aware, surrender to this heresy by the optimistic Christian radicals amounted to no less than the abrupt suicide of an eighteen-hundred-year-old theology. No wonder that Noyes and Finney had to deal with the charge that they were arrogant!

Part Two, entitled "Rationalists," presents a more diverse sample of people. Working alongside the evangelical Christians, these varied advocates of pronounced social change shared a common debt to the ideas of justice, equality, and humanitarianism found in the European Enlightenment of the eighteenth century. Since many of these figures also betrayed a deep sense of attachment to the Christian tradition as they understood it, it must be recognized that there is a certain arbitrariness about the dividing line between the first two sections. Yet it can be defended. The second group of spokesmen includes both agnostics and religious believers, but the believers have all been far more deeply influenced by secular social thought than those of the first group—they are more cosmopolitan, more in touch with the rationalist heritage in human thought that underlay the French Revolution and then spawned the socialist movement. Noah Worcester and Dorothea Dix were both Unitarians, and Unitarianism, more than any other Christian sect, reflected the impact of the Age of Reason. Charles Sumner's beliefs were also vaguely Unitarian; he did not regularly attend any church. Thomas Skidmore, Albert Brisbane, and Stephen Pearl Andrews had seceded from Christianity entirely, while Horace Greeley flirted with spiritualism. Among these reformers Biblical language was sometimes invoked, but essentially as a device to gain wider popular approval. (To be sure, many Christian liberals earnestly believed that the teachings of natural reason coincided, if not with the whole Bible, at least with the message of Christ as presented in the four gospels.) The social thinkers within this range were often unclear as to the ultimate source of intellectual authority in their lives. But if writers like Voltaire, Diderot, and Beccaria had not preceded them, it is difficult to conceive of them saying what they did. Most revealingly, these radicals may be identified by the primary emphasis they placed on alleviating human misery in the here and now, without waiting even for a Kingdom of God to be established. Nothing is so indicative of this shift as their frequent invocation of a distinctly human posterity.

The Transcendentalists, who are represented in Part Three, formed a highly special group, more clearly set apart from the others. Their literary fame may make one forget that in their own day they comprised a tiny elite, almost all physically in touch with each other, in the environs of Boston. They were America's first intellectual avant-garde. Except perhaps in the case of Emerson, one turns to them not for their contemporary influence, nor for a "typical" expression of radical views, but instead for their intrinsic worth and interest. More cosmopolitan and well-educated than most other reformers, the Transcendentalists were at the same time the most self-absorbed, the least firmly connected with specific social causes and organizations. In part this was an effect of their peculiar religious outlook, which stemmed from German romanticism and Asian philosophy. Intensely spiritual without being recognizably Christian, this small band of free spirits gravitated toward nature-worship and pantheistic mysticism. But at the same time its members shared the optimism, the sense of an imminent breakthrough onto new terrain, of the other radicals of their age.

We have, then, three fairly distinct kinds of people who were involved in promoting drastically new ideas and social projects in early nineteenth-century America. Though historians tend to agree that the Transcendentalists were highly unusual, they have argued about the relative impact of the Christian evangelical and secular rationalist sources of the reform impulse. Close study of the readings in this anthology may help to define the limits of this argument. Clearly men of both persuasions already existed in the America of the 1820s, on the eve of the major radical outburst. As evangelical Christianity gained dramatically in strength for fifteen years or so after 1826, it temporarily overshadowed secular radicalism of the kind represented by Thomas Skidmore and the New York Working Men's Party. But thereafter secular currents of thought began once again increasingly coming to the fore. It is remarkable, in fact, the extent to which abolitionist leaders who began their adult lives as evangelicals gradually broke with that version of Christianity, sometimes, as in the case of Gerrit Smith, openly gravitating into the rationalist camp.[2] The logic of the reform argument might seem to dictate this. If the Bible could be quoted in defense of slavery, as it often was by southerners, then the Bible itself might be wrong, and a new source of ultimate intellectual authority required. Human reason, advocated during the Enlightenment, was conveniently available. In a broader sense, the trend of the times in Europe and America was back toward rationalism and positivist skepticism for several decades after 1840, and the American reformers echoed this tendency.

Finally, Part Four demonstrates this important process of rethinking during the course of the slavery controversy, while showing the simultaneous rise in political passions engendered by the sectional conflict of the 1850s. The heat of events helped move leading reformers toward reason in a formal sense, while it was tempting them to applaud violent conflict in the name of social justice on another level of their minds. But the growing abandonment of historic Christianity that is registered in this process could scarcely be termed a small matter. Darwin's subsequent victory in American thought was being prepared in the forge of these other issues.

If the flames of social conflict melted away some of the distinctions that earlier had seemed meaningful in the reform camp, it must still be asked what all these individuals had in common that might set them apart from other Americans of the same time. In the 1960s it was generally conceded that Jesus freaks, followers of Asian mysticism, and political radicals of the New Left did somehow form a single "counterculture." This judgment was usually based on two factors—the strikingly uniform physical appearance of the radicals, and their generational identity in the under-thirty age group. In the pre-Civil War period, neither of these indicators was nearly as pronounced, though there were some symptoms, interestingly enough, of each. Even then flowing hair was the widely understood mark of unconventional opinions, though many of the radicals preferred to retain a neat appearance, and Garrison was something of a dandy. Again the radicals often had a youthful image, as the selections from Emerson and Whitman illustrate, but it was a youth that

[2]See Bertram Wyatt-Brown, *Lewis Tappan and the Evangelical War Against Slavery* (New York: Atheneum, 1971), p. 311.

extended freely upward toward middle life, as the varied birth dates of the writers in this volume testify. Ideas rather than life-style figured most strongly in self-definitions, though the first indications of a concern for life-style, as proof of fidelity to one's principles, were present. Sexual radicalism came to the fore in such communities as Oneida, in the women's rights movement, and among the Mormons. For Thoreau, the daily pattern of existence contained the whole kernel of life. But compared with more recent times, the reliance on high-flown rhetoric and formal constitution-making was certainly very high.

The common identity of these early radicals must be sought in key aspects of what they believed in. Increasingly historians are attracted to the term "perfectionism" to sum up the spirit of social activism in the years after 1830. Though "ultraism" was a more widely accepted contemporary label, the term "perfection" was indeed then used; it appears many times in the documents below, including those by such diverse authors as Adin Ballou and Margaret Fuller. And when it is not explicitly used it is strongly implied, as in the last paragraphs of the essays by Thomas Skidmore and Horace Greeley.

What does "perfectionism" mean? It must first of all be divorced from its twentieth-century connotation of personal finickiness in small details. The liability of using the word stems from this fact that in our own day it has become an uncomplimentary epithet with purely psychological implications. In the 1830s the term referred instead to the belief that individuals, groups, or entire nations might make themselves morally blameless through a sudden, conscious act of will. Its original context was religious, in the theology of John Humphrey Noyes and Charles G. Finney, but its easy transference to the secular realm is again shown by the wide use the word received beyond evangelical circles. The assumptions underlying perfectionism were perhaps never stated more clearly than by Adin Ballou:

"Man as a religious being and moral agent acts more or less in three general spheres or departments of effort and responsibility, viz.:—The individual, the social, and the civil or governmental spheres. . . . It follows, therefore, that there are individual duties, virtues, sins; social duties, virtues, sins; and governmental duties, virtues, sins. In each sphere our religious and moral obligations are the same. Right and wrong confront human beings at every step. To be perfect, one must think, say, and do what is right in each and all the spheres of responsibility named."[3]

[3]Adin Ballou, *Autobiography* (Lowell, Mass.: Vox Populi Press, 1896), p. 340.

Though Ballou carefully distinguishes among these several spheres of life, the implication is that private and public morality are ultimately identical; nations are to be judged by the same standards that weigh on the individual. Another implication, repugnant to our own age of relativism, is that in all spheres, right and wrong are total or absolute. There can be, or ought to be, no mixing of the two. Anything that is not morally right is utterly wrong.

Viewed more dynamically, perfectionism is the belief that a state of total righteousness may be achieved all at once—by the individual Christian in the brief experience of conversion or regeneration, and by the whole society in the immediate renunciation of such obvious wrongs as slavery or the consumption of alcohol. It is easier to go the whole route toward moral victory in a single swoop, argues Noyes, than to crawl toward it by painfully slow increments. Such a leap can be made thanks to the intensity of the individual's willful desire to bring about the change. It can be seen, then, how closely perfectionism is tied to a supreme optimism about human nature, an optimism first broached during the Enlightenment and seemingly verified by the facts of life on the American continent. It appears highly doubtful that without either the Enlightenment or this more local and recent mood of exhilaration, Christian theology would have veered in so striking and uncharacteristic a direction.

Stripped of some of these extreme religious connotations, which even then were fast beginning to fade, perfectionism may be seen as faith in man's capacity to improve himself drastically, to achieve a qualitatively better pattern of life on earth. The social evils that the radicals of the nineteenth century apprehended often remain those of our own time, as several of the selections below reveal—war, patriotism, racial and sexual discrimination, unequal distribution of wealth, inhumanity toward deprived or unfortunate people. Legal slavery is the great contrary example of an evil that was indeed utterly exterminated. But as regards all such evils, the perfectionist is one who retains an unshakable conviction that sudden movement for the better is possible. It was easier to hold to this faith in the nineteenth century, before the frailty of repeated appeals to man's reason and conscience had become so evident. In the 1950s the conservative sociologist Edward A. Shils could declare: "A few perfectionists here and there in society are vital to our well-being: a movement of perfectionists of any sort is dangerous."[4] Yet the lives of many millions would be incomparably gloomier today if no persons of such

[4] Edward A. Shils, *The Torment of Secrecy* (Glencoe, Ill.: Free Press, 1956), p. 17.

pronounced convictions had ever appeared. The logical alternative to perfectionism is the belief that all improvement occurs by accident, a philosophy even more repugnant to most modern people, who do believe that we can will ourselves into better conditions, but happen to disagree with the specific blueprints for happiness offered by the radicals, or perhaps with the speed of the timetable for their achievement.

What first caused the radical or perfectionist movement to come into being in America at that particular time? It arose independently of the sectional controversy that led to the Civil War, because it gathered steam long before slavery emerged as a burning political issue, and it was internally too diverse and many-faceted to be seen as a response to that single problem, although it eventually added much fuel to it, since all the reformers lived in the north and early became committed to abolition.

The radical spirit was too sweepingly universalistic for it to make much sense in terms of the national political life. (Indeed, many of the radicals had a strongly international perspective.) For this reason, it was not closely related to Jacksonianism, nor inseparably linked with the "democratic" tendency of the times. It always bisected the major political parties, or moved far beyond them; if anything it tended at first to attract religious-minded New Englanders who were Whigs. It also affected individuals at many points on the social scale, excluding only the Catholic immigrants. Thomas Skidmore, the author of a major work of social philosophy, was a machinist. Men from humble backgrounds, such as William Lloyd Garrison, Horace Greeley, and Joseph Smith, became leading figures. Run-of-the-mill rural preachers, like Adin Ballou, could also be found. On the other hand, the economic elite of the day was represented by such radical spokesmen as Albert Brisbane and Gerrit Smith. This diversity of circumstances is certainly striking. Nor were the views of most of these writers "democratic," in the best understood sense of majoritarian. It was more usual for them to defend the rights of unpopular minorities. To be sure, they often looked ahead to a day when all mankind would be converted to their views and customary social distinctions would be modified or erased, but only if they were very naively optimistic—like Skidmore and Walt Whitman—could they identify themselves with the aspirations of the existing common man in America.

In fact the movement bears the symptoms of a much more persistent tendency in human societies, toward millennialism. Many times and in many places all over the world, small bands of men have seceded from the conventional life that flows around them and announced a new vision that calls for a general social reordering.[5] Centuries ago in Europe, sects such as the Anabaptists promoted communism of goods and unusual sexual practices that undercut the private family. Usually these movements were quickly exterminated by the surrounding society. But their dream of a millennium to be achieved suddenly has lived on as a kind of underground tradition that may correspond to certain deeply embedded human aspirations. In this sense, the utopian movement of the early nineteenth century is at bottom the child neither of the Enlightenment nor of Christianity; instead it marks a recurring tendency toward social revitalization whose wellsprings are inadequately understood. American historians have too seldom paid attention to cross-cultural comparisons in viewing our own radical tradition, or they have focused too narrowly on differences between the American and European political atmospheres. Anthropology, world history, and psychology might tell us a great deal about the meaning of the extreme search for "freedom," though the quest for more immediate sources in political and religious thought (for instance, the impact of British abolitionism on American antislavery leaders) must of course continue.

The broader literature suggests that the tendency to "come out," in a posture of open separation from the larger society, may be crucial, for the erection of a clear boundary between "ourselves" and outsiders is the first step in the creation of a new culture that seeks to replace the old order. But in this respect American history handed the radicals an ambiguity. Was the new culture embodied in a single, small utopian sect or community, or was it embodied in the northern United States as a whole? As the slavery controversy advanced, radicals increasingly turned in the latter direction, only to find themselves eventually co-opted into the patriotism of the Civil War.

In pursuing a topic as wide in its implications as this one, an anthology possesses a great virtue. By its very nature, it can probe an area, suggesting themes and tones of voice without insisting on their final adequacy in furnishing an explanation. Immersion in the rich remains of an earlier time offers the surest help in getting beyond the oversimplifications, including the concept of "perfectionism," that historians love to construct.

[5]See Anthony F. C. Wallace, "Revitalization Movements," *American Anthropologist*, LVIII (April 1956), 264-281; Sylvia Thrupp, ed., *Millennial Dreams in Action: Essays in Comparative Study*, (Supplement II, *Comparative Studies in Society and History* (The Hague: Mouton & Co., 1962); and Norman Cohn, *The Pursuit of the Millennium*, 2d ed., (New York: Harper Torchbooks, 1961).

Part One

EVANGELICALS

1

CHRISTIAN PERFECTIONISM

John Humphrey Noyes
THREE PERFECTIONIST SELECTIONS

The term "perfectionist" originally referred to the beliefs of a small band of
"ultraist" Christians, scattered across western New England and upstate
New York in the early 1830s. Stimulated by the universal promise of
regeneration in the post-Calvinist revivalism exemplified by Charles G.
Finney, these few men and women began to declare that God made them
inwardly perfect from the moment of their conversion, though they admitted
they might go on improving in externals. Christians had always believed in
the attainment of such a perfect state after death; the new inspiration merely
moved the site of the Kingdom of God to earth itself, aided by a
postmillennial interpretation of the New Testament. But this theological
change certainly registered a sense of the utopian possibilities of life on the
American continent, as well as a sudden enthusiasm for recapturing the spirit
of very early Christianity. From the beginning the Perfectionists were
communally oriented, even to the point of renouncing traditional marriage
ties, for such exclusive pairing conflicted with the goal of total equality and
sharing among believers. The first Perfectionists were often ill-educated and
itinerant, and inclined toward great sexual freedom. But John Humphrey
Noyes (1811–1886) gave them direction and a certain precarious measure of
respectability. Noyes was from a well-to-do Vermont family. He graduated
from Dartmouth, became converted by Finney, studied theology for three
years at Andover and Yale, and then announced his Perfectionist beliefs. First
at Putney, Vermont, and after 1847 at Oneida, New York, he led a community
that put into practice an austere regime of "complex marriage." People slept
together only with Noyes' approval and after negotiations through intermedi-
aries; the birth rate was regulated by male continence. In all its highly

SOURCE. John Humphrey Noyes, "Perfectionism," *The Berean: A Manual for
the Help of Those Who Seek the Faith of the Primitive Church* (Putney, Vt.:
The Spiritual Magazine, 1847), pp. 178–181; John Humphrey Noyes, "Bible
Communism" and "The Kingdom of God Has Come," in George
Wallingford Noyes, ed., *John Humphrey Noyes: The Putney Community*
(Oneida, N.Y.: by the editor, 1931), pp. 116–122, 235–239, first published in
1847 and 1849.

organized social arrangements, which included mutual criticism sessions and communal child-rearing, the Oneida community became the most interesting utopian experiment in nineteenth-century America. Ultimately a huge economic success, it endured in its original form until 1880. Noyes consciously tried to blend Christianity with communitarian socialism, and he eventually adopted a less literal view of the Bible, but the documents show the awesome religious primitivism that underlay his vision. Their publication to an often scornful and threatening audience was an act of bravery.

PERFECTIONISM

Perceiving nothing in the sound or form of the word Perfectionist, essentially odious, and assuredly anticipating the time of its redemption from infamy, we will take the liberty to explain the meaning of it, as used by those who consent to bear it.

We will not attempt to state what a Perfectionist *is not*; for this would require us to dissect and disclaim all the varying and incongruous images of perfection conjured up by the word in the various fancies of men, from a picture of a monk in sackcloth and ashes, to that of a seraph with six wings. It is sufficient to say, that in the minds of those who consent to bear the name, so far as we know, perfection is predicated of only a single attribute, viz., holiness; and of that only in a limited sense. We find in the Bible, as well as in the nature of the case, three modifications of *perfect holiness:* perfection of obedience; perfection of security of obedience; and perfection of holiness by experience or suffering. . . .

The holiness of Christ, the second Adam, was perfect, both as present obedience to law, and as prospectively secure. Yet in another sense it was imperfect, during his residence on earth. For "though he were a *son*, yet *learned he obedience* by the things which he suffered; and *being made perfect*, he became the author of eternal salvation to all them that obey him." "For it became him, by whom are all things, and for whom are all things, in bringing many sons unto glory to make the captain of their salvation *perfect through sufferings*." Previous to his crucifixion, this captain of our salvation was perfectly successful in his conflict with sin, both presently and prospectively; yet the battle was before him. So Paul . . . denied that he had already attained the victory, or was already perfect; and yet in the next breath, falling back upon an inferior meaning of the word, he could say, "Let us therefore, as many as be perfect be thus minded."

The present holiness of Christ, on the throne of his glory, and of those who, having overcome by his blood, have attained that likeness of his resurrection toward which Paul was urging his way, is perfected in the highest sense. The battle is fought; the victory won; their holiness is perfect as obedience—perfect in security—and perfect by victory over suffering. Perfectionists, then, if they may be allowed to designate the place which they suppose they hold on the scale of perfection, universally disclaim the profession of attainments above those of the *suffering* Son of God. They covet not the premature glory of victory before battle. They stand with Paul on the middle ground, between the perfection of Adam and of Christ, saved from sin—eternally saved—yet "saved by hope, waiting for the adoption, to wit, the redemption of their bodies." . . .

The truth is too simple to need expansion, that every individual action is either wholly sinful or wholly righteous; and that every being in the universe, at any given time, is either entirely wicked or entirely holy, i. e. either conformed to law or not conformed to law: yet the prevailing modes of thought and speech force us to recognize a quality of action and character, called *imperfect holiness*, which takes rank somewhere indefinitely below what may seem the lowest possible or conceivable modification of holiness. So that, with reference to this, we must name *mere* holiness, *perfect* holiness—consigning the censure due to the impropriety of our language, to those who maintain the possibility of serving God and mammon, i.e. of being holy and sinful, at the same time. A profession, then, of *perfect* holiness, thus understood, is in truth merely a profession of holiness, without which, confessedly, none can claim the name of sons or servants of God; and instead of deserving the charge of arrogance should rather be censured, if at all, for conveying, in the language of it, the implication that men may be less than perfectly holy, and yet not perfectly sinful. But we take higher ground. The first Adam was holy; the second Adam was, in a more proper sense, perfectly holy—his holiness was secure. The gospel platform is as much above the ground of mere holiness, as a deed in fee simple is above mere possession.

As obedience is the test of all holiness, so we believe, under the gospel, *perpetuity of obedience* is the test of all holiness. Here we may speak, without solecism, of perfect holiness; and here we are exposed to a more plausible charge of arrogance. Let us examine the ground of this charge. Without entering the wide field of scripture argument, it is sufficient for our purpose to notice a single fact in relation to the views of those who most freely stigmatize the supposed self-righteousness of Perfectionists. These very persons universally and confessedly expect, at death, to become Perfectionists, and that not merely of the second, but of the third degree: in other words, while earthly Perfectionists claim only secure deliverance from sin, their accusers anticipate, within a brief space, secure deliverance from sin and all evil. What is the consideration which exempts their anticipation from the charge of self-righteous presumption, and yet leaves the burden upon our claim? Their answer assuredly must be—"We anticipate, at death, secure redemption from sin and evil, as the *gift of the grace of God.*" But the self-same apology relieves our claim. We *receive* present redemption from sin as the gift of the grace of God; we only enter, "by a new and living way," upon the possession of a portion of that gratuitous inheritance which they expect to receive at death. We must be permitted, then, to say boldly, that the same rule which allows men to *hope* for heaven without presumption, allows us to *receive* heaven here without self-righteousness: and the charge of arrogance is due to those who hope for the gift, while they daily displease the Giver. The same Christ who will be the believer's portion in heaven, is our righteousness and sanctification here. While, therefore, we shrink not from the odium connected with the name *Perfectionist*, we cannot despair of disabusing all honest men, ere long, of a portion of their prejudices against it, by convincing them that we join in the testimony of our living head, that "there is none good but one, that is God," and believe that by the energy of his goodness alone we are delivered from sin.

The standard by which every man judges of the nature of true humility, and of its opposite, spiritual pride, is determined by the answer which his heart gives to the question—"Who is the author of righteousness?" If the credit of holiness is due to him who professes it, then his profession exalts himself at the expense of God, and justly exposes him to the charge of spiritual arrogance, however high or low may be his claim. But if God alone is acknowledged as the author of righteousness, a profession of holiness is only the acknowledgment of a gift—and not only consistent with, but necessary to, the exercise of true humility. The man who has no conception of any righteousness other than his own, may well count the confession of imperfection—-genuine modesty. From such we expect no mercy. But if there are any who ascribe all righteousness to God, we hope to convince them that the arrogance which boasts of the "Lord our righteousness" is the perfection of humility; and that the profession of humility which delights in the confession of sin and in the expectation of a continued commission of it, is only a modest way of robbing Christ of the crown of his glory.

Is it imagined that the man to whom God in truth has given perfect holiness, has done some great thing? He has done nothing. The great achievement of his will which, be it remembered, the grace of God has secured, is the cessation from his own works, and the commencement of an everlasting repose on the energy of the living God, as the basis and hope of his righteousness. He has simply died—and with his dying breath bequeathed his body, soul and spirit to his Maker, rolling the responsibility of his future and eternal obedience upon the everlasting arm.

We believe it is incomparably easier to receive deliverance from all sins, than to conquer one. Paul clearly presents the principle in Romans 1:21–32, which accounts for the difficulty men find in obtaining freedom from sin. Because they refuse to glorify God, he *gives them up* to vile affections. The affections of men are rightfully under the perfect control of God. When he is dethroned, he abandons his kingdom, and anarchy ensues; every effort to quell the rebellion of desires, which falls short of a reinstatement of God in his sovereignty over the heart, must result in disheartening failure. But why should it be difficult for Him who "stands at the door," if his petition for entrance is heard, and his claim for dominion admitted, to restore peace and security to the ruined kingdom? Why should it be thought an incredible thing, that God should raise the dead? Pride, envy, anger, sensuality, etc., are but limbs of the tree of sin, the stock of which is that *unbelief which rejects the righteousness of God.* The man who commences the work of exterminating sin at the top of the tree, or among any of the branches, will soon be disheartened by the discovery that the branches he has once lopped off, soon grow again, or send their juice into other limbs. We say, therefore, it is easier to lay the ax at the root and fell the whole tree at once, than to exterminate effectually a single limb. In view of these considerations, though we object not to the name, Perfectionist—and though we verily believe and unblushingly maintain that we are free from sin—we beg to be relieved of the glory, and of the shame of the achievement; as we have been taught with the scourge, that the day has come when "all the haughtiness of men shall be brought low, and the Lord alone exalted."

BIBLE COMMUNISM

1. The Bible predicts that the Kingdom of God will come on earth. Daniel 2:44, Isaiah 25:6–9.

2. The administration of the will of God in his kingdom on earth will be the same as the administration of his will in heaven. Matthew 6:10, Ephesians 1:10.

3. God's plan at the beginning of the Christian era was not to establish immediately his kingdom on earth, but to march an isolated church through the world, establish the kingdom in the heavens, and prepare the way for the kingdom on earth by giving the Gentiles the Bible, and religious training. Hence the apostolic church was directed to submit to "the powers that be." But at the end of the "times of the Gentiles" God will call his church to break in pieces the powers that be and take their place.

4. The institutions of the Kingdom of God are such that a disclosure of them in the apostolic age would have been inconsistent with God's plan of continuing the institutions of this world through the times of the Gentiles. Hence the Bible must not be asked to lead us into the institutions of the Kingdom of God step by step, but only to point the way, consigning us to the specific guidance of "the spirit of wisdom and revelation."

5. In the Kingdom of God marriage does not exist. On the other hand there is no proof in the Bible nor in reason that the distinction of sex will ever be abolished. Matthew 22:29–30.

6. In the Kingdom of God the intimate union that in the world is limited to the married pair extends through the whole body of communicants; without however excluding special companionships founded on special adaptability. John 17:21.

7. The situation on the day of Pentecost shows the practical tendency of heavenly influences. "All that believed were together, and had all things common; and sold their possessions and goods, and parted them to all, as every man had need.". . .

The communism of the day of Pentecost is not to be regarded as temporary and circumstantial. The seed of heavenly unity fell into the earth and was buried for a time, but in the harvest at the second coming of Christ it was reproduced and became the universal, eternal principle of the invisible church.

8. The abolishment of appropriation is involved in the very nature of a true relation to Christ. Appropriation is a branch of egotism. But the grand mystery of the gospel is vital union with Christ, which is the extinguishment of egotism at the center.

9. The abolishment of worldly restrictions on sexual union is involved in the anti-legality of the gospel. It is incompatible with the perfected freedom, toward which Paul's gospel of "grace without law" leads, that a person should be allowed to love in all directions, and yet be forbidden to express love except in one direction.

10. The abolishment of marriage is involved in Paul's doctrine of the end of ordinances. Marriage is a worldly ordinance. Christians are

dead to the world by the death of Christ. The same reasoning which authorized the abolishment of the Jewish ordinances makes also an end of marriage.

11. The abolishment of the Jewish ordinances was the "offense of the cross" in the apostolic age. It brought the church into collision with the civil as well as the ecclesiastical authorities, compelled Christians to die substantially to the world at the outset, and exposed them to constant persecution and the hazard of literal death. If Christ and the unbelieving world are as hostile to each other now as ever (which is certainly true), the cross of Christ must have a development today as offensive to the Gentiles as the nullification of the Sinai law was to the Jews. Where then shall the death-blow of the flesh fall in the Gentile world? We answer, on marriage. That is a civil as well as religious ordinance, common to all Christian sects. The nullification of marriage in the modern world will be just such an offense of the cross as the nullification of the ordinances of Judaism was in the apostolic age.

12. The plea that marriage is founded in nature will not bear investigation. Experience testifies that the human heart is capable of loving more than one at the same time. It is not the loving heart but the green-eyed claimant of the loving heart that sets up the one-love theory.

13. A system of complex marriage will open the prison doors to the victims both of marriage and celibacy: to the married who are oppressed by lust, tied to uncongenial natures, separated from their natural mates; to the unmarried who are withered by neglect, diseased by unnatural abstinence, or plunged into prostitution by desires that find no lawful outlet.

14. The Kingdom of God on earth is destined to abolish death.

15. The abolition of death is to be the last triumph of the Kingdom of God. Christ cannot save the body until he has "put down all [present] authority and rule," and organized society anew. It is true that, since life works legitimately from within outward, the social revolution ought not to be commenced until the resurrection power is established in the heart. The shell ought not to be broken until the chick itself is strong enough to make the breach. Yet in the order of nature the shell bursts before the chick comes forth. Just so the breaking up of the fashion of the world must precede the resurrection of the body.

16. The chain of evils which holds humanity in ruin has four links: first, a breach with God; second, a disruption of the sexes, involving a special curse on woman; third, oppressive labor, bearing specially on

man; fourth, death. The chain of redemption begins with reconciliation with God, proceeds to a restoration of true relations between the sexes, then to a reform of the industrial system, and ends with victory over death.

It was the special function of the apostolic church to break up the worldly ecclesiastical system and reopen full communication with God. It is the special function of the present church, availing itself first of the work of the apostolic church by union with it and a re-development of its theology, to break up the worldly social system and establish true sexual and industrial relations.

From what precedes it is evident that no one should attempt to revolutionize sexual morality before settlement with God. Holiness, communism of love, association in labor, and immortality must come in their true order.

17. The amative branch of the sexual relation is favorable to life. The propagative branch is expensive of life. The problem that must be solved before redemption can be carried forward to immortality is to secure the benefits of amativeness while reducing the expenses of propagation to what life can afford. This can be done through male continence.

18. Sexual shame is factitious and irrational. The moral reform that arises from the sentiment of shame attempts a hopeless war with nature. Its policy is to prevent pruriency by keeping the mind in ignorance of sexual subjects, while nature is constantly thrusting those subjects upon the mind. The only way to elevate love is to clear away the false, debasing associations that usually crowd around it, and substitute true, beautiful ones.

19. The foregoing principles furnish motives for association. They develop in a larger partnership the same attractions that draw and bind together a marriage partnership. A community home, where love is honored and cultivated, will be as much more attractive than an ordinary home as the community outnumbers a pair.

These principles also remove the chief obstruction to association. There is a strong tendency to crossing love even in marriage. Association inevitably increases this. A confederation of contiguous states with custom-house lines around each is sure to be quarrelsome. The only way to prevent smuggling and strife in such a confederation is to abolish custom-house lines from the interior, and collect revenues by one custom-house line around the whole. The Shakers avoid this stumblingblock, but they sacrifice the life of society in securing its peace.

20. Association to be valuable must be not mere compaction of

material but community of life. A congeries of loose particles cannot make a living body; no more can a congeries of loose double particles. Just so in association individuals and pairs as well as all larger combinations must be knit together organically and pervaded by one common life. Association of this kind will be to society what regeneration is to the individual, a resurrection from the dead. Bible communism, as this kind of association may properly be called, demands the surrender not only of property and conjugal interests but of life itself to the use of the whole. If this is the "grave of liberty," as the Fourierists say, it is the grave of the liberty of war, which has done mischief enough to deserve death; and it is the birth of the liberty of peace.

21. In Bible communism excessive labor will be done away. Labor is excessive or not according to the proportion between strength and work. Bible communism increases strength by placing the individual in an organization which receives life from its source and distributes it with the highest activity. It reduces work by reducing the needed amount of food, raiment and shelter. As society becomes vital and refined, drawing its best nourishment from happiness, the grosser kinds of food, especially animal food, will go out of use, and the fruits of trees will become staple. Woman's dress will be simple and beautiful and nearly the same as man's. Buildings too will be more compact, and much labor now expended in accommodating egotism and exclusiveness will be saved.

In Bible communism labor, no longer excessive, will become naturally attractive. Loving companionship will contribute to this result. When the partition between the sexes is taken away, when fashion follows nature in dress and vocation, men and women will mingle like boys and girls in their employments, and labor will become sport.

22. We can now see our way to victory over death. Reconciliation with God opens the way for reconciliation of the sexes. Reconciliation of the sexes excludes shame, and opens the way for Bible communism. Bible communism increases strength, diminishes work, and makes work attractive. Thus the antecedents of death are removed. First we abolish sin, then shame, then the curse on woman of exhausting childbearing, then the curse on man of excessive labor, and so we arrive regularly at the tree of life. Genesis 3.

23. The men and women who are called to usher in the Kingdom of God will be guided not merely by theoretical truth, but by direct communication with the heavens, as were Abraham, Moses, David, [and] Paul. This will be called a fanatical principle. But it is clearly a

Bible principle, and we must place it on high above all others as the palladium of conservatism in the introduction of the new social order.

We hereby notify all that we neither license nor encourage any one to attempt the practice of this theory without clear directions from the government in the heavens. No movement in these matters can be made safely in the way of imitation, nor on the mere ground of acquaintance with the theory of the new order. Other qualifications besides theory are required for the construction and handling of a locomotive, and much more for the management of such tremendous machinery as that of Bible communism. Whoever meddles with the affairs of the inner sanctuary without true spirituality securing inspiration will plunge himself into consuming fire.

THE KINGDOM OF GOD HAS COME:
OUTLINE OF REMARKS BY J.H. NOYES AT A MEETING
OF BELIEVERS AT PUTNEY ON THE EVENING OF JUNE 1, 1847

The testimony of John the Baptist, and of Christ, and of the apostles down to the second coming of Christ in 70 A.D. was "The Kingdom of Heaven is at hand." This has been our testimony since the reappearance in our day of the primitive gospel, salvation from sin. We believe that the kingdom now coming is the same that was established in heaven at the second coming of Christ. God then commenced a kingdom in human nature independent of the laws of this world. That kingdom, withdrawn to heaven, has been strengthening and enlarging itself ever since. We look for its re-establishment here, and this extension of an existing government into this world is what we mean by the coming of the Kingdom of God.

But we have expected that the manifestation of this kingdom after a successful career of eighteen hundred years in the invisible world will be by a process different from the original one.

The difference may be illustrated thus: If it is understood that on the 21st day of March at noon spring begins, the natural declaration before that time is "Spring is at hand," and immediately afterward, "Spring is come." This was the situation of the primitive church. The second coming of the Lord Jesus was to mark the exact time of their translation to the invisible kingdom. "Now is come salvation, and strength, and the kingdom of our God, and the power of his Christ" was the new testimony that was raised in heaven at that time.[1] But if it is understood that spring coincides not with a fixed astronomical

[1] Revelation 12:10.

period but with a particular stage of the sun's power over the earth, it is impossible to refer the advent of spring to any precise point of time. To determine the presence of spring in this case is more difficult than in the other, but within a moderate latitude of time and with a certain accumulation of data it is easily done. Through the month of March the progress of the sun up the heavens is distinctly visible, though there is yet a prevalence of wintry weather. Later when we begin to have mild, springlike days there are also occasional ones in which the ground is covered with snow. Yet we are certain that sometime within the limits of April spring will have come. Such is our problem with reference to the coming of the Kingdom of God on earth. The evidence goes to show that the Kingdom of God will be established here not in a formal, dramatic way, but by a process like that which brings the seasonal spring. The primitive church like the sun will come near to us, and the judgment and resurrection will be effected by an infusion of the light and energy of God.

I will put the question: is not now the time for us to commence the testimony that the Kingdom of God has come? We must not do this on insufficient grounds; nor should we be withheld from it by merely apparent difficulties.

I think there is abundant evidence, especially in the last year, that the judgment has begun. He that searcheth the hearts and trieth the reins has been among us cutting between the righteous and the wicked and between good and evil in our own characters. So of the resurrection. We have seen that there is a power among us that can conquer death. Some of us have lived for a long time in the jaws of death, and also in the jaws of the resurrection; dying daily and rising daily.

With a mighty hand and marvelous wisdom God has gathered us together here. We have been able to cut our way through the isolation and selfishness in which the mass of men exist, and have attained a position in which before heaven and earth we trample under foot the domestic and pecuniary fashions of the world. Separate households, property exclusiveness have come to an end with us. Our association is established on principles opposed at every point to the institutions of the world.

If our spiritual attainments are inferior to those of the primitive church before 70 A.D., on the other hand our political and corporate position is in advance of theirs. The fact that communism is developed with us at an earlier period of experience than with them corresponds with the advancing purpose of God. They were not destined to remain an organized body in the world. A future branch of the church was to be the medium of establishing on earth the institutions of heaven, and of extending God's everlasting dominion over men.

Statement by the editor of *The Spiritual Magazine.* A discussion followed in which the nature and effect of the proposed act were fully examined. The new relation which such a declaration would bring us into with the primitive church was shown by the following illustration: Suppose it a fact that the government of the United States is destined to prevail over the American continent. The inhabitants of certain provinces in Mexico get this persuasion. They study the principles and laws of our government, they correspond with our citizens and obtain correct ideas of our designs. After a proper time they declare their annexation and put themselves under our protection. These provinces might not be as civilized in every respect as our states were when they obtained their independence, yet all their political relations would be vastly superior; they would come in on a constitutional level with the states as they exist now, and would have for all purposes of defense and public necessity the strength, experience and revenue which this nation has accumulated during sixty years. So, although we are not equal to the primitive church as they were in 70 A.D., yet by the act of annexation we shall be admitted to a full partnership with them as they exist now.

All expressed themselves deliberately and freely. The indivisible unity and unfeigned brotherly love, the growing momentum of improvement, the increasing intimacy of communication with God's invisible kingdom, which have been conferred upon this body, were mentioned among the proofs of God's purpose concerning us. Respecting the fire of judgment and the power of the resurrection among us there was but one belief and one voice. It was seen that a new and further confession of truth was necessary. Therefore it was unanimously adopted as the declaration of the believers assembled, that *The Kingdom of God has come.*

Paper by Noyes August 28, 1872. The declaration [that has been reported above] was made at an important crisis. It bore the same relation to the Oneida Community as the Declaration of Independence did to the United States. We had commenced the practice of our present institutions a year before, but the movement had been somewhat private. Now we were approaching public cognizance in various ways. . . .

A singular incident occurred at the close of the meeting. At the exact moment when the vote was taken a sublime clap of thunder like a cannon salvo startled us. It was the only clap that evening, and was so entirely unexpected that it seemed like Heaven's response to our act.

2

THE COMMUNITARIAN DREAM

Adin Ballou
CONSTITUTION OF THE PRACTICAL
CHRISTIAN REPUBLIC

*Another figure who approached social reform primarily from within the
evangelical mold was Adin Ballou (1803–1890). Ballou was raised on a farm
where Rhode Island joins Massachusetts. He was unable to attend college or
train formally for the ministry. Not especially religious in his early youth, he
experienced a nocturnal vision at the age of nineteen, commanding him to
preach the gospel of Christ to his fellowmen. Most of his life was spent in
small-town surroundings, where he doggedly pursued a self-directed course.
Only once did he have a chance to meet Emerson. Thus his intellectual career
illustrates the largely indirect impact of broader impulses on the mind of an
earnest provincial. Theologically, Ballou soon went over to Universalism but
always remained in its most conservative wing. He and a small band of
people who called themselves Restorationists accepted the universality of
salvation, but on narrow biblical grounds, abhorring the tendency among
other Universalists and Unitarians to wander far away from the scriptures.
Delicately straddling the domains of revelation and reason, he further split
his tiny sect in the mid-1830s by ardently embracing the causes of antislavery
and pacifism. He claimed that in 1840 his sudden inspiration to found a
community came to him with no knowledge that others were doing the same
thing. Hopedale, located on a farm at Milford, Massachusetts, lasted with fair
success from 1842 to 1856. Legal formalities were its undoing. Ballou had
made it a joint-stock venture, and two brothers quietly bought up
three-quarters of the stock, then announced they were disenchanted with
socialism and proceeded to dissolve the enterprise, leaving everyone else
helpless.*

*Ballou enjoyed devising intricately formal constitutional schemes, as did
many other communitarian leaders of the day. The most grandiose, though
not the longest, is printed below. Written in 1854, it reveals the final extent of
Ballou's vision of a new social order ultimately enveloping the globe.*

SOURCE. Adin Ballou, "Constitution of the Practical Christian Republic,"
History of the Hopedale Community (Lowell, Mass.: Thompson & Hill,
1897), pp. 397–410; first written in 1854.

A new Order of Human Society is hereby founded, to be called The Practical Christian Republic. It shall be constituted, organized and governed in accordance with the following fundamental articles, to wit:

ARTICLE I. OBJECTS.

The cardinal objects of this Republic are and shall be the following, viz.:

1. To institute and consolidate a true order of human society, which shall harmonize all individual interests in the common good and be governed by Divine Principles as its Supreme Law.

2. To establish local Communities of various grades and peculiarities, all acknowledging the sovereignty of Divine Principles and so constituted as to promote the highest happiness of their respective associates.

3. To confederate all such local Communities wheresoever existing throughout the earth by an ascending series of combinations in one common Social Republic.

4. To insure to every orderly citizen of this Republic a comfortable home, suitable employment, adequate subsistence, congenial associates, a good education, proper stimulants to personal righteousness, sympathetic aid in distress, and due protection in the exercise of all natural rights.

5. To give mankind a practical illustration of civil government maintained in just subordination to Divine Principles; which shall be powerful without tyranny, benignant without weakness, dignified without ostentation, independent without defiance, invincible without resorting to injurious force, and pre-eminently useful without being burdensome.

6. To institute and sustain every suitable instrumentality for removing the causes of human misery and promoting the conversion of the world to true righteousness.

7. To multiply, economize, distribute and apply beneficently, wisely and successfully, all the means necessary to harmonize the human race with each other, with the heavenly world and with the universal Father; that in one grand communion of angels and men the will of God may be done "on earth as it is in heaven."

ARTICLE II. PRINCIPLES.

We proclaim the absolute sovereignty of Divine Principles over all human beings, combinations, governments, institutions, laws, customs, habits, practices, actions, opinions, intentions and affections. We recognize in the religion of Jesus Christ as he taught and exemplified it a complete annunciation and attestation of essential Divine Principles.

We accept and acknowledge the following as Divine Principles of Theological Truth, viz.:

1. The existence of one all-perfect, infinite God.
2. The mediatorial manifestation of God through Christ.
3. Divine revelations and inspirations given to mankind.
4. The immortal existence of human and angelic spirits.
5. The moral agency and religious obligation of mankind.
6. The certainty of a perfect divine retribution.
7. The necessity of man's spiritual regeneration.
8. The final universal triumph of good over evil.

We accept and acknowledge the following as Divine Principles of Personal Righteousness; viz.:

1. Reverence for the Divine and spiritual.
2. Self-denial for righteousness' sake.
3. Justice to all beings.
4. Truth in all manifestations of mind.
5. Love in all spiritual relations.
6. Purity in all things.
7. Patience in all right aims and pursuits.
8. Unceasing progress toward perfection.

We accept and acknowledge the following as Divine Principles of Social Order; viz.:

1. The supreme Fatherhood of God.
2. The universal Brotherhood of man.
3. The declared perfect love of God to man.
4. The required perfect love of man to God.
5. The required perfect love of man to man.
6. The required just reproof and disfellowship of evil-doers.
7. The required non-resistance of evil doers with evil.
8. The designed unity of the righteous.

We hold ourselves imperatively bound by the sovereignty of these acknowledged Divine Principles, never, under any pretext whatsoever, to kill, injure, envy or hate any human being, even our worst enemy.

Never to sanction chattel slavery or any obvious oppression of man by man.

Never to countenance war or capital punishment, or the infliction of injurious penalties, or the resistance of evil with evil in any form.

Never to violate the dictates of chastity by adultery, polygamy, concubinage, fornication, self-pollution, lasciviousness, amative abuse, impure language, or cherished lust.

Never to manufacture, buy, sell, deal out or use any intoxicating liquor, *as a beverage.*

Never to take or administer an oath.

Never to participate in a sword-sustained human government, either as voters, office holders or subordinate assistants, *in any case prescriptively involving the infliction of death* or *any absolute injury whatsoever by man on man;* nor to invoke governmental interposition in any such case, even for the accomplishment of good objects.

Never to indulge self-will, bigotry, love of pre-eminence, covetousness, deceit, profanity, idleness or an unruly tongue.

Never to participate in lotteries, gambling, betting or pernicious amusements.

Never to resent reproof or justify ourselves in a known wrong.

Never to aid, abet or approve others in anything sinful; but, through divine assistance, always to recommend and promote with our entire influence the holiness and happiness of all mankind.

ARTICLE III. RIGHTS.

No member of this Republic, nor Association of its members, can have a right to violate any one of its acknowledged Divine Principles; but all the members, however peculiarized by sex, age, color, native country, rank, calling, wealth or station, have indefeasible rights as human beings to do, to be and to enjoy whatsoever they are personally capable of that is not in violation of those Principles. Within these just limits no person shall be restricted or interfered with by this Republic, nor by any constituent Association thereof, in the exercise of the following declared rights; viz.:

1. The right to worship God, with or without external ceremonies and devotional observances, according to the dictates of his or her own conscience.

2. The right to exercise reason, investigate questions, form opinions and declare convictions, by speech, by pen and by the press, on all subjects within the range of human thought.

3. The right to hold any official station to which he or she may be elected, to pursue any avocation or follow any course in life, according to genius, attraction and taste.

4. The right to be stewards, under God, of his or her own talents, property, skill and personal endowments.

5. The right to form and enjoy particular friendships with congenial minds.

6. The right to contract marriage and sustain the sacred relationships of family life.

7. The right to unite with, and also to withdraw from, any Community or Association, on reciprocal terms, at discretion.

8. In fine, the right to seek happiness in all rightful ways and by all innocent means.

ARTICLE IV. MEMBERSHIP.

Section 1. Membership in this Republic shall exist in seven Circles; viz.: the Adoptive, the Unitive, the Preceptive, the Communitive, the Expansive, the Charitive, and the Parentive. The Adoptive Circle shall include all members living in isolation, or not yet admitted into the membership of an integral Community. The Unitive Circle shall include all members of Rural and Joint-Stock Communities. The Preceptive Circle shall include all members specially and perseveringly devoted to Teaching; whether it be teaching religion, morality or any branch of useful knowledge, and whether their teaching be done with the living voice, or with the pen, or through the press, or in educative institutions. All such teachers, after having proved themselves competent, devoted and acceptable in the Communities to which they belong, shall be considered in this Circle. The Communitive Circle shall include all members of integral Common-Stock Communities or Families, whose internal economy excludes individual profits on capital, wages for labor and separate interests. The Expansive Circle shall include all members who are especially devoted to the extension of this Republic, by founding and strengthening new integral Communities; who have associated in companies for that express purpose and are employing the principal portion of their time, talents or property in that work. The Charitive Circle shall include all members who are especially devoted to the reformation, elevation, improvement and welfare of the world's suffering classes, by furnishing them homes, employment, instruction and all the requisite helps to a better condition; who are associated in companies for that express purpose and are employing the principal portion of their time, talents or property in such works. The Parentive Circle shall include all members who, on account of their mature age, faithful services, great experience, sound judgment or unquestionable reliability, are competent to advise, arbitrate and recommend measures in cases of great importance. They shall be declared worthy of a place in the Parentive Circle by their respective integral Communities, in a regular meeting notified for that purpose, by a unanimous vote.

Section 2. The members of no Circle shall ever assume to exercise any other than purely moral or advisory power, nor claim any exclusive prerogatives, privileges, honors or distinctions whatsoever over members of other Circles; but shall be entitled to respect and influence in consideration of intrinsic worth alone. Nor shall there be any permanent general organization of these Circles *as such.* But the members of either may unite in co-operative associations, companies and partnerships, for the more efficient prosecution of their peculiar objects; and may also hold public meetings, conferences and conventions, at pleasure, for the promotion of these objects.

Section 3. Any person may be admitted a member of this Republic by any constituent Community or other authorized body thereof in regular meeting assembled. And any twelve or more persons adopting this Constitution from conviction may render themselves members of the Republic by uniting to form a constituent and confederate Community thereof.

Section 4. Any person may resign or withdraw membership at discretion, or may recede from either of the other Circles to the Adoptive Circle, by giving written notice to the body or principal persons concerned. Any person uniting with a society of any description radically opposed in principle, practice or spirit to this Republic, shall be deemed to have relinquished membership; likewise any person who shall have ceased to manifest any interest in its affairs for the space of three years.

Section 5. Any constituent Community or other organized body of this Republic competent to admit members shall have power to dismiss or discharge them for justifiable reasons. And no person shall be retained a member after persistently violating or setting at naught any one of the sovereign Divine Principles declared in Art. II of this Constitution.

ARTICLE V. ORGANIZATION.

Section 1. The constituent and confederate bodies of this Social Republic shall be the following; viz.: Parochial Communities, Integral Communities, Communal Municipalities, Communal States and Communal Nations.

Section 2. Parochial Communities shall consist each of twelve or more members belonging chiefly to the Adoptive Circle, residing promiscuously in a general neighborhood, associated for religious and moral improvement and to secure such other social advantages as may be found practicable.

Section 3. Integral Communities shall consist each of twelve or more members inhabiting an integral territorial Domain, so held in possession and guaranteed that no part thereof can be owned in fee by any person not a member of this Republic.

There shall be three different kinds of Integral Communities; viz.: Rural, Joint-Stock and Common-Stock Communities. Rural Communities shall hold and manage the major portion of their respective Domains in separate Homesteads, adapted to the wants of families and to small associations under a system of individual proprietorship. Joint-Stock Communities shall hold and manage the major part of their respective Domains in Joint-Stock proprietorship, with various unitary economies, under a system of associative co-operation; laying off the minor portion into Village House Lots, to be sold to individual members under necessary restrictions. Common-Stock Communities shall hold and manage their respective Domains and property in Common-Stock, without paying individual members profits on capital or stipulated wages for labor. . . .

Section 4. Communal Municipalities shall consist each of two or more Communities, whether Parochial or Integral, combined, as in a town or city, for municipal purposes necessary to their common welfare, and impracticable or extremely difficult of accomplishment without such a union.

Section 5. Communal States shall consist each of two or more Communal Municipalities. . . .

Section 6. Communal Nations shall consist each of two or more Communal States. . . .

Section 7. When there shall be two or more Communal Nations, they shall be represented equitably, according to population, in a Supreme Unitary Council by Senators elected for the term of — years.

Section 8. The several constituent bodies of this Republic herein before named shall be organized under written Constitutions, Compacts or Fundamental Laws not inconsistent with this General Constitution, and shall exercise the governmental prerogatives and responsibilities defined in the next ensuing Article.

ARTICLE VI. GOVERNMENT.

Section 1. Self-government in the Individual, the Family and the primary congenial Association, under the immediate sovereignty of

Divine Principles, being the basis of moral and social order in this Republic, shall be constantly cherished as indispensable to its prosperity. Therefore all governmental powers vested in the confederate bodies of this Republic shall be such as are obviously beneficent and such as cannot be conveniently exercised by the primary Communities or their component Circles. And such confederate bodies shall never assume to exercise governmental powers not clearly delegated to them by their constituents. . . .

Section 5. The duties and powers of the Supreme Unitary Council shall be defined in a Fundamental Compact, to be framed by delegates from all the Communal Nations then existing and adopted by at least two-thirds of the citizen members of the Republic present and acting in their respective primary Communities, at meetings duly notified for that purpose. And all questions throughout this Republic, excepting the election of officers, shall be determined by a two-thirds vote.

Section 6. No official servant of any grade in this Republic shall ever assume to distinguish him or herself by external display of dress, equipage or other artificial appliances above the common members; nor shall receive compensation for official services beyond the average paid to the first class of operatives at large, with a reasonable allowance for incidental expenses; but every official servant shall be considered bound to exemplify the humility, modesty and benevolence inculcated in the Christian precept. "Whosoever will be chief among you, let him be the servant of all." Nor shall it be allowable for any of the constitutional bodies of this Republic to burden the people with governmental expenses for mere worldly show or for any other than purposes of unquestionable public utility.

ARTICLE VII. RELIGION.

Section 1. Acknowledging the Christian religion as one of fundamental Divine Principles, to be practically carried out in all human conduct, this Republic insists only on the essentials of faith and practice affirmed in Article II of this Constitution. Therefore, no uniform Religious or Ecclesiastical system of externals shall be established; nor shall any rituals, forms, ceremonies or observances whatsoever be either instituted or interdicted; but each Community shall determine for itself, with due regard for the conscientious scruples of its own members, all matters of this nature.

Section 2. Believing that the Holy Christ-Spirit will raise up competent Religious and Moral Teachers, and commend them, by substantial demonstration of their fitness, to the confidence of those to whom they minister, this Republic shall not assume to commission, authorize or forbid any person to preach or to teach Religion; nor shall any constituent body thereof assume to do so. But each Community may invite any person deemed worthy of confidence to be their religious teacher, on terms reciprocally satisfactory to the parties concerned.

Section 3. It shall be the privilege and duty of members of this Republic to hold general meetings, at least once in three months, for religious improvement and the promulgation of their acknowledged divine principles. In order to this, Quarterly Conferences shall be established in every general region of country inhabited by any considerable number of members. Any twenty-five or more members wheresoever resident shall be competent to establish a Quarterly Conference whenever they may deem the same necessary to their convenience. In so doing they shall adopt a written Constitution subsidiary to this general Constitution and no wise incompatible therewith, under which they may make such regulations as they may deem promotive of the objects they have in view. All such Conferences shall have power to admit members into the Adoptive Circle of this Republic, and also, for sufficient reasons, to discharge them. And each Quarterly Conference shall keep reliable records of its proceedings, with an authentic copy of this general Constitution prefixed.

ARTICLE VIII. MARRIAGE.

Section 1. Marriage, being one of the most important and sacred of human relationships, ought to be guarded against caprice and abuse by the highest wisdom that is available. Therefore within the membership of this Republic and the dependencies thereof, Marriage is specially commended to the care of the Preceptive and Parentive Circles. These are hereby designated as the confidential counsellors of all members and dependents who may desire their mediation in cases of matrimonial negotiation, contract or controversy; and shall be held pre-eminently responsible for the prudent and faithful discharge of their duties. But no person decidedly averse to their interposition shall be considered under obligation to solicit or accept it. And it shall be considered the perpetual duty of the Circles named to enlighten the public mind relative to the requisites of true matrimony, and to elevate the marriage institution within this Republic to the highest possible plane of purity and happiness.

Section 2. Marriage shall always be solemnized in the presence of two or more witnesses, by the distinct acknowledgment of the parties before some member of the Preceptive or Parentive Circle selected to preside on the occasion. . . .

Section 3. Divorce from the bonds of matrimony shall never be allowable within the membership of this Republic except for adultery conclusively proved against the accused party. But separations for other sufficient reasons may be sanctioned, with the distinct understanding that neither party shall be at liberty to marry again during the natural life-time of the other.

ARTICLE IX. EDUCATION.

Section 1. The proper education of the rising generation being indispensable to the prosperity and glory of this Republic, it shall be amply provided for as a cardinal want; and no child shall be allowed to grow up anywhere under the control of its membership without good educational opportunities.

Section 2. Education shall be as comprehensive and thorough as circumstances in each case will allow. It shall aim in all cases to develop harmoniously the physical, intellectual, moral and social faculties of the young: to give them, if possible, a high-toned moral character based on scrupulous conscientiousness and radical Christian principles; a sound mind, well stored with useful knowledge and capable of inquiring, reasoning and judging for itself; a healthful, vigorous body, suitably fed, exercised, clothed, lodged and recreated; good domestic habits, including personal cleanliness, order, propriety, agreeableness and generous social qualities; industrial executiveness and skill in one or more of the avocations necessary to a comfortable subsistence; and, withal, practical economy in pecuniary matters. In fine, to qualify them for solid usefulness and happiness in all the rightful pursuits and relations of life. . . .

ARTICLE X. PROPERTY.

Section 1. All property, being primarily the Creator's and provided by Him for the use of mankind during their life on earth, ought to be acquired, used and disposed of in strict accordance with the dictates of justice and charity. Therefore, the members of this Republic shall consider themselves stewards in trust, under God, of all property coming into their possession, and as such imperatively bound not to consume it in the gratification of their own inordinate lusts, nor to hoard it up as a mere treasure, nor to employ it to the injury of any human being, nor withhold it from the relief of distressed fellow creatures; but always to use it, as not abusing it, for strictly just, benevolent and commendable purposes.

Section 2. It shall not be deemed compatible with justice for the people of this Republic, in their pecuniary commerce with each other, to demand, in any case, as a compensation for their mere personal service, labor or attendance, a higher price per cent., per piece, per day, week, month or year than the average paid to the first class of operatives in the Community, or general vicinity where the service is rendered. Nor shall it be deemed compatible with justice for the members, in such commerce, to demand, as a price for anything sold or exchanged, more than the fair cost value thereof, as nearly as the same can be estimated, reckoning prime cost, labor or attention, incidental expenses, contingent waste, depreciation and average risks of sale; nor to demand for the mere use of capital, except as partners in the risks of its management, any clear interest or profit whatsoever exceeding four per cent. per annum.

Section 3. It shall not be deemed compatible with the welfare, prosperity and honor of this Republic for the people thereof to owe debts outside of the same exceeding three-fourths of their available property rated at moderate valuation by disinterested persons; nor to give or receive long credits, except on real estate security; nor to manufacture, fabricate or sell sham and unreliable productions; nor to make business engagements, or hold out expectations, which are of doubtful fulfillment.

Section 4. Whenever the population and resources of this Republic shall warrant the formation of the first Communal Nation, and the government thereof shall have been organized, a uniform system of Mutual Banking shall be established, based mainly on real estate securities, which shall afford loans at the mere cost of operations. Also, a uniform system of Mutual Insurance, which shall reduce all kinds of insurance to the lowest terms. Also, a uniform system of reciprocal Commercial Exchange, which shall preclude all needless intervention between producers and consumers, all extra risks of property, all extortionate speculation, all inequitable profits on exchanges, and all demoralizing expedients of trade. Also, Regulations providing for the just encouragement of useful industry and the practical equalization of all social advantages, so far as the same can be done without infringing on individual rights. And all the members shall be considered under sacred moral obligations to co-operate adhesively and persistently in every righteous measure employed for the accomplishment of these objects.

ARTICLE XI. POLICY.

It shall be the fundamental, uniform and established Policy of this Republic:

1. To govern, succor and protect its own people to the utmost of its ability, in all matters and cases whatsoever not involving anti-Christian conflict with the sword-sustained governments of the world under which its members live.

2. To avoid all unnecessary conflicts whatsoever with these governments, by conforming to all their laws and requirements which are not repugnant to the Sovereignty of Divine Principles.

3. To abstain from all participation in the working of their political machinery and to be connected as little as possible with their systems of governmental operation.

4. To protest, remonstrate and testify conscientiously against their sins on moral grounds alone; but never to plot schemes of revolutionary agitation, intrigue or violence against them, nor be implicated in countenancing the least resistance to their authority by injurious force.

5. If compelled in any case by Divine Principles to disobey their requirements, or passively to withstand their unrighteous exactions and thus incur their penal vengence, to act openly and suffer with true moral heroism.

6. Never to ask their protection, even in favor of injured innocence or threatened rights, when it can be interposed only by means which are condemned by Divine Principles.

7. To live in peace, so far as can innocently be done, with all mankind outside of this Republic, whether individuals, associations, corporations, sects, classes, parties, states or nations; also to accredit and encourage whatever is truly good in all; yet to fellowship iniquity in none, be enslaved by none, be amalgamated with none, be morally responsible for none; but ever be distinctly, unequivocally and uncompromisingly *The Practical Christian Republic* until the complete regeneration of the world. . . .

3

A MORMON POLITICAL PLATFORM

Joseph Smith
VIEWS ON THE POWERS AND POLICY
OF THE GOVERNMENT OF THE UNITED STATES

The most rough-hewn version of an evangelical social ideal came from the pen of Joseph Smith (1805–1844), founder of the Mormon religious sect. Smith was born into an obscure family that moved from Vermont to upstate New York. As a young man, he began experimenting with necromancy. He then claimed that an angel appeared to him delivering a lengthy message on a series of golden tablets. The resulting Book of Mormon extended the Christian Bible in the direction of North American prehistory. It prophesied the establishment of a new Kingdom of Jerusalem to be located in Missouri. With his followers, Smith traveled westward, remaining for several years in Nauvoo, Illinois. The Mormons never adopted a completely communal social scheme, but many of their arrangements leaned in this direction. Their practice of polygamy aroused enormous opposition among their neighbors, leading to the murder of Smith at Nauvoo by a lynch mob in mid-1844, after which the surviving faithful traveled to Utah to establish a new base of operations. Shortly before his death, Smith had proclaimed himself a presidential candidate in the election of 1844. His statement of political aims, part of which appears below, reveals the populistic rhetoric—sweeping, turgid, often apparently contradictory—that could issue from an "inspired" Christian leader without worldly education.

No honest man can doubt for a moment but the glory of American liberty is on the wane, and that calamity and confusion will sooner or later destroy the peace of the people. Speculators will urge a national

SOURCE. Joseph Smith, *Views on the Powers and Policy of the Government of the United States* (Salt Lake City, Utah: J.H. Parry & Co., 1886), pp. 15–22; written in 1844.

bank as a savior of credit and comfort. A hireling pseudo-priesthood will plausibly push abolition doctrines and doings and "human rights" into Congress, and into every other place where conquest smells of fame, or opposition swells to popularity; Democracy, Whiggery, and cliquery will attract their elements and foment divisions among the people, to accomplish fancied schemes and accumulate power, while poverty, driven to despair, like hunger forcing its way through a wall, will break through the statutes of men to save life, and mend the breach in prison glooms.

A still higher grade of what the "nobility of nations" call "great men" will dally with all rights, in order to smuggle a fortune at "one fell swoop," mortgage Texas, possess Oregon, and claim all the unsettled regions of the world for hunting and trapping; and should an humble, honest man, red, black, or white, exhibit a better title, these gentry have only to clothe the judge with richer ermine, and spangle the lawyer's finger with finer rings, to have the judgment of his peers and the honor of his lords as a pattern of honesty, virtue, and humanity, while the motto hangs on his nation's escutcheon—"*Every man has his price!*"

Now, O people! people! turn unto the Lord and live, and reform this nation. Frustrate the designs of wicked men. Reduce Congress at least two-thirds. Two senators from a state and two members to a million of population will do more business than the army that now occupy the halls of the national legislature. Pay them two dollars and their board per diem (except Sundays). That is more than the farmer gets, and he lives honestly. Curtail the officers of government in pay, number, and power; for the Philistine lords have shorn our nation of its goodly locks in the lap of Delilah.

Petition your state legislatures to pardon every convict in their several penitentiaries, blessing them as they go, and saying to them, in the name of the Lord, *Go thy way, and sin no more.*

Advise your legislators, when they make laws for larceny, burglary, or any felony, to make the penalty applicable to work upon roads, public works, or any place where the culprit can be taught more wisdom and more virtue, and become more enlightened. Rigor and seclusion will never do as much to reform the propensities of men as reason and friendship. Murder only can claim confinement or death. Let the penitentiaries be turned into seminaries of learning, where intelligence, like the angels of heaven, would banish such fragments of barbarism. Imprisonment for debt is a meaner practice than the savage tolerates, with all his ferocity. *"Amor vincit omnia."* (Love conquers all.)

Petition, also, ye goodly inhabitants of the slave states, your legislators to abolish slavery by the year 1850, or now, and save the abolitionist from reproach and ruin, infamy and shame.

Pray Congress to pay every man a reasonable price for his slaves out of the surplus revenue arising from the sale of public lands, and from the deduction of pay from the members of Congress.

Break off the shackles from the poor black man, and hire him to labor like other human beings; for "an hour of virtuous liberty on earth is worth a whole eternity of bondage." Abolish the practice in the army and navy of trying men by court-martial for desertion. If a soldier or marine runs away, send him his wages, with this instruction, that *his country will never trust him again; he has forfeited his honor.*

Make honor the standard with all men. Be sure that good is rendered for evil in all cases, and the whole nation, like a kingdom of kings and priests, will rise up in righteousness, and be respected as wise and worthy on earth, and as just and holy for heaven, by Jehovah, the author of perfection.

More economy in the national and state governments would make less taxes among the people; more equality through the cities, towns, and country, would make less distinction among the people; and more honesty and familiarity in societies, would make less hypocrisy and flattery in all branches of the community; and open, frank, candid decorum to all men, in this boasted land of liberty, would beget esteem, confidence, union and love; and the neighbor from any state, or from any country, of whatever color, clime or tongue, could rejoice when he put his foot on the sacred soil of freedom, and exclaim, The very name of *"American"* is fraught with *friendship*. Oh, then, create confidence! restore freedom! break down slavery! banish imprisonment for debt, and be in love, fellowship, and peace, with all the world! Remember that honesty is not subject to law: the law was made for transgressors; wherefore, a Dutchman might exclaim—*"Ein ehrlicher name ist besser als Reichthum."* (A good name is better than riches.)

For the accommodation of the people in every state and territory, let Congress show their wisdom by granting a national bank, with branches in each state and territory, where the capital stock shall be held by the nation for the mother bank, and by the states and territories for the branches; and whose officers and directors shall be elected yearly by the people, with wages at the rate of two dollars per day for services; which several banks shall never issue any more bills than the amount of capital stock in her vaults and the interest.

The net gain of the mother bank shall be applied to the national revenue, and that of the branches to the states and territories' revenues. And the bills shall be par throughout the nation, which will mercifully cure that fatal disorder known in cities as *brokerage,* and leave the people's money in their own pockets.

Give every man his constitutional freedom, and the president full power to send an army to suppress mobs, and the states authority to repeal and impugn that relic of folly which makes it necessary for the governor of a state to make the demand of the president for troops, in case of invasion or rebellion.

The governor himself may be a mobber; and instead of being punished, as he should be, for murder or treason, he may destroy the very lives, rights, and property he should protect. Like the good Samaritan, send every lawyer, as soon as he repents and obeys the ordinances of heaven, to preach the Gospel to the destitute, without purse or scrip, pouring in the oil and the wine. A learned priesthood is certainly more honorable than *"an hireling clergy."*

As to the contiguous territories to the United States, wisdom would direct no tangling alliance. Oregon belongs to this government honorably; and when we have the red man's consent, let the Union spread from the east to the west sea; and if Texas petitions Congress to be adopted among the sons of liberty, give her the right hand of fellowship, and refuse not the same friendly grip to Canada and Mexico. And when the right arm of freemen is stretched out in the character of a navy for the protection of rights, commerce, and honor, let the iron eyes of power watch from Maine to Mexico, and from California to Columbia. Thus may union be strengthened, and foreign speculation prevented from opposing broadside to broadside.

Seventy years have done much for this goodly land. They have burst the chains of oppression and monarchy, and multiplied its inhabitants from two to twenty millions, with a proportionate share of knowledge keen enough to circumnavigate the globe, draw the lightning from the clouds, and cope with all the crowned heads of the world.

Then why—oh, why will a once-flourishing people not arise, phoenixlike, over the cinders of Martin Van Buren's power, and over the sinking fragments and smoking ruins of other catamount politicians, and over the windfalls of Benton, Calhoun, Clay, Wright, and a caravan of other equally unfortunate law doctors, and cheerfully help to spread a plaster and bind up the *burnt, bleeding wounds* of a sore but blessed country?

The southern people are hospitable and noble. They will help to rid so *free* a country of every vestige of slavery, whenever they are assured of an equivalent for their property. The country will be full of money and confidence when a national bank of twenty millions, and a state bank in every state, with a million or more, gives a tone to monetary matters, and make a circulating medium as valuable in the purses of a whole community, as in the coffers of a speculating banker or broker.

The people may have faults, but they should never be trifled with. . . .

We have had Democratic presidents, Whig presidents, a pseudo-Democratic-Whig president, and now it is time to have a *president of the United States;* and let the people of the whole Union, like the inflexible Romans, whenever they find a *promise* made by a candidate that is not *practiced* as an officer, hurl the miserable sycophant from his exaltation, as God did Nebuchadnezzar, to crop the grass of the field with a beast's heart among the cattle.

Mr. Van Buren said, in his inaugural address, that he went "into the presidential chair the inflexible and uncompromising opponent of every attempt, on the part of Congress, to abolish slavery in the District of Columbia, against the wishes of the slave-holding states, and also with a determination equally decided to resist the slightest interference with it in the states where it exists."

Poor little Matty made this rhapsodical sweep with the fact before his eyes, that the state of New York, his native state, had abolished slavery without a struggle or a groan. Great God, how independent! From henceforth slavery is tolerated where it exists, constitution or no constitution, people or no people, right or wrong: *Vox Matti—vox Diaboli* ("the voice of Matty—the voice of the Devil)." And, peradventure, his great "sub-treasury" scheme was a piece of the same mind. But the man and his measures have such a striking resemblance to the anecdote of the Welshman and his cart-tongue, that when the Constitution was so long that it allowed slavery at the capitol of a free people, it could not be cut off; but when it was so short that it needed a *sub-treasury* to save the funds of the nation, *it could be spliced!* Oh, granny, granny, what a long tail our puss has got! As a Greek might say, *Hysteron proteron,* (the cart before the horse). But his mighty whisk through the great national fire, for the presidential chestnuts, *burnt the locks of his glory with the blaze of his folly!*

In the United States the people are the government, and their united voice is the only sovereign that should rule, the only power that should be obeyed, and the only gentlemen that should be honored at home and abroad, on the land and on the sea. Wherefore, were I the president of the United States, by the voice of a virtuous people, I would honor the old paths of the venerated fathers of freedom; I would walk in the tracks of the illustrious patriots who carried the ark of the government upon their shoulders with an eye single to the glory of the people; and when that people petitioned to abolish slavery in the slave states, I would use all honorable means to have their prayers granted, and give liberty to the captive by paying the southern gentlemen a reasonable equivalent for his property, that the whole nation might be free indeed! . . .

And when a neighboring realm petitioned to join the union of the sons of liberty, my voice would be, *Come*—yea, come, Texas; come, Mexico; come, Canada; and come, all the world; let us be brethren, let us be one great family, and let there be a universal peace.

Abolish the cruel custom of prisons (except certain cases), penitentiaries, court-martials for desertion; and let reason and friendship reign over the ruins of ignorance and barbarity; yea, I would, as the universal friend of man, open the prisons, open the eyes, open the ears, and open the hearts of all people, to behold and enjoy freedom—unadulterated freedom; and God, who once cleansed the violence of the earth with a flood, whose Son laid down His life for the salvation of all His Father gave Him out of the world, and who has promised that He will come and purify the world again with fire in the last days, should be supplicated by me for the good of all people.

With the highest esteem, I am a friend of virtue and of the people,

JOSEPH SMITH.

Nauvoo, Illinois, Feb. 7, 1844.

4

AN EVANGELICAL VIEW OF POLITICS AND SALVATION

Charles G. Finney
SYSTEMATIC THEOLOGY

Undoubtedly the most influential figure in the evangelical drive toward perfectionist beliefs, Charles Grandison Finney (1792–1875) retained a prudence lacking in such figures as Noyes or Smith, while at the same time carving himself out a role far more prominent than Ballou's. Finney was born in Connecticut, studied in academies, and initially began reading law in upstate New York. After eighteen months of soul-searching and several religious visions, he switched to theology. He was ordained in the Presbyterian church in 1824. Soon his highly emotional revivalistic methods began to cause great controversy within the denomination. He broke conspicuously with the traditional Calvinist emphasis on predestination, adopting the view that all men could freely claim eternal life through the salvation experience. Though this outlook was essentially perfectionist, Finney carefully dissociated himself from the extreme adherents of the label, such as Noyes. (So that Finney may be compared with Noyes in this central respect, a few paragraphs by Finney on the subject of regeneration appear at the beginning of this selection.) By 1835 a Congregationalist, Finney obtained a secure base of operations at Oberlin, where he served as professor of theology and after 1851 as president of the college. A man of truly unusual magnetic force, Finney inspired a growing audience to link abolitionism with the new style of religious and moral regeneration, dividing churchmen in the process, but ultimately galvanizing northern determination to stand firm against the south. Yet Finney did not allow himself to be diverted into the social causes of the day. Indeed, he was personally not an extremist on the subject of antislavery, fearing that it would distract attention from the saving of individual souls. (At Oberlin his occasional lapses into racial bigotry became something of a local scandal.) In the portion of the selection that deals with civil government, Finney adopts a notably conservative stand on a theoretical plane, before abruptly switching to a condemnation of the unjust war against Mexico. In this, one can see how particular events might lead

SOURCE. Charles G. Finney, *Lectures on Systematic Theology* (Oberlin, Ohio: James M. Fitch, 1846), pp. 441–446, 496, 499–501, 535.

men like Finney into a more extreme attitude of opposition to established authority than their original instincts would have dictated. Yet in the end Finney's views open the door both to war as divine retribution and to an abandonment of the Bible as the highest source of moral authority—themes more openly developed by Gerrit Smith in the final selection of this anthology.

Regeneration, to have the characteristics ascribed to it in the Bible, must consist in a change in the attitude of the will, or a change in its ultimate choice, intention, or preference; a change from selfishness to benevolence; from choosing self-gratification as the supreme and ultimate end of life to the supreme and ultimate choice of the highest well-being of God and of the universe; from a state of entire consecration to self-interest, self-indulgence [and] self-gratification for its own sake or as an end, and as the supreme end of life to a state of entire consecration to God and to the interests of his kingdom as the supreme and ultimate end of life. . . .

In regeneration the subject is both passive and active. . . . The spirit acts upon him through or by the truth. Thus far he is passive. He closes with the truth. Thus far he is active. What a mistake those theologians have fallen into who represent the sinner as altogether passive in regeneration! This rids the sinner at once of the conviction of any duty or responsibility about it. It is wonderful that such an absurdity should have been so long maintained in the church. . . . Why, while the sinner believes this, it is impossible if he has it in mind that he should be regenerated. He stands and waits for God to do what God requires him to do, and which no one can do for him. Neither God nor any other being can regenerate him if he will not turn. If he will not change his choice, it is impossible that it should be changed. . . .

The nature of the change shows that it must be *instantaneous.* . . . It implies an entire present change of moral character, that is, a change from entire sinfulness to entire holiness. . . . The Bible represents regeneration as a dying to sin and becoming alive to God. Death *in* sin is total depravity. This is generally admitted. Death *to* sin and becoming alive to God must imply entire present holiness.

The scriptures represent regeneration as the condition of salvation in a sense that if the subject should die immediately after regeneration and without any further change, he would immediately go to heaven.

Again: the scripture requires only perseverance in the first love as the condition of salvation, in case the regenerate soul should live long in the world subsequent to regeneration. . . .

Oh, how much all classes of persons need to have clearly defined ideas of what really constitutes sin and holiness. A false philosophy of the mind, and especially of the will and of moral depravity, has covered the world with gross darkness on the subject of sin and holiness, of regeneration, and of the evidences of regeneration, until the true saints on the one hand are kept in a continual bondage to their false notions, and on the other the church swarms with unconverted professors, and is cursed with many deceived ministers.

To the rights and duties of government in relation to mobs, riots, etc. It is plain that the right and duty to govern for the security and promotion of the public interests implies the right and duty to use any means necessary to this result. It is absurd to say that the ruler has the right to govern, and yet that he has not a right to use the necessary means. Some have taken the ground of the inviolability of human life, and have insisted that to take life is wrong *per se*, and of course that governments are to be sustained without taking life. Others have gone so far as to assert that governments have no right to resort to physical force to sustain the authority of law. But this is a most absurd philosophy, and amounts to just this: the ruler has a right to govern while the subject is pleased to obey; but if the subject refuse obedience, why then the right to govern ceases, for it is impossible that the right to govern should exist when the right to enforce obedience does not exist. This philosophy is in fact a denial of the right to use the necessary means for the promotion of the great end for which all moral agents are bound to live. And yet strange to tell, this philosophy professes to deny the right to use force and to take life in support of government on the ground of benevolence, that is, that benevolence forbids it. What is this but maintaining that the law of benevolence demands that we should love others too much to use the indispensable means to secure their good? Or that we should love the whole too much to execute the law upon those who would destroy all good? Shame on such a philosophy. It overlooks the foundation of moral obligation and of all morality and religion. Just as if an enlightened benevolence could forbid the due, wholesome and necessary execution of law. This philosophy impertinently urges the commandment, "Thou shalt not kill," as prohibiting all taking of human life. But it may be asked, why say *human* life. The commandment, so far as the letter is concerned, as fully prohibits the killing of animals or vegetables as it does of men. The question is what kind of killing does this commandment prohibit? Certainly not all killing of human beings, for in the next chapter we are commanded to kill human beings for certain crimes. The ten commandments are precepts, and the lawgiver, after laying down the precepts, goes on to specify the penalties that are to be inflicted by men for a violation of these precepts. Some of these penalties are death, and the penalty for the violation of the precept under consideration is death. It is certain that this precept was not intended to prohibit the taking of life for murder. A consideration of the law in its tenor and spirit renders it most evident that the precept in question prohibits murder, and the penalty of death is added by the lawgiver to the violation of this precept. Now how absurd and impertinent it is to quote this precept in prohibition of taking life under all circumstances!

Men have an undoubted right to do whatever is plainly indispensable to the highest good of man, and therefore nothing can by any possibility be law that should prohibit the taking of human life when it became indispensable to the great end of government. This right is every where recognized in the Bible, and if it were not, still the right would exist. . . .

It will be seen that the same principles are equally applicable to insurrections, rebellion, etc. While government is right, it is duty, and while it is right and duty because necessary as a means to the great end upon which benevolence terminates, it must be both the right and the duty of government, and of all the subjects, to use any indispensable means for the suppression of insurrections, rebellion, etc., as also for the due administration of justice in the execution of law.

These principles will guide us in ascertaining the rights, and of course the duty of governments in relation to war.

War is one of the most heinous and horrible forms of sin unless it be evidently demanded by and prosecuted in obedience to the moral law. Observe, war to be in any case a virtue or to be less than a crime of infinite magnitude, must not only be honestly believed by those who engage in it, to be demanded by the law of benevolence, but it must also be engaged in by them with an eye single to the glory of God and the highest good of being. That war has been in some instances demanded by the spirit of the moral law there can be no reasonable doubt, since God has sometimes commanded them, which he could not have done had they not been demanded by the highest good of the universe. In those cases, if those who were commanded to engage in them had benevolent intentions in prosecuting them as God had in commanding them, it is absurd to say that they sinned. Rulers are represented as God's ministers to execute wrath upon the guilty. If in the Providence of God He should find it duty to destroy or to rebuke a nation for his own glory and the highest good of being, he may, beyond question, command that they should be chastised by the hand of man. But in no case is war any thing else than a most horrible crime unless it is plainly the will of God that it should exist, and unless it be actually engaged in in obedience to his will. This is true of all, both of rulers and of subjects who engage in war. Selfish war is wholesale murder. For a nation to declare war or for persons to enlist or in any way to designedly aid or abet in the declaration or prosecution of war upon any other conditions than those just specified involves the guilt of murder.

There can scarcely be conceived a more abominable and fiendish maxim than "our country right or wrong." Recently this maxim seems to have been adopted and avowed in relation to the present war of the United States with Mexico.

It seems to be supposed by some that it is the duty of good subjects to sympathize with and support government in the prosecution of a war in which they have unjustly engaged, and to which they have committed themselves, upon the ground that since it is commenced it must be prosecuted as the less of two evils. The same class of men seem to have adopted the same philosophy in respect to slavery. Slavery, as it exists in this country, they acknowledge to be indefensible on the ground of right; that it is a great evil and a great sin, but it must be let alone as the less of two evils. It exists, say they, and it can not be abolished without disturbing the friendly relations and federal union of the states, therefore the institution must be sustained. The philosophy is this: war and slavery as they exist in this nation are unjust, but they exist, and to sustain them is duty, because their existence, under the circumstances, is the less of two evils. To this I answer:

1. That of moral evils or sins we can not know which is the least, that is, which involves the least or the greatest guilt.

2. I would ask, do these philosophers intend to admit that the prosecution of a war unjustly waged is sin, and that the support of slavery in this country is sin, but that the sin of supporting them is less than would be the sin of abandoning them under the circumstances? If they mean this, to be sure this were singular logic. To repent of a sin and forsake it were a greater sin than to persist in it! . . . To repent and forsake all sin is always right, always duty and can in no case be sin. If war has been unjustly waged, if slavery or any thing else exists that involves injustice and oppression or sin in any

form, it cannot be sin to abandon it. To abhor and reject it at once must be duty, and to persevere in it is only to add insult to injury.

Nothing can sanctify any crime but that which renders it no crime, but a virtue. But the philosophers whose views I am examining, must if consistent, take the ground that since war and slavery exist, although their commencement was unjust and sinful, yet since they exist, it is no crime but a virtue to sustain them as the least of two *natural* evils. But I would ask to whom are they the least of two evils? To ourselves or to being in general? The least of two present, or of two ultimate evils? Our duty is not to calculate the evils in respect merely to ourselves or to this nation and those immediately oppressed and injured, but to look abroad upon the world and the universe, and inquire what are the evils resulting and likely to result to the world, to the church, and to the universe from the declaration and prosecution of such a war, and from the support of slavery by a nation professing what we profess; a nation boasting of liberty; who have drawn the sword and bathed it in blood in defence of the principle that all men have an inalienable right to liberty; that they are born free and equal. Such a nation proclaiming such a principle and fighting in the defence of it, standing with its proud foot on the neck of three millions of crushed and prostrate slaves! O horrible! This a less evil to the world than emancipation or even than the dismemberment of our hypocritical union! "O shame, where is thy blush!" The prosecution of a war unjustly engaged in a less evil than repentance and restitution! It is impossible. Honesty is always and necessarily the best policy. Nations are bound by the same law as individuals. If they have done wrong it is always duty and honorable for them to repent, confess, and make restitution. To adopt the maxim, "Our country right or wrong," and to sympathise with the government in the prosecution of a war unrighteously waged must involve the guilt of murder. To adopt the maxim, "Our union even with perpetual slavery," is an abomination so execrable as not to be named by a just mind without indignation. . . .

5. The same principles apply to slavery. No human constitution or enactment can, by any possibility, be *law* that recognizes the right of one human being to enslave another in a sense that implies selfishness on the part of the slaveholder. Selfishness is wrong *per se*. It is therefore always and unalterably wrong. No enactment, human or Divine, can *legalize* selfishness and make it right, under any conceivable circumstances. . . . God can not authorize it. The Bible can not sanction it, and if both God and the Bible were to sanction it, it could not be *lawful*. God's arbitrary will is not law. The moral law,

as we have seen, is as independent of his will as his own necessary existence is. He can not alter or repeal it. He could not sanctify selfishness and make it right. Nor can any book be received as of Divine authority that sanctions selfishness. God and the Bible quoted to sustain and sanctify slaveholding in a sense implying selfishness! 'Tis blasphemous! That slaveholding, as it exists in this country, implies selfishness at least, in almost all instances, is too plain to need proof. The sinfulness of slaveholding and war, in almost all cases, and in every case where the terms slaveholding and war are used in their popular signification, will appear irresistible, if we consider that sin is selfishness, and that all selfishness is necessarily sinful. Deprive a human being of liberty who has been guilty of no crime! Rob him of himself—his body—his soul—his time and his earnings to promote the interest of his master, and attempt to justify this on the principles of moral law! It is the greatest absurdity, and the most revolting wickedness.

Part Two

RATIONALISTS

1

THE ARGUMENT AGAINST WAR

Noah Worcester
SOLEMN REVIEW OF THE CUSTOM OF WAR

The idea that human suffering can be prevented through an act of will is more a product of the European Enlightenment than of the Christian tradition. In the early nineteenth century, some Americans began to push this idea very strongly in a number of directions. Though usually intertwined with some version of religious belief, the style of the argument betrayed its heavy debt to the Age of Reason. Thus it might seem important that Noah Worcester (1758–1837) had been a Congregational minister in New Hampshire and Massachusetts. But he was converted to Unitarianism, and the grounds of his lucid exposition are quite independent of the conventional Christian heritage. The meaning of barbarity, as contrasted with civilization, he takes for granted in a frame of reference that really demands no theological assumptions. For this reason, his words may well seem as powerful now as when first written. Their early date also reminds us that the upsurge of radical reform activity after 1830 did not spring fullblown from nothing.

We regard with horror the custom of the ancient heathens in offering their children in sacrifice to idols. We are shocked with the customs of the Hindus, in prostrating themselves before the car of an idol to be crushed to death; in burning women alive on the funeral piles of their husbands; in offering a monthly sacrifice, by casting living children into the Ganges to be drowned. We read with astonishment of the sacrifices made in the papal crusades, and in the Mahometan and Hindu pilgrimages. We wonder at the blindness of Christian nations, who have esteemed it right and honorable to buy and sell Africans as property, and reduce them to bondage for life. But that which is

SOURCE. Philo Pacificus [Noah Worcester], *A Solemn Review of the Custom of War* (Cambridge, Mass.: Hilliard and Metcalf, 1816), pp. 3–7, 11, 15, 17, 20, 24–25, 28–29, 31; first published 1814.

fashionable and popular in a country is esteemed right and honorable, whatever may be its nature in the views of men better informed.

But while we look back with a mixture of wonder, indignation and pity on many of the customs of former ages, are we careful to inquire whether some customs, which we deem honorable, are not the effect of popular delusion? and whether they will not be so regarded by future generations? Is it not a fact that one of the most horrid customs of savage men is now popular in every nation in Christendom? What custom of the most barbarous nations is more repugnant to the feelings of piety, humanity and justice, than that of deciding controversies between nations by the edge of the sword, by powder and ball, or the point of the bayonet? What other savage custom has occasioned half the desolation and misery to the human race? And what but the grossest infatuation could render such a custom popular among rational beings?

When we consider how great a part of mankind have perished by the hands of each other, and how large a portion of human calamity has resulted from war; it surely cannot appear indifferent, whether this custom is or is not the effect of delusion. Certainly there is no custom which deserves a more thorough examination, than that which has occasioned more slaughter and misery, than all the other abominable customs of the heathen world.

War has been so long fashionable among all nations that its enormity is but little regarded; or when thought of at all, it is usually considered as an evil necessary and unavoidable. Perhaps it is really so in the present state of society, and the present views of mankind. But the question to be considered is this; cannot the state of society and the views of civilized men be so changed as to abolish a barbarous custom, and render wars unnecessary and avoidable?

If this question may be answered in the affirmative, then we may hope "the sword will not devour forever."

Some may be ready to exclaim, none but God can produce such an effect as the abolition of war; and we must wait for the millennial day. We admit that God only can produce the necessary change in the state of society, and the views of men; but God works by human agency and human means. God only could have overthrown the empire of Napoleon; but this he did by granting success to the efforts of the allied powers. He only could have produced such a change in the views of the British nation, as to abolish the slave trade; yet the event was brought about by a long course of persevering and honorable exertions of benevolent men. . . .

As to waiting for the millennium to put an end to war, without any exertions on our own part; this is like the sinner's waiting God's time for conversion, while he pursues his course of vice and impiety. If ever there shall be a millennium in which the sword will cease to devour, it will probably be effected by the blessing of God on the benevolent exertions of enlightened men. Perhaps no one thing is now a greater obstacle in the way of the wished for state of the church, than the *spirit* and *custom* of war, which is maintained by Christians themselves. Is it not then time that efforts should be made to enlighten the minds of Christians on a subject of such infinite importance to the happiness of the human race?

It is not the present object to prove that a nation may not defend their lives, their liberties and their property against an invading foe; but to inquire whether it is not possible to effect such a change in the views of men, that there shall be no occasion for *defensive* war. . . .

The whole amount of property in the United States is probably of far less value than what has been expended and destroyed within two centuries by wars in Christendom. Suppose, then, that one-fifth of this amount had been judiciously laid out by peace associations in the different states and nations, in cultivating the spirit and art of peace, and in exciting a just abhorrence of war; would not the other four-fifths have been in a great measure saved, besides many millions of lives, and an immense portion of misery? Had the whole value of what has been expended in wars been appropriated to the purpose of peace, how laudable would have been the appropriation, and how blessed the consequences!

That it is possible to produce such a state of society, as to exclude national wars, may appear probable from the following facts.

1. It is impossible for the rulers of any one nation to do much in carrying on a war with another, without the aid of subjects, or the common people.

2. A war between two nations is generally produced by the influence of a small number of ambitious and unprincipled individuals; while the greater part of the nation has no hand in the business until war is proclaimed.

3. A vast majority of every civilized nation have an aversion to war; such an aversion that it requires much effort and management, to work up their passions so far, that they are willing personally to engage in such hazardous and bloody conflicts. The more any people are civilized and christianized, the greater is their aversion to war; and the more powerful exertions are necessary to excite what is called the *war spirit*. Were it not for the influence of a few ambitious or revengeful men, an offensive war could not be undertaken with any

prospect of success, except when the mass of the people are either uncivilized, or slaves. If then, as great exertions should be made to excite a just abhorrence of war, as have often been made to excite a war spirit, we may be very certain that rulers would find little encouragement to engage in any war, which is not strictly defensive. And as soon as offensive wars shall cease, defensive wars will of course be unknown.

4. It is an affront to common sense to pretend that military officers and soldiers have no right to inquire whether a war be just or unjust; and that all they have to do is to obey the orders of government. Such a doctrine is fit to be taught only to slaves without souls. If a man is called to fight, he should be faithfully informed, and fully satisfied, that he is not to act the part of a murderer, that the blood of men may not be required at his hands. Every soldier ought to be impressed with the idea that offensive war is murderous, and that no government on earth has any right to compel him to shed blood in a wanton and aggressive war. Yet in the present state of general delusion, the soldiers and most of the citizens are treated as having no more right to judge of the justice or the injustice of a war than the horses employed in military service. . . .

5. National wars often originate from such petty offences, as would not justify the taking of a single life, and from false principles of honor, which every Christian should abhor. What can be more perfect delusion than to suppose the *honor* of a nation requires a declaration of war, for such offences as would not justify one individual in taking the life of another? Or what can be more absurd than to suppose the honor of a nation requires going to war, while there is not even the prospect of advantage? Is such petulance, as would disgrace a common citizen, or such a revengeful spirit, as would disgrace a savage, becoming the dignity of a national government, or the ruler of a christian people?

To sacrifice human beings to false notions of national honor, or to the ambition or avarice of rulers, is no better than to offer them to Moloch, or any other heathen deity. As soon as the eyes of people can be opened to see that war is the effect of delusion, it will then become as unpopular as any other heathenish mode of offering human sacrifices. . . .

But if the eyes of people could be opened in regard to the evils and delusions of war, would it not be easy to form a confederacy of nations, and organize a high court of equity, to decide national controversies? Why might not such a court be composed of some of the most eminent characters from each nation; and a compliance with the decision of the court be made a point of national honor, to prevent the effusion of blood, and to preserve the blessings of peace? Can any considerate person say, that the probability of obtaining right in such a court, would be *less* than by an appeal to arms? . . .

Among the evil effects of war, a wanton undervaluing of human life ought to be mentioned. This effect may appear in various forms. When a war is declared for the redress of some wrong, in regard to property, if nothing but property be taken into consideration, the result is not commonly better than spending five hundred dollars in a law suit to recover a debt of ten. But when we come to estimate human lives against dollars and cents, how are we confounded! "All that a man hath will he give for his life." Yet by the custom of war men are so deluded that a ruler may give fifty or a hundred thousand lives, when only a trifling amount of property is in question, and when the probabilities are as ten to one against him that even that small amount will not be secured by the contest. It must however again be remarked that war makers do not usually give their *own lives*, but the *lives of others*. How often has a war been declared with the prospect that not less than 50,000 lives must be sacrificed; and while the chief agent in making the war would not have given his own life to secure to his nation every thing that he claimed from the other? And are rulers to be upheld in thus gambling away the lives of others, while they are careful to secure their own? If people in general could obtain just views of this species of gambling, rulers would not make offensive wars with impunity. How little do they consider the misery and wretchedness which they bring on those, for whom they should exercise the kindness and care of a father! Does it not appear that they regard the lives of soldiers as mere property, which they may sacrifice, or barter away at pleasure? War is in truth the most dreadful species of gambling. Rulers are the gamblers. The lives and property of their subjects are the things they put to hazard in the game; and he that is most successful in doing mischief, is considered as the best gamester. . . .

Perhaps some apologist may rise up . . . and plead, that it appears from the history of our times, that it was supposed necessary to the safety of a nation, that its government should be quick to assume a warlike tone and attitude, upon every infringement of their rights; that magnanimous forbearance was considered as pusillanimity, and that Christian meekness was thought intolerable in the character of a ruler.

To this others may reply: Could these professed christians imagine, that their safety depended on displaying a spirit the reverse of their

Master's? . . . Did they not know that wars were of a demoralizing tendency, and that the greatest danger of a nation resulted from its corruption and depravity? Did they not also know, that a haughty spirit of resentment in one government was very sure to provoke a similar spirit in another? that one war usually paved the way for a repetition of similar calamities, by depraving each of the contending parties, and by fixing enmities and jealousies, which would be ready to break forth on the most frivolous occasions? . . .

It is an awful feature in the character of war, and a strong reason why it should not be countenanced, that it involves the innocent with the guilty in the calamities it inflicts; and often falls with the greatest vengeance on those, who have had no concern in the management of national affairs. It surely is not a crime to be born in a country, which is afterwards invaded; yet in how many instances do war makers punish or destroy, for no other crime than being a native or resident of an invaded territory. . . .

As there is an aversion to war in the breast of a large majority of people in every civilized community; and as its evils have been recently felt in every Christian nation; is there not ground to hope, that it would be as easy to excite a disposition for peace, as a disposition for war? If then, peace societies should be formed, . . . is it not very certain, that the most beneficial effects would result? Would they not gradually produce an important change in the views and state of society, and give a new character to Christian nations? What institution or project would more naturally unite all pious and virtuous men? And on what efforts could we more reasonably hope for the blessing of the God of peace? . . .

If men must have objects for the display of heroism, let their intrepidity be shown in firmly meeting the formidable prejudices of a world in favor of war. . . .

That there is nothing in the nature of mankind, which renders war necessary and unavoidable—nothing which inclines them to it, which may not be overcome by the power of education, may appear from what is discoverable in the two sects already [devoted to peace]. The Quakers and Shakers are of the same nature with other people, "men of like passions" with those who uphold the custom of war. All the difference between them and others results from education and habit. The principles of their teachers are diffused through their societies, impressed on the minds of old and young; and an aversion to war and violence is excited, which becomes habitual, and has a governing influence on their hearts, their passions and their lives.

If then it has been proved to be *possible*, by the force of education, to produce such an aversion to war, that people will not even *defend* their own lives by acts of violence; shall it be thought impossible by similar means to destroy the popularity of *offensive* war, and exclude the deadly custom from the abodes of men?

It will perhaps be pleaded, that mankind are not yet sufficiently enlightened, to apply the principles of the gospel for the abolition of war; and that we must wait for a more improved state of society. *Improved in what?* in the science of blood? Are such improvements to prepare the way for peace? Why not wait a few centuries, until the natives of India become more improved in their idolatrous customs, before we attempt to convert them to Christianity? Do we expect that by continuing in the practice of idolatry, their minds will be prepared to receive the gospel? If not, let us be consistent, and while we use means for the conversion of heathens, let means also be used for the conversion of Christians. For war is in fact a heathenish and savage custom, of the most malignant, most desolating, and most horrible character. It is the greatest curse, and results from the grossest delusions that ever afflicted a guilty world.

2

THE ARGUMENT AGAINST INHUMANE
TREATMENT OF THE UNFORTUNATE

Dorothea L. Dix
MEMORIAL TO THE LEGISLATURE
OF MASSACHUSETTS

The father of Dorothea L. Dix (1802–1877) was a religious fanatic who made her early childhood so unhappy as possibly to give her a lifelong interest in the prevention of unnecessary suffering. While mistress at a private school in Boston and an admirer of the Unitarian William Ellery Channing, she became interested in what was then known as charity. A comfortable legacy enabled her to develop this interest without hindrance. In 1841 she was asked to teach a Sunday school class in the women's department of the House of Correction in East Cambridge. Horrified by the conditions she found, she began to campaign publicly to change them. Her report to the Massachusetts legislature, excerpted below, followed a two-year secret investigation of all the jails and almshouses of the state. It is important to recognize the place of her style of down-to-earth eyewitness inquiry in the social ferment of the period. Not everyone who carried the banner of reform was a writer of high-flown constitutions or a creator of impeccable utopian communities. A few, like her, anticipated the empirical approach to social realities and the direct appeal to existing structures of power that gained renewed headway during major seasons of humanitarian awareness in the twentieth century. Yet what could be more "perfectionist" than her belief in the power of a changed environment to transform the minds even of the insane? Regeneration was open to all.

This particular plea was uttered on the eve of a nationwide crusade that was to last a decade and take her thirty thousand miles to inspect and denounce countless jails and hospitals. Her proposal for a federal system of hospitals, pragmatic in its acceptance of the need to work within the framework of established authority, won the approval of Congress but ran afoul of the states' rights scruples of President Franklin Pierce, who vetoed the

SOURCE. Dorothea L. Dix, *Memorial to the Legislature of Massachusetts, 1843* Old South Leaflets, VI, No. 148 (Boston: Old South Meeting House, n.d.) pp. 489–491, 493–495, 504, 505, 506–508, 511, 512–513.

measure. Temporarily crushed, she rebounded to labor tirelessly for the wounded during the Civil War.

Gentlemen—I respectfully ask to present this memorial, believing that the *cause,* which actuates to and sanctions so unusual a movement, presents no equivocal claim to public consideration and sympathy. Surrendering to calm and deep convictions of duty my habitual views of what is womanly and becoming; I proceed briefly to explain what has conducted me before you unsolicited and unsustained, trusting, while I do so, that the memorialist will be speedily forgotten in the memorial.

About two years since leisure afforded opportunity and duty prompted me to visit several prisons and almshouses in the vicinity of this metropolis. I found, near Boston, in the jails and asylums for the poor, a numerous class brought into unsuitable connection with criminals and the general mass of paupers. I refer to idiots and insane persons, dwelling in circumstances not only adverse to their own physical and moral improvement, but productive of extreme disadvantages to all other persons brought into association with them. I applied myself diligently to trace the causes of these evils, and sought to supply remedies. As one obstacle was surmounted, fresh difficulties appeared. Every new investigation has given depth to the conviction that it is only by decided, prompt, and vigorous legislation the evils to which I refer, and which I shall proceed more fully to illustrate, can be remedied. I shall be obliged to speak with great plainness, and to reveal many things revolting to the taste, and from which my woman's nature shrinks with peculiar sensitiveness. But truth is the highest consideration. *I tell what I have seen*—painful and shocking as the details often are—that from them you may feel more deeply the imperative obligation which lies upon you to prevent the possibility of a repetition or continuance of such outrages upon humanity. If I inflict pain upon you, and move you to horror, it is to acquaint you with sufferings which you have the power to alleviate, and make you hasten to the relief of the victims of legalized barbarity.

I come to present the strong claims of suffering humanity. I come to place before the legislature of Massachusetts the condition of the miserable, the desolate, the outcast. I come as the advocate of helpless, forgotten, insane, and idiotic men and women; of beings sunk to a condition from which the most unconcerned would start with real horror; of beings wretched in our prisons, and more wretched in our almshouses. And I cannot suppose it needful to employ earnest persuasion, or stubborn argument, in order to arrest and fix attention upon a subject only the more strongly pressing in its claims because it is revolting and disgusting in its details. . . .

I proceed, gentlemen, briefly to call your attention to the *present* state of insane persons confined within this commonwealth, in *cages, closets, cellars, stalls, pens! Chained, naked, beaten with rods,* and *lashed* into obedience.

As I state cold, severe *facts,* I feel obliged to refer to persons, and definitely to indicate localities. But it is upon my subject, not upon localities or individuals, I desire to fix attention; and I would speak as kindly as possible of all wardens, keepers, and other responsible officers, believing that *most* of these have erred not through hardness of heart and willful cruelty so much as want of skill and knowledge, and want of consideration. Familiarity with suffering, it is said, blunts the sensibilities, and where neglect once finds a footing other injuries are multiplied. This is not all, for it may justly and strongly be added that, from the deficiency of adequate means to meet the wants of these cases, it has been an absolute impossibility to do justice in this matter. Prisons are not constructed in view of being converted into county hospitals, and almshouses are not founded as receptacles for the insane. And yet, in the face of justice and common sense, wardens are by law compelled to receive, and the masters of almshouses not to refuse, insane and idiotic subjects in all stages of mental disease and privation.

It is the commonwealth, not its integral parts, that is accountable for most of the abuses which have lately and do still exist. I repeat it, it is defective legislation which perpetuates and multiplies these abuses. In illustration of my subject, I offer the following extracts from my notebook and journal:[1]

Danvers. November. Visited the almshouse. A large building, much out of repair. Understand a new one is in contemplation. Here are from fifty-six to sixty inmates, one idiotic, three insane; one of the latter in close confinement at all times.

Long before reaching the house, wild shouts, snatches of rude songs, imprecations and obscene language, fell upon the ear, proceeding from the occupant of a low building, rather remote from the principal building to which my course was directed. Found the mistress, and was conducted to the place which was called *"the home"* of the *forlorn* maniac, a young woman, exhibiting a condition of neglect and misery blotting out the faintest idea of comfort, and outraging every

---

[1]Her original address contained several dozen authenticated instances, of which only a few of the most vivid have been retained here. Ed.

sentiment of decency. She had been, I learnt, "a respectable person, industrious and worthy. Disappointments and trials shook her mind, and, finally, laid prostrate reason and self-control. She became a maniac for life. She had been at Worcester Hospital for a considerable time, and had been returned as incurable." The mistress told me she understood that, "while there, she was comfortable and decent." Alas, what a change was here exhibited! She had passed from one degree of violence to another, in swift progress. There she stood, clinging to or beating upon the bars of her caged apartment, the contracted size of which afforded space only for increasing accumulations of filth, a *foul* spectacle. There she stood with naked arms and dishevelled hair, the unwashed frame invested with fragments of unclean garments, the air so extremely offensive, though ventilation was afforded on all sides save one, that it was not possible to remain beyond a few moments without retreating for recovery to the outward air. Irritation of body, produced by utter filth and exposure, incited her to the horrid process of tearing off her skin by inches. Her face, neck, and person were thus disfigured to hideousness. She held up a fragment just rent off. To my exclamation of horror, the mistress replied: "Oh, we can't help it. Half the skin is off sometimes. We can do nothing with her; and it makes no difference what she eats, for she consumes her own filth as readily as the food which is brought her."

It is now January. A fortnight since two visitors reported that most wretched outcast as "wallowing in dirty straw, in a place yet more dirty, and without clothing, without fire. Worse cared for than the brutes, and wholly lost to consciousness of decency." . . . These gross exposures are not for the pained sight of one alone. All, all, coarse, brutal men, wondering, neglected children, old and young, each and all, witness this lowest, foulest state of miserable humanity. . . .

Some may say these things cannot be remedied, these furious maniacs are not to be raised from these base conditions. I *know* they are. Could give *many* examples. Let *one* suffice. A young woman, a pauper, in a distant town, Sandisfield, was for years a raging maniac. A cage, chains, and *the whip* were the agents for controlling her, united with harsh tones and profane language. Annually, with others (the town's poor), she was put up at auction, and bid off at the lowest price which was declared for her. One year, not long past, an old man came forward in the number of applicants for the poor wretch. He was taunted and ridiculed. "What would he and his old wife do with such a mere beast?" "My wife says yes," replied he, "and I shall take her." She was given to his charge. He conveyed her home. She was washed, neatly dressed, and placed in a decent bedroom, furnished for comfort and opening into the kitchen. How altered her condition! As yet *the chains* were not off. The first week she was somewhat restless, at times violent, but the quiet, kind ways of the old people wrought a change. She received her food decently, forsook acts of violence, and no longer uttered blasphemies or indecent language. After a week the chain was lengthened, and she was received as a companion into the kitchen. Soon she engaged in trivial employments. "After a fortnight," said the old man, "I knocked off the chains and made her a free woman." She is at times excited, but not violently. They are careful of her diet. They keep her very clean. She calls them "father" and "mother." Go there now, and you will find her "clothed," and, though not perfectly in her "right mind," so far restored as to be a safe and comfortable inmate.

Newburyport. Visited the almshouse in June last. Eighty inmates. Seven insane, one idiotic. Commodious and neat house. Several of the partially insane apparently very comfortable. Two very improperly situated; namely, an insane man, not considered incurable, in an out-building, whose room opened upon what was called "the dead room," affording, in lieu of companionship with the living, a contemplation of corpses. The other subject was a woman in a *cellar.* I desired to see her. Much reluctance was shown. I pressed the request. The master of the house stated that she was *in the cellar;* that she was *dangerous to be approached;* that she had lately attacked his wife, and *was often naked.* I persisted, "If you will not go with me, give me the keys and I will go alone." Thus importuned, the outer doors were opened. I descended the stairs from within. A strange, unnatural noise seemed to proceed from beneath our feet. At the moment I did not much regard it. My conductor proceeded to remove a padlock, while my eye explored the wide space in quest of the poor woman. All for a moment was still. But judge my horror and amazement, when a door to a closet *beneath* the *staircase* was opened, revealing in the imperfect light a female apparently wasted to a skeleton, partially wrapped in blankets, furnished for the narrow bed on which she was sitting. Her countenance furrowed, not by age, but suffering, was the image of distress. In that contracted space, unlighted, unventilated, she poured forth the wailings of despair. Mournfully she extended her arms and appealed to me: "Why am I consigned to hell? dark—dark—I used to pray, I used to read the Bible—I have done no crime in my heart. I had friends. Why have all forsaken me!—my God, my God, why hast *thou* forsaken me!" Those groans, those wailings, come up daily, mingling with how many others, a perpetual and sad memorial.

When the good Lord shall require an account of our stewardship, what shall all and each answer?

Perhaps it will be inquired how long, how many days or hours, was she imprisoned in these confined limits? *For years!* . . .

Groton. A few rods removed from the poorhouse is a wooden building upon the roadside, constructed of heavy board and plank. It contains one room, unfurnished, except so far as a bundle of straw constitutes furnishing. There is no window, save an opening half the size of a sash, and closed by a board shutter. In one corner is some brick-work surrounding an iron stove, which in cold weather serves for warming the room. The occupant of this dreary abode is a young man, who has been declared incurably insane. He can move a measured distance in his prison; that is, so far as a strong, heavy chain, depending from an *iron collar which invests his neck* permits. In fine weather—and it was pleasant when I was there in June last—the door is thrown open, at once giving admission to light and air, and affording some little variety to the solitary in watching the passers-by. But that portion of the year which allows of open doors is not the chiefest part; and it may be conceived, without drafting much on the imagination, what is the condition of one who for days and weeks and months sits in darkness and alone, without employment, without object. It may be supposed that paroxysms of frenzy are often exhibited, and that the tranquil state is rare in comparison with that which incites to violence. This, I was told, is the fact. . . .

I have been asked if I have investigated the causes of insanity. I have not; but I have been told that this most calamitous overthrow of reason often is the result of a life of sin: it is sometimes, but rarely, added, they must take the consequences; they deserve no better care. Shall man be more just than God, he who causes his sun and refreshing rains and life-giving influence to fall alike on the good and the evil? Is not the total wreck of reason, a state of distraction, and the loss of all that makes life cherished a retribution sufficiently heavy, without adding to consequences so appalling every indignity that can bring still lower the wretched sufferer? Have pity upon those who, while they were supposed to lie hid in secret sins, "have been scattered under a *dark veil of forgetfulness,* over whom is spread a heavy night, and who unto themselves are more grievous than the darkness." . . .

Bolton. Late in December, 1842; thermometer 4° above zero; visited the almshouse; neat and comfortable establishment; two insane women, one in the house associated with the family, the other *"out of doors."* . . . I asked to see the subject who was "out of doors"; and, following the mistress of the house through the deep snow, shuddering and benumbed by the piercing cold, several hundred yards, we came in rear of the barn to a small building, which might have afforded a degree of comfortable shelter, but it did not. About two-thirds of the interior was filled with wood and peat. The other third was divided into two parts; one about six feet square contained a cylinder stove, in which was no fire, the rusty pipe seeming to threaten, in its decay, either suffocation by smoke, which by and by we nearly realized, or conflagration of the building, together with destruction of its poor crazy inmate. My companion uttered an exclamation at finding no fire, and busied herself to light one; while I explored, as the deficient light permitted, the cage which occupied the undescribed portion of the building. "Oh, I'm so cold, so cold," was uttered in plaintive tones by a woman within the cage; "oh, so cold, so cold!" And well might she be cold. The stout, hardy driver of the sleigh had declared 'twas too hard for a man to stand the wind and snow that day, yet here was a woman caged and imprisoned without fire or clothes, not naked, indeed, for one thin cotton garment partly covered her, and part of a blanket was gathered about the shoulders. There she stood, shivering in that dreary place; the gray locks falling in disorder about the face gave a wild expression to the pallid features. Untended and comfortless, she might call aloud, none could hear. She might die, and there be none to close the eye. But death would have been a blessing here. "Well, you shall have a fire, Axey. I've been so busy getting ready for the funeral!" One of the paupers lay dead. "Oh, I want some clothes," rejoined the lunatic; "I'm so cold." "Well, Axey, you shall have some as soon as the children come from school; I've had so much to do." "I want to go out, do let me out!" "Yes, as soon as I get time," answered the respondent. "Why do you keep her here?" I asked. "She appears harmless and quiet." "Well, I mean to take her up to the house pretty soon. The people that used to have care here kept her shut up all the year; but it is cold here, and we take her to the house in hard weather, The only danger is her running away. I've been meaning to this good while." The poor creature listened eagerly: "Oh, I won't run away. Do take me out!" "Well, I will in a few days." . . . Pretty soon I moved to go away. "Stop, did you walk?" "No." "Did you ride?" "Yes." "Do take me with you, do, I'm so cold. Do you know my sisters? They live in this town. I want to see them so much. Do let me go"; and, shivering with eagerness to get out, as with the biting cold, she rapidly tried the bars of the cage.

The mistress seemed a kind person. Her tones and manner to the lunatic were kind; but how difficult to unite all the cares of her household, and neglect none! Here was not willful abuse, but great, very great suffering through undesigned negligence. . . .

Could we in fancy place ourselves in the situation of some of these poor wretches, bereft of reason, deserted of friends, hopeless, troubles without, and more dreary troubles within, overwhelming the wreck of the mind as "a wide breaking in of the waters"—how should we, as the terrible illusion was cast off, not only offer the thank-offering of prayer, that so mighty a destruction had not overwhelmed our mental nature, but as an offering more acceptable devote ourselves to alleviate that state from which we are so mercifully spared? . . .

In Worcester has for several years resided a young woman, a lunatic pauper of decent life and respectable family. I have seen her as she usually appeared, listless and silent, almost or quite sunk into a state of dementia, sitting one amidst the family, "but not of them." A few weeks since, revisiting that almshouse, judge my horror and amazement to see her negligently bearing in her arms a young infant, of which I was told she was the unconscious parent. Who was the father, none could or would declare. Disqualified for the performance of maternal cares and duties, regarding the helpless little creature with a perplexed or indifferent gaze, she sat a silent, but, oh, how eloquent, a pleader for the protection of others of her neglected and outraged sex! Details of that black story would not strengthen the cause. Needs it a mightier plea than the sight of that forlorn creature and her wailing infant? Poor little child, more than orphan from birth, in this unfriendly world! A demented mother, a father on whom the sun might blush or refuse to shine!

Men of Massachusetts, I beg, I implore, I demand pity and protection for these of my suffering, outraged sex. Fathers, husbands, brothers, I would supplicate you for this boon; but what do I say? I dishonor you, divest you at once of Christianity and humanity, does this appeal imply distrust. If it comes burdened with a doubt of your righteousness in this legislation, then blot it out; while I declare confidence in your honor, not less than your humanity. Here you will put away the cold, calculating spirit of selfishness and self-seeking; lay off the armor of local strife and political opposition; here and now, for once, forgetful of the earthly and perishable, come up to these halls and consecrate them with one heart and one mind to works of righteousness and just judgment. Become the benefactors of your race, the just guardians of the solemn rights you hold in trust. Raise up the fallen, succor the desolate, restore the outcast, defend the helpless, and for your eternal and great reward receive the benediction, "Well done, good and faithful servants, become rulers over many things!" . . .

3
THE ARGUMENT AGAINST RACIAL DISCRIMINATION

Charles Sumner
PLAINTIFF'S CASE IN ROBERTS VS. BOSTON

Institutionalized racism came under attack in a few quarters, almost invariably in New England or northern Ohio, during the early nineteenth century. This issue went beyond the immediate evil of slavery; it anticipated the problems of definition facing a multiracial society in which everyone claimed to be legally free. Thus it posed questions still cogent during the debates over school bussing in the 1970s. If all men are equal, then any customary arrangement that separates some men constitutes a grievous social imperfection. Again the argument stems more from the humanistic frame of reference of the Enlightenment than from a specifically Christian conscience. Here we see the appeal for equal treatment being put forward by Charles Sumner (1811–1874), two years before he began representing Massachusetts in the United States Senate. Sumner's keen awareness of this issue, so far in advance of his time, may have been quickened by a private difficulty in adjusting to the realities of life in his own day, as some have suggested. In the later stages of the slavery controversy he showed signs of an emotional self-righteousness lacking in balance. But in this argument before the court, his is the voice of reason, also attempting to be the voice of history. (The opposition case was presented in narrow legalistic terms.) The white schools of Boston had four times refused to admit Benjamin Roberts' daughter. This court suit was lost by Roberts in a unanimous decision that set the precedent for the "separate but equal" doctrine in later decades. But after continued agitation by blacks and interested white reformers, the Massachusetts legislature in 1855 passed a law prohibiting racial or religious distinctions in the admission of public school students. That fall, blacks were admitted to Boston schools without violence. It was an isolated victory; no general trend toward school integration occurred in the north.

SOURCE. *Argument of Charles Sumner, Esq., Against the Constitutionality of Separate Colored Schools, in the Case of Sarah C. Roberts vs. The City of Boston, Before the Supreme Court of Massachusetts, December 4, 1849* (Boston: B.F. Roberts, 1849), pp. 3–7, 9–15, 20, 22, 23–26, 28–30, 32.

May it please your Honors:

Can any discrimination, on account of color or race, be made, under the constitution and laws of Massachusetts, among the children entitled to the benefit of our public schools? This is the question which the Court is now to hear, to consider, and to decide.

Or, stating the question with more detail and with a more particular application to the facts of the present case, are the committee, having the superintendence of the public schools of Boston, entrusted with the *power*, under the constitution and laws of Massachusetts, to exclude colored children from these schools, and to compel them to resort for their education to separate schools, set apart for colored children only, at distances from their homes less convenient than those open to white children?

This important question arises in an action by a colored child, only five years old, who, by her next friend, sues the city of Boston for damages, on account of a refusal to receive her into one of the public schools. . . .

This little child asks at your hands her *personal rights*. So doing, she calls upon you to decide a question which concerns the personal rights of other colored children; which concerns the constitution and laws of the Commonwealth; which concerns that peculiar institution of New England, the common schools; which concerns the fundamental principles of human rights; which concerns the Christian character of this community. Such parties, and such interests, so grand and various, may justly challenge your most earnest attention.

Though this discussion is now for the first time brought before a judicial tribunal, it is no stranger to the public. For five years it has been an occasion of discord to the School Committee. No less than four different reports—two majority reports, and two minority reports, forming pamphlets of solid dimensions—devoted to this question have been made to this committee, and afterwards published. The opinions of learned counsel have been enlisted in the cause. The controversy, leaving these regular channels, has overflowed the newspaper press, and numerous articles have appeared espousing opposite sides. At last it has reached this tribunal. It is in your power to cause it to subside for ever.

Forgetting many of the topics, and all of the heats which have heretofore mingled with the controversy, I shall strive to present the question in its juridical light, as becomes the habits of this tribunal. It is a question of jurisprudence on which you are to give judgment. But I cannot forget that the principles of morals and of natural justice lie at the foundation of all jurisprudence. Nor can any reference to these be inappropriate in a discussion before this Court. . . .

I begin with the principle, that, according to the spirit of American institutions, and especially of the constitution of Massachusetts, *all men, without distinction of color or race, are equal before the law.*

I might, perhaps, leave this proposition without one word of comment. The equality of men will not be directly denied on this occasion, and yet it has been so often assailed of late, that I trust I shall not seem to occupy your time superfluously in endeavoring to show what is understood by this term, when used in laws, or constitutions, or other political instruments. Mr. [John C.] Calhoun, in the Senate of the United States, and Lord Brougham, in his recent work on *Political Philosophy* (Part 2. chap. 4), have characterized equality as impossible and absurd. If they had chosen to comprehend the true extent and application of the term, as employed on such occasions, something, if not all of the force of their objections, would have been removed. That we may better appreciate its character and its limitations, let me develop with some care the origin and growth of this sentiment, until it finally ripened into a formula of civil and political right.

The *sentiment* of equality among men was early cherished by generous souls. It showed itself in the dreams of ancient philosophy. It was declared by Seneca; when writing to a friend a letter of consolation on death, he said, *Prima enim pars Equitatis est Equalitas* (Epist. 30). The first part of equity is equality. But it was enunciated with persuasive force in the truths of the Christian religion. Here we learn that God is no respecter of persons; that he is the father of all; and that we are all his children, and brethren to each other. When the Saviour taught the Lord's prayer, he taught the sublime doctrine of the brotherhood of mankind, enfolding the equality of men.

Slowly did this sentiment enter the *state.* The whole constitution of government in modern times was inconsistent with it. An hereditary monarchy, an order of nobility, and the complex ranks of superiors and inferiors established by the feudal system, all declared, not the equality, but the inequality of men, and they all conspired to perpetuate this inequality. Every infant of royal blood, every noble, every vassal, was a present example, that, whatever might be the truths of religion, or the sentiments of the heart, men living under these institutions were not born equal.

The boldest political reformers of early times did not venture to proclaim this truth; nor did they truly perceive it. Cromwell beheaded his king, but caused the supreme power to be secured in hereditary succession to his eldest son. . . . The Revolution of 1688 . . . brought . . . the establishment, according to the boast of loyal Englishmen, of the freedom of the land. But the Bill of Rights did not declare, nor did the genius of Somers or Maynard conceive the political axiom, that all men are born equal. It may find acceptance in our day from individuals in England, but it is disowned by English institutions.

It is to France that we must pass for the earliest development of this idea, for its amplest illustration, and for its most complete, accurate, and logical expression. In the middle of the last century appeared the renowned *Encyclopedie*, edited by D'Alembert and Diderot. This remarkable production, where science, religion and government were all discussed with a revolutionary freedom, contains an article on equality, which was published in 1755. Here we find the boldest expression which had then been given to this sentiment. "Natural Equality," says the Encyclopedia, "is that which exists between all men by the constitution of their nature only. This equality is the principle and the foundation of liberty. Natural or moral equality is then founded upon the constitution of human nature, common to all men, who are born, grow, subsist, and die in the same manner. Since human nature finds itself the same in all men, it is clear, that according to nature's law, each ought to esteem and treat the others as beings who are naturally equal to himself; that is to say, who are men as well as himself." . . .

At such a period the Encyclopedia did well in uttering such important and effective truth. The *sentiment* of equality was here fully declared. Nor could it be expected at that early day that it should adequately perceive, or if it perceived, that it should dare to utter, our axiom of liberty, that all men are born equal in civil and political rights.

It is thus with the history of all moral and political ideas. First appearing merely as a sentiment, they animate those who receive them with a noble impulse, filling them with generous sympathies, and encouraging them to congenial efforts. Slowly recognized, they finally pass into a formula to be acted upon, to be applied, to be defended in the concerns of life. . . .

The French Revolution was now at hand. This great movement for enfranchisement was the expression of this sentiment. Here it received a distinct and authoritative enunciation. In the constitutions of government which were successively adopted, amidst the throes of bloody struggles, the equality of men was constantly proclaimed. King, nobles, and all distinctions of birth, passed away before this mighty and triumphant truth. . . .

At a later day, after France had passed through an unprecedented series of political vicissitudes, in some of which the rights of equality had been trampled under foot, when, at the revolution of 1830, Louis

Philippe was called to a "throne surrounded by republican institutions," the charter which was then promulgated repeated this phrase. In its first article, it declared, that "Frenchmen are *equal before the law*, whatever may be their titles or ranks."

While recognizing this peculiar enunciation of the equality of men as more specific and satisfactory than the naked statement that all men are born equal, it is impossible not to be reminded that this form of speech finds its prototype in the ancient Greek language. In the history of Herodotus, we are told that "the government of the many has the most beautiful name of *isonomia*"—or *equality before the law* (Book 3, § 80). Thus this remarkable language, by its comprehensiveness and flexibility, in an age when equality before the law was practically unknown, nevertheless supplied a single word, which is not to be found in modern tongues, to express an idea which has been practically recognized only in modern times. Such a word in our own language, as a substitute for equality, might have superseded some of the criticism to which this political doctrine has been exposed.

After this review, the way is now prepared to consider the nature of equality, as secured by the constitution of Massachusetts. The Declaration of Independence, which was put forth after the French Encyclopedia, and the political writings of Rousseau, places among self-evident truths this proposition—"*that all men are created equal*, and that they are endowed by the Creator with certain unalienable rights; that among these are life, liberty, and the pursuit of happiness." The constitution of Massachusetts repeats the same idea in a different form. In the first article it says: "*All men are born free and equal*, and have certain natural, essential and unalienable rights, among which may be reckoned the right of enjoying and defending their lives and liberties." The sixth section further explains the doctrine of equality. It says: "*No man, nor corporation, or association of men, have any other title to obtain advantages, or particular and exclusive privileges, distinct from those of the community, than what arises from the consideration of services rendered to the public;* and this title being in nature neither hereditary, nor transmissible to children, or descendants, or relations by blood, the idea of a man being born a magistrate, law-giver, or judge, is absurd and unnatural." The language here employed, in its natural signification, condemns every form of inequality, in civil and political institutions. . . .

It is a palpable truth that men are not born equal in physical strength, or in mental capacities; in beauty of form or health of body. Diversity or inequality, in these respects, is the law of creation. From this difference springs divine harmony. But this inequality is in no particular inconsistent with a complete civil and political equality.

The equality which was declared by our fathers in 1776, and which was made the fundamental law of Massachusetts, in 1780, was *equality before the law*. Its object was to efface all political or civil distinctions, and to abolish all institutions founded upon *birth*. . . . This is the Great Charter of every person who draws his vital breath upon this soil, whatever may be his condition, and whoever may be his parents. He may be poor, weak, humble, black—he may be of Caucasian, of Jewish, of Indian, or of Ethiopian race—he may be of French, of German, of English, of Irish extraction—but before the constitution of Massachusetts all these distinctions disappear. He is not poor, or weak, or humble, or black—nor Caucasian, nor Jew, nor Indian, nor Ethiopian—nor French, nor German, nor English, nor Irish; he is a man—the equal of all his fellowmen. He is one of the children of the state, which, like an impartial parent, regards all its offspring with an equal care. To some it may justly allot higher duties, according to their higher capacities, but it welcomes all to its equal, hospitable board. The state, imitating the divine justice, is no respecter of persons.

Here nobility cannot exist, because it is a privilege from birth. But the same anathema which smites and banishes nobility, must also smite and banish every form of discrimination founded on birth. . . .

The legislature of Massachusetts, in entire harmony with the constitution, has made no discrimination of color or race, in the establishment of public schools.

The provisions of the law regulating this subject are entitled, *Of the Public Schools* (Revised Statutes, chap. 23). . . . The language here employed does not recognize any discrimination of color or race. Thus in every town, whether there be one or more schools, they are all to be "schools for the instruction of *children*" generally—not children of any particular class, or color, or race, but children—meaning the children of the town where the schools are.

The 5th and 6th sections provide for the establishment, in certain cases, of a school, in which additional studies are to be pursued, "which shall be kept *for the benefit of all the inhabitants* of the town." Here the language not only does not recognize any discrimination among the children, but seems directly to exclude it.

In conformity with these sections is the peculiar phraseology of the memorable law of the Colonies in 1647, founding public schools. . . . This law obliged towns having fifty families "forthwith to appoint one" within their limits "to teach *all such children as shall resort to him*, to write and read" (Ancient charters, 186). . . .

There are a few decisions only of our court bearing on this subject, but they all breathe one spirit. The sentiment of equality animates them. In the case of *Commonwealth* vs. *Davis*, 6 Mass. R. 146, while declaring the equal rights of all the inhabitants, both in the grammar and district schools, the court said: "The schools required by the statute are to be maintained for the benefit of the whole town, *as it is the wise policy of the law to give all the inhabitants equal privileges for the education of their children in the public schools.* Nor is it in the power of the majority to deprive the minority of this *privilege.* * * * * Every inhabitant of the town has a right to participate in the benefits of both descriptions of schools, and it is not competent for a town to establish a grammar school for the benefit of one part of the town to the exclusion of the other, although the money raised for the support of schools may be in other respects fairly apportioned."

In the case of *Withington* vs. *Eveleth*, 7 Pick. 106, the court said, they "were all satisfied that the power given to towns to determine and define the limits of school districts, can be executed only by a geographical division of the town for that purpose." A limitation of the district, which was merely *personal,* was held invalid. This same principle was again recognized in *Perry* vs. *Dove*, 12 Pick. R. 213, where the court said, "Towns, in executing the power to form school districts, are bound so to do it as to include *every inhabitant* in some of the districts. They cannot lawfully omit any, and thus deprive them of *the benefits of our invaluable system of free schools.*" . . .

The exclusion of colored children from the public schools, open to white children, is a source of practical inconvenience to them and their parents, to which white persons are not exposed, and is, therefore, a violation of equality. The black and the white are not equal before the law.

It appears . . . that among the rules of the Primary School Committee, is one to this effect: *"Scholars to go to the school nearest their residence.* Applicants for admission to our schools (with the exception and provision referred to in the preceding rule) are especially entitled to enter the schools nearest to their places of residence." The exception here is "of those for whom special provision has been made" in separate schools; that is, colored children.

In this rule—without the exception—is seen a part of the beauty of our public school system. . . . Education in Boston, through the multitude of schools, is brought to every *white* man's door. But it is not brought to every black man's door. He is obliged to go for it—to travel for it—often a great distance. . . .

The two primary schools open to these [African] children are in Belknap street and in Sun court. . . . The colored parents, anxious that their children should have the benefit of education, are compelled to live in the neighborhood of the schools, to gather about them, as in the East people come from a distance to rest near a fountain or a well. They have not, practically, the same liberty of choosing their homes, which belongs to the white man. Inclination, or business, or economy, may call them to another part of the city; but they are restrained on account of their children. There is no such restraint upon the white man, for he knows that wherever in the city inclination, or business, or economy, may call him, he will find a school open to his children near his door. Surely this is not equality before the law.

Or if a colored person, yielding to the necessities of his position, removes to a distant part of the city, his children may be compelled, at an inconvenience which will not be called trivial, to walk a long distance in order to enjoy the advantages of the school. In our severe winters, this cannot be disregarded by children so tender in years as those of the primary schools. There is a respectable colored person, I am told, who became some time since a resident at East Boston, separated by the water from the main land. There are, of course, proper public schools at East Boston, but none that were then open to colored children. This person, therefore, was obliged to send his children, three in number, daily, across the ferry to the distant African school. The tolls for these children amounted to a sum which formed a severe tax upon a poor man. . . .

It is unquestionably true that there is a distinction between the Ethiopian and Caucasian races. Each has received from the hand of God certain characteristics of color and form. The two may not readily intermingle, although we are told by Homer that Jupiter "did not disdain to grace / The feast of Ethiopia's blameless race." One may be uninteresting or offensive to the other, precisely as different individuals of the same race and color may be uninteresting or offensive to each other. *But this distinction can furnish no ground for any discrimination before the law.*

We abjure nobility of all kinds; but here is a nobility of the skin. We abjure all hereditary distinctions; but here is an hereditary distinction, founded not on the merit of the ancestor, but on his color. We abjure all privileges derived from birth; but here is a privilege which depends solely on the accident, whether an ancestor is black or white. We abjure all inequality before the law; but here is an inequality which touches not an individual, but a race. We revolt at the relation of caste; but here is a caste which is established under a constitution, declaring that all men are born equal. . . .

But it is said that the committee are intrusted with a discretion, in the exercise of their power, and that, in this discretion, they may distribute, assign, and classify all children belonging to the schools of the city, *according to their best judgment,* making, if they think proper, a discrimination of color or race. Without questioning that they are intrusted with a discretion, it is outrageous to suppose that it can go to this extent. The committee can have no discretion which is not in harmony with the constitution and laws. Surely, they cannot, in their mere discretion, nullify a sacred and dear-bought principle of human rights which is expressly guaranteed by the constitution. . . .

It is clear that the committee may classify scholars, according to their age and sex; for the obvious reasons that these distinctions are inoffensive, and especially recognized as *legal* in the law relating to schools (Revised Statutes, chap. 23, § 63). They may also classify scholars according to their moral and intellectual qualifications, because such a power is necessary to the government of schools. But the committee cannot assume, *a priori,* and without individual examination, that an *entire race* possess certain moral or intellectual qualities, which shall render it proper to place them all in a class by themselves. Such an exercise of the discretion with which the committee are intrusted, must be unreasonable, and therefore illegal.

But it is said that the committee, in thus classifying the children, have not violated any principle of equality, inasmuch as they have provided a school with competent instructors for the colored children, where they have equal advantages of instruction with those enjoyed by the white children. . . .

A separate school, though well endowed, would not secure to them that precise equality, which they would enjoy in the general public schools. The Jews in Rome are confined to a particular district, called the Ghetto. In Frankfort they are condemned to a separate quarter, known as the Jewish quarter. It is possible that the accommodations allotted to them are as good as they would be able to occupy, if left free to choose throughout Rome and Frankfort; but this compulsory segregation from the mass of citizens is of itself an *inequality* which we condemn with our whole souls. It is a vestige of ancient intolerance directed against a despised people. It is of the same character with the separate schools in Boston. . . .

In determining that the committee have no *power* to make a discrimination of color or race, we are strengthened by yet another consideration. If the power exists in the present case, it must exist in many others. It cannot be restrained to this alone. The committee may distribute all the children into classes—merely according to their discretion. They may establish a separate school for the Irish or the Germans, where each may nurse an exclusive spirit of nationality alien to our institutions. They may separate Catholics from Protestants, or, pursuing their discretion still further, they may separate Protestants, different sects of Protestants, and establish one school for Unitarians, another for Presbyterians, another for Baptists, and another for Methodists. They may establish a separate school for the rich, that the delicate taste of this favored class may not be offended by the humble garments of the poor. They may exclude the children of mechanics from the public schools, and send them to separate schools by themselves. All this, and much more, can be done by the exercise of the high-handed power which can make a discrimination on account of color or race. The grand fabric of our public schools, the pride of Massachusetts—where, at the feet of the teacher, innocent childhood should meet, unconscious of all distinctions of birth —where the equality of the constitution and of Christianity should be inculcated by constant precept and example—may be converted into a heathen system of proscription and caste. . . .

The whites themselves are injured by the separation. Who can doubt this? With the law as their monitor, they are taught to regard a portion of the human family, children of God, created in his image, co-equals in his love, as a separate and degraded class—they are taught practically to deny that grand revelation of Christianity, the brotherhood of mankind. Their hearts, while yet tender with childhood, are necessarily hardened by this conduct, and their subsequent lives, perhaps, bear enduring testimony to this legalized uncharitableness. Nursed in the sentiment of caste, receiving it with the earliest food of knowledge, they are unable to eradicate it from their natures, and then weakly and impiously charge upon their Heavenly Father the prejudice which they have derived from an unchristian school, and which they continue to embody and perpetuate in their institutions. Their characters are debased, and they become less fit for the magnanimous duties of a good citizen. . . .

Who can say, that this does not injure the blacks? Theirs, in its best estate, is an unhappy lot. Shut out by a still lingering prejudice from many social advantages, a despised class, they feel this proscription from the public schools as a peculiar brand. Beyond this, it deprives them of those healthful animating influences which would come from a participation in the studies of their white brethren. It adds to their discouragements. It widens their separation from the rest of the community, and postpones that great day of reconciliation which is sure to come. . . .

Nothing is more clear than that the welfare of classes, as well as of individuals, is promoted by mutual acquaintance. . . . Prejudice is the child of ignorance. It is sure to prevail where people do not know each other. Society and intercourse are means established by Providence for human improvement. They remove antipathies, promote mutual adaptation and conciliation, and establish relations of reciprocal regard. Whoso sets up barriers to these, thwarts the ways of Providence, crosses the tendencies of human nature, and directly interferes with the laws of God.

The civilization of the age joins in this appeal. It is well known that this prejudice of color is peculiar to our country. You have not forgotten that two youths of African blood only recently gained the highest honors in the college at Paris, and dined on the same day with the king of France, the descendant of St. Louis, at the palace of the Tuileries. And let me add, if I may refer to my own experience, that in Paris, I have sat for weeks, at the School of Law, on the same benches with colored persons, listening, like myself, to the learned lectures . . .; nor do I remember observing in the throng of sensitive young men by whom they were surrounded, any feeling towards them except of companionship and respect. . . . In these examples may be discerned the Christian spirit.

And, finally, it is this spirit that I invoke. Where this prevails there is neither Jew nor Gentile, Greek nor barbarian, bond nor free; but all are alike. It is from this that we derive new and solemn assurances of the equality of mankind, as an ordinance of God. The bodies of men may be unequal in beauty or strength; these mortal cloaks of flesh may differ, as do these worldly garments; these intellectual faculties may vary, as do the opportunities of action and the advantages of position; but amidst all unessential differences there is an essential agreement and equality. . . .

But this is not all. The vaunted superiority of the white race imposes upon it corresponding duties. The faculties with which they are endowed, and the advantages which they possess, are to be exercised for the good of all. If the colored people are ignorant, degraded, and unhappy, then should they be the especial objects of your care. From the abundance of your possessions you must seek to remedy their lot. And this Court, which is as a parent to all the unfortunate children of the Commonwealth, will show itself most truly parental, when it reaches down, and, with the strong arm of the law, elevates, encourages, and protects its colored fellow citizens.

4

PRE-MARXIAN SOCIALISM

Thomas Skidmore
THE RIGHTS OF MAN TO PROPERTY

Another distinct source of agitation for change in the direction of social perfection that owed little if anything to the Christian tradition lay in the workingmen's movement. Thomas Skidmore (1790–1832) was a leading figure in the creation of the Working Men's Party of New York in 1829, though his ideas so frightened conservatives that they infiltrated the party and rapidly deposed him. He was born in rural Connecticut, spent his youth as a schoolteacher and inventor, and then moved to New York, where he earned his living as a machinist. He was influenced in his young manhood by the radical views in the Jeffersonian newspaper The Aurora. Much of his social philosophy came from reading Thomas Paine and the English agrarian radicals. A child of the Enlightenment, Skidmore rested his faith on the intrinsic moral goodness of man. Though he never used the term "socialist," he divided mankind into two distinct classes, proprietors and nonproprietors. Clearly the most radical American social thinker of his day, he alone advocated immediate confiscation of all existing property by the state and its equal redistribution, through the device of a new state convention. This call for direct action was what frightened so many of his hearers. Independent and self-assured, Skidmore dismissed all rival thinking as "quackery." Yet when he died during the cholera epidemic of 1832 his few remaining admirers mourned him as a man of rare integrity. It is conceivable, though not clearly proved, that he influenced the much later proposals of Henry George. Whether or not this is true, it is highly interesting that someone of his uncompromising views about the distribution of wealth appeared at so early a date.

Perhaps, among all the subjects that have received human investigation, there is none that has occupied so much of the time, and

SOURCE. Thomas Skidmore, The Rights of Man to Property (New York: by the author, 1829), pp. 30–40, 126–130, 388–390.

exercised so severely, the intellectual faculties of man, as his inquiries into the origin and nature of the rights of property. And perhaps it is equally true, that no inquiry whatever, has been attended with so little success. It may seem to be the height of egotism, of vanity, of arrogance, of ignorance perhaps, and I know not what else, to make such a charge against the wisdom of past ages. But I confidently point to all that has been, and all that is, and ask if there be, or have been, any two governments of the world, that now have, or that ever have had their laws alike each other, on the subject of the rights of property? Not any two, even of the states of our Union, can say as much; though among them, one would think, was the place to look for such a similarity, if it were any where to be found. No wonder then, that Voltaire, on some occasion should have said that rights change character, as often as a traveller changes post-horses. It was, in truth, no exaggeration; for the fact is still worse than his representation makes it. In the same nation, even, those rights, at two different periods of time are not the same. And, as if this were not a sufficient satire upon our understanding of the subject, I believe that there may be cases of the litigation of the rights of property in any country now known, where, if one hundred tribunals were simultaneously to try them, each of the greatest eminence for talents in judicial investigation, and each having before them precisely the same means of arriving at the facts, but having, however, no knowledge of each others' deliberations, they would, nevertheless, give a hundred different decisions.

This "uncertainty of the law," glorious as it has been proverbially called, by way of ridicule, I take it, is evidence that the subject is not understood. If it were so, these varying decisions could never happen. Rights are like truths, capable of being understood alike by all men—as much so as the demonstrations of Euclid. If, what are called so, are not so understood, it is proof that they are not rights; for it is scarcely to be presumed that they could not be rendered apparent to our perception—and that they are rather the arbitrary commands of power, than anything else.

But it is better to supply the deficiency of understanding on this subject, which seems to prevail, than to make it a matter of reproach. Let us see if it is possible to do it. It will be an achievement of no small importance to mankind, inasmuch, as it will, in my apprehension, go far to exterminate all the moral and political evils, with which they are now afflicted.

There seem to be three things which have an intimate and inseparable connection with each other.

These are property, persons and rights.

Out of these materials are built, or ought to be built, all the governments in the world. These are all the necessary and proper elements of their constitution; and these being applied as they have been, have caused, in my estimation, more evil to mankind, than any one can pretend that governments have done good; and, being applied as they may be, will fulfill the destiny of man, by reversing the results of the past.

What, then, is property? I answer; the whole material world: just as it came from the hands of the Creator.

What are persons? The human beings, whom the same Creator placed, or formed upon it, as inhabitants.

What are rights? The title which each of the inhabitants of this globe has to partake of and enjoy, equally with his fellows, its fruits and its productions.

Let no one pretend that there is yet other property. Let him ascend with me to the earliest ages; to periods of time, anterior to the formation of all governments; when our race existed, but when political institutions did not. For it is to these periods we must ascend if we mean to arrive at a true understanding of the theory of all just governments: and it is to these all my remarks will apply, until I come to offer my sentiments as to the principles of property which *ought* to enter into their formation. Let no one, then tell me that the *labor* which the savage of the forest has employed in the manufacture of his bow is property. That only is *property* which belongs to some one. Now it cannot belong to the race, collectively, for they did not produce it. It cannot belong to the individual who prepared the bow —because *it cannot be separated from it;* and because, if it could, it could have no physical existence whatever; and having no such existence, he would possess nothing more, than if he had never made it. Besides, the *material,* of which the bow is made, is the property of mankind. It is a property, too, which, previous to the existence of government, has never been alienated to any one. If it has not been alienated, it cannot belong to another. Another cannot have any right to make use of it. Before he does so, he must obtain the consent of all. What right, then had that other, to bestow his labor upon it? What right had he to convert it into a bow, or into any thing else? Instead of acquiring a right, thereby, to the bow, he has rather committed a trespass upon the great community of which he is a member. He is rather, of right, subject to punishment, than invested with title, to that which he has taken without consent, and appropriated to his own use. At least, then, it is evident that *his labor,* bestowed upon the *material* of the bow, does not give him a title to the latter? Does the mere act of *taking possession* of it, give it? Most certainly not. For here, as well as elsewhere, consent is necessary. Otherwise, it would be quite as correct, for example (all the members having put in an equal share of the capital), for a member of a banking company to appropriate to his own use the contents or any part thereof of the iron chest containing the gold and silver belonging to the whole. Nor is it an objection to the force of this argument to say that the iron chest is already in possession of the company, by its agents or otherwise, while the domain of nature is not. It is here that I deny the truth of the declaration. The domain *is* in possession. The owners—and they are *equal* owners too, are already present, and upon it. They have not , it is true, *divided* it, among themselves and given to each what he may call his own, anymore than the banking company mentioned, has done the same thing: but they are nevertheless in possession. The analogy therefore is full and complete.

Will it be said, then, someone may ask, that if an Indian kill a deer, it is not, therefore, his? Most certainly it is not. What, in my turn I would ask, is to become of other Indians, if there be actually fewer deer, than are needed? Must the mere accidental, or even sought for, circumstance, of any Indian's meeting with and killing a deer make such Indian the owner of it, to the exclusion of his fellows, who have an equal claim to it by the right of nature? Shall one of the species feast upon it and the remainder hunger? Besides as in the case of the bow, may not trespass have been committed in killing the deer also? As, in that case, the *animal is the property of the whole*, and if consent have not been given, it still remains their property, whatever *one* of their number may have thought or done to the contrary. For the owners of this deer are only to be divested of their right and title to it by their *own* act—and not by the act of another.

Again if an Indian collect wood and make a fire, it may be asked, is it not *therefore* his? By no means. For by the same right that one Indian may gather fuel into a heap, another may take it and scatter it to the four winds. The right is as good in the one case as in the other. The materials are as much the property of the one as of the other. They belong to neither. They belong to the *whole community*—and certainly not to any part less than a majority. Besides, the *ground* upon which the one has built a fire, or prepared to build it, is as much at the pleasure of the occupancy of him who has not built it, as of him who has. Each has an equal, and of course a conflicting title to such ground, for such purposes and in such a manner, and for such time, as to him shall seem fit. The *ground* also, as we have just said of the materials of the fire, belongs to neither. It is the property of the whole. So that if one may do, another may undo. If one may build up, another may pull down. If one may appropriate, another may dispossess. If one may do any thing without the consent of the whole, another without the same consent may go and destroy it altogether. The fire being built, *the space adjacent* to it is of the same common right, and whoever pleases may approach and warm himself as much as he chooses, without hindrance or obstruction from anyone. And this too, on the same principles which we see prevail throughout the previous cases.

Lastly, let us suppose this Indian, to cultivate a field. He plants it. Is it therefore his, in opposition to another, who, it may be, desires it for another use? May not this latter eject the other from his possession with the same propriety that this other attempts to make an exclusive use of it? Most undoubtedly. That which belongs to a thousand cannot be made the property of a single person, without their consent. Why then will not *possession* give title? Because that which is taken into possession belongs to another, and not to him who takes it: and because the *consent* of that other must give title; possession, if it be just, growing out of consent. Why will not *labor* bestowed upon property in possession give title? Because the property *itself* is another's and before any *labor* can be honestly bestowed upon it, that other, who alone owns it, must give his consent. Why will not occupancy give title? Because it is only another species of possession: and because, here, as before, the consent of him who owns, must be first had and obtained. And if it be so had and obtained, then is *title* given even though possession or occupancy be not had. It is *consent,* therefore, and nothing but the consent, of those who own, which can accord title. And yet it is very plain, that if possession, occupancy, or labor bestowed, in consequence of either, is sufficient to give title, then consent is not necessary; and then it would follow, that those who are truly the rightful owners could be stripped of that which beyond all dispute belongs to them without any act on their part to divest themselves of their right and, in fact, in opposition to their will and consent. If then possession, occupancy, or labor superadded is insufficient to convey title, then is my position established; and consent of the owners of property is the only requisite to title to its possession by another. That the making a bow, the killing a deer, the building a fire, or the planting a field, or any similar act or acts, cannot give title is self-evident; from this, that *before any of these acts were performed,* there was a proprietor in actual existence, to whom, and to whom alone they belonged, and not to those who undertake surreptitiously to obtain the title.

In all these cases, it is apparent that industry has added *value* to the materials and productions of nature, and therefore if any one desire it, it may be said by way of complaisance, that there is more *property* in the world than there was as it came from the hands of the Creator. This, it is not so much my purpose to deny, although it may seem to controvert the definition I have already given to the term *property*, as it is to assert that *whenever this Indian is permitted to retain exclusive possession of his bow, his deer, his fire and his field, or either of them, government has actually begun;* and of course the supposition has vanished upon which I began my consideration of the rights of property. For it was to a period of time anterior to the formation of all governments, the reader will recollect, to which I confined my remarks. If government had not then thus begun, consent could not have been given. There would have been none to give it. Without this he could not possess aught. With it, he is enabled to exclude all others from the use or enjoyment of what otherwise they could enjoy as well as he, and with as much propriety. Nor does it alter the principle of the thing that his possession is granted for a limited time, be it long or short, instead of being rendered perpetual. For the time being, his right of possession is as absolute and unconditional as anything can be. If he have his field for one season only, the exclusive right he has over it is as perfect, *for the time,* as if he held it in perpetuity. I know there are those who are disposed to consider such possession, as it were, for a year, to be nothing more than, as it is called, a *usufruct,* for that time. But what I ask is a fee-simple deed, but a perpetual *usufruct?* Certainly, when a piece of land is sold forever, nothing more is sold than the fruits, which can be drawn from the *use* of it for ever. And this is what is meant by the term *usufruct.* There seems, then, in such an idea to be more of distinction than difference. All the difference which I am able to perceive is that in one case, the *use* of land is given for a single year; in the other, it is given without limitation of years, or in other words for ever.

It may seem very rigid in me, to insist that no individual of his species, previous to the first establishment of any government, has a right to appropriate to himself, exclusively, anything; such, for example, as the articles which have been mentioned, or whatever else it may be, without the consent of those who are joint owners with him. But I apprehend it is nevertheless true. Investigations of right are necessarily of the rigid character in question. In this consists their impartiality; and in this again is found the guarantee of their truth. If the fact were not so, there would be much reason to suspect the soundness of the conclusions at which we might arrive. An Egyptian king was once told "there was no royal road to Geometry." Neither is there any such road to a full understanding of the rights of property. They must be deeply and patiently investigated, or they will never be understood.

But an illustration of the necessity and propriety of these truths may be drawn from what is very familiar to us all. An estate is left to a number of heirs, in equal right, and an executor is appointed to make the distribution. Before the distribution is made, would any one of the heirs be allowed to help himself to what he might wish of the estate? Would not everyone see the impropriety of this? Would not everyone understand that the proper course to be pursued was to call upon the executor and obtain his consent? The executor, having the power of acting for the benefit of all, is the only one competent to grant, if to him it shall appear proper, what may be desired. So, in the case in which this example is offered as an illustration, the whole community stand in the place of the executor, and have the power, and they *alone* have it, to alienate to any one, or more of their own number, temporarily or otherwise, any portion of the property in possession. . . .

The truth is, *all* governments in the world have begun wrong; in the *first appropriation* they have made, or suffered to be made, of the domain, over which they have exercised their power, and in the *transmission* of this domain to their posterity. Here are the two great and radical evils, that have caused all the misfortunes of man. These and these alone, have done the whole of it. I do not class among these misfortunes the sufferings with which sickness afflicts him, because these have a natural origin; capable, however, of being nearly annihilated by good governments, but greatly aggravated by those that are bad.

If these remarks be true, there would seem, then, to be no remedy but by commencing anew. And is there any reason why we should not? That which is commenced in error and injustice, may surely be set right, when we know how to do it. There is *power* enough in the hands of the people of the state of New York, or of any other state, to rectify any and every thing which requires it, when they shall see wherein the evil exists, and wherein lies the remedy. These two things it is necessary they should see before they can possess the moral power and motive to act. I have succeeded, I think, in showing, for that is self-evident, that man's *natural* right to an equal portion of property is indisputable. His artificial right, or right in society, is not less so. For it is not to be said that any power has any right to make our artificial rights unequal, any more than it has to make our *natural* rights unequal. And inasmuch as a man, in a state of nature, would have a right to resist, even to the extremity of death, his fellow, or his fellows, whatever might be their number, who should undertake to give him less of the property, common to all, than they take each to themselves; so also has man now, in society, the same right to resist a similar wrong done him. Thus, today, if property had been made equal among all present, right would have taken place among them; but if tomorrow a new member appear, and provision be not made to give him a quantity substantively equal with all his fellows, injustice is done him, and if he had the power, he would have the perfect right, to dispossess all those who have monopolized to themselves not only their own shares, but his also. For it is not to be allowed even to a majority, to contravene equality, nor, of course, the right, even though it be a single individual. And if, alone, he has not power sufficient to obtain his rights, and there be others, also, in like condition with him, they may unite their efforts, and thus accomplish it if within their power. And, if this may be lawfully done, upon the supposition that yesterday, only, a government was made, and an equal enjoyment of property guaranteed to all, how much more proper is it when, unjust government existing, it has never been done at all. When the whole mass of people, as it were, ninety-nine out of every hundred, have never had this equal enjoyment, in any manner or shape, whatever? If still there be those who shall say that these unjust and unequal governments ought not to be destroyed, although they may not give to man, in society, the same equality of property as he would enjoy in a state of nature; then I say, that *those are the persons* who, in society, *if anybody,* should be deprived of all their possessions, inasmuch as it is manifestly as proper for them to be destitute of property as it is for anyone else. If slavery and degradation are to be the result, they are the proper victims. After an equal division has been once made, there seems nothing wanting but to secure an equal transmission of property to posterity. And to this, there is no irremovable objection. For, I think I have succeeded in showing, that the right of a testator to give, and of an heir to receive, is a mere creature of the imagination; and that these rights, as they are called, ought to be abolished as interfering with the real rights of the succeeding generation. Had it not been for these, we should not have seen a Van Rensallaer possessing that which would make hundreds, and perhaps thousands, of families as happy as they could wish to be, and to which they have as good a *natural right,* and ought to have as good an *artificial title* as himself. It would be of no consequence for him to say that he derived his right from some old Dutch charter, obtained some twenty years after Hudson's first discovery of the river which now bears his name. The rights of nature, which can never be alienated, which can never pass out of our hands but through ignorance or force and which may be claimed again whenever ignorance and force disappear, are superior to any and to all chartered rights, as they are called, let them be of what government they may, even of our own government; and much more so, to those of any that is or was foreign. . . .

Let the poor and middling classes understand that their oppressions come from the overgrown wealth that exists among them, on the one hand, and from entire destitution on the other; and that as this overgrown wealth is continually augmenting its possessions, in a rapid ratio, the public sufferings are continually augmenting also; and must continue to augment, until the equal and unalienable rights of the people shall order otherwise. Let the parent reflect, if he be now a man of toil, that his children must be, ninety-nine cases in a hundred, slaves *and worse* to some rich proprietor; and that there is no alternative, but the change proposed. Let him not cheat himself with empty pretensions; for *he who commands the property of a state, or even an inordinate portion of it, has the liberty and the happiness of its citizens in his own keeping.* And if there be some dozen, or fifty, or five hundred of these large proprietors, they are neither more nor less than so many additional keepers. He who can feed me, or starve me, give me employment, or bid me wander about in idleness, is my master, and it is the utmost folly for me to boast of being anything but a slave.

In fine, let the people awake to their rights; let them understand in what they consist; let them see the course they must pursue to obtain them; let them follow up that course, by informing each as many as he can, his fellow citizens, of the truth which this work contains; let all cooperate in the early and effectual accomplishment of the objects it recommends, and these objects will easily and speedily be achieved, and none will have labored in vain.

At the moment of taking leave of the reader, it occurs to me, that it would be well to add a single remark. If ever the principles of this work are to prevail; if ever they are to find their way among men and to restore to them their rights, it is only to be done by each doing all he can, single and separately, to open the eyes of his fellows, to the perception of the evil that oppresses him, its origin and cure. While this is doing, and doing too in many parts of the state, of the Union, and the world at one and the same time; for such is the coextensive and cotemporary energy, with which the productions of the press operate; the rich, now and then, will cast their eyes on this work; and they, too, will see that the system which it proposes, must, sooner or later, take place. Ultimately, the whole of them will come to the same conclusion. So many of them as shall dread its approach, and shall not have the moral honesty to surrender up to the disposition of their fellow citizens all that they have, will, of course, conceal as much as they can. And that which is the most desirable to conceal, and the easiest concealed, is money. Now, whenever it shall appear, correctly or otherwise it is no matter, to the rich generally that the great mass of the people have very nearly awakened to the determination to resume their rights, and pursuant thereto, to order a general division of property, these concealments will take place very suddenly; and, perhaps, to such an extent as to withdraw the precious metals entirely from circulation, out of the banks, as well as elsewhere. In such an event, the banks would be broken; and as there would be no circulating medium, all business would be instantly suspended. Those who now carry on extensive business would have nothing with which to pay off their hands; and if they had, *they* might be as willing as others to bury it in the earth for the purpose of defrauding the community out of it.

In such an event, which is far from being impossible, the wished-for change would arrive earlier, than is already anticipated in this work; and in manner somewhat different. For the reader understands, that I have intended, that a state convention to be chosen by the people for the purpose shall order the suspension of all business, which, by this operation of withdrawing all the gold and silver from circulation, and burying it in the earth by the rich, would be anticipated. If it should so happen, it will not be the fault of this work, or of the great mass of the people, and may not be that even, of the majority of the rich; for even a very few of them would be able to put away all the precious metals that are to be found in the state; and as to other states, they could no more spare *their* precious metals than ourselves, without coming in contact with a similar catastrophe; and of which, they too, will be in similar danger. Besides, as to personal property in the city of New York, alone, there is probably more in value than all the specie money in the United States, twice, or even thrice told. So that it will be no difficult thing, if dishonesty prevail, even to a small extent among the rich, to bring about the withdrawal of which I am speaking.

Under such circumstances, it may be said, that the government has suddenly ceased to exist; that it has expired, as it were, in a fit of apoplexy; and it will then be incumbent on the people to organize a temporary commitee of safety; and take care, immediately, that no property leaves the state or is wasted or destroyed further than is necessary for subsistence; until a state convention can be assembled to form a new government on principles corresponding with *all* the rights of man; and which, as it ensures his happiness, by preserving his equality, and that of all succeeding generations, we may confidently hope will be eternal.

5

FOURIERISM

Albert Brisbane
SOCIAL DESTINY OF MAN

When a socialist movement emerged in America around 1840, its inspiration was middle- and upper-class rather than proletarian. The central figure in promoting it was Albert Brisbane (1809–1890), a disciple of the French utopian thinker Charles Fourier (1772–1837), under whom Brisbane had studied for two years in France. Brisbane was the son of a prominent landowner in Batavia, New York. He received an education from private tutors and then spent seven years traveling and studying in Europe, where a developing sense of needless social misery finally led him to Fourier's philosophy. In 1839 Brisbane began lecturing in Philadelphia and New York; soon he was given enthusiastic publicity by Horace Greeley. Some forty Fourierist phalanxes were begun by Americans in the next few years, though without Brisbane's blessing. Although one of these communities lasted for eighteen years, most of them failed quickly. Brisbane was a modest, self-distrusting man, ill-suited to take command of a movement; in this respect he was quite unlike John Humphrey Noyes or Joseph Smith. This phase of American socialism proved to be no more than a brief epiphenomenon, geared more to a European than to a local perception of social realities. Still, the sudden flare of interest in the founding of intentional communities on the part of Americans in the early 1840s, in which Fourierism so largely figured, was a major aspect of the contemporary impulse toward social perfection.

Man becomes so accustomed to the society in which he has passed his life, that its institutions, laws, and customs grow upon him until they become a second nature. His feelings, views and prejudices are so interwoven with its whole mechanism, that he looks upon it as

SOURCE. Albert Brisbane, *Social Destiny of Man: Or, Association and Reorganization of Industry* (Philadelphia: C. F. Stollmeyer, 1840), pp. 1–6, 76–79, 81–83.

natural, unchangeable and perfect. So great is this illusion, that the evils he labors under are attributed to every cause but the true one— the defective organization of society; and while the government, the administration, and even religion are doubted and criticized, the social system, as if it were some thing superior to human imperfection and error, alone commands the respect and reverence of all. . . .

This veil of prejudice must be torn away. We assert that the evil, misery and injustice, now predominant on the earth, have not their foundation in political or administrative errors, in the defects of this or that institution, in the imperfection of human nature, or in the depravity of the passions; but in the false organization of society alone. We assert that the present social mechanism is not adapted to the nature of man and to his passions; that its laws are in flagrant opposition to those which regulate or govern their action; that it perverts, misdirects and develops them subversively, and that the selfishness, oppression, fraud, injustice, and crime, which mark the course of his societies, are attributable to that artificial or social misdirection and perversion, and not to any inborn, inherent depravity in the human being himself.

The passions tend from their nature (and how could they do otherwise since they are the work of the Divinity?) to social unity, concord, and the development of all the sympathies. *But the great mistake which has been made, has been to confound the false developments, which the passions receive from our subversive societies, with their real essence and their true nature:* the effect has been mistaken for the cause. Science has fallen into this gross error; it has sought for the cause of social evil and misery in the perverted action of the passions, without going any further, whereas, had it taken one step more, it would have found in the vicious organisation of the social mechanism, the cause of their perverted action, consequently the real source of misery and evil. This it has not done; it has left the social mechanism as it was, and applied correctives to the passions; these having failed entirely, it has declared their depravity and the permanency of evil, and advised an apathetic resignation to its sway. This advice has been but too faithfully followed, and the belief in the fatality of evil has sunk so deeply into the minds of men, that it has eradicated all hope of the possibility of general and collective happiness on this earth. As a proof of the fact, ask the learned or the ignorant, ask the world in general, and they will answer alike that happiness is not the lot of man, that it is a boon which has not been granted him by the Divinity.

But, between this theory and practice, there exists a strange contradiction which should have led to a further examination of the subject.

While the supremacy of evil is acknowledged on all sides, every individual in his sphere is in ardent pursuit of happiness, which he feels to be the law of his nature, and which he believes, if his plans succeed, possible and attainable.

The secret instinct of the individual is truer than the reasonings of science. The destiny of man is to be happy on this earth, but not in our subversive societies, characterized by indigence and discord. The realization of happiness requires a different social order; and to induce its research, to awaken a desire for that realization, we wish to excite, not a war of the poor against the rich—as a certain political party is accused of doing—but the just indignation, of all those who suffer, not from causes inherent in the nature of things, but from the circumstances of society, against the insidious social mechanism which, like a Divinity, stands undoubted and unsuspected.

If we descend to a more positive and practical sphere, we ask how it has happened that the present social system, termed civilization, has not been the object of scientific investigation. Had its mechanism been analyzed, it would necessarily have been discovered that it is full of complication and waste, and devoid of the three principal characteristics which mark all nature's operations: *economy of means, distributive justice, unity of system;* characteristics which should not be banished from the social relations of man.

But civilization in its various branches is based upon the incoherent, conflicting efforts of individuals, between whom, not only no connection and combination exist, but on the contrary opposition and competition full of hatred and envy. If we take agriculture, for example, the present condition of which calls so loudly for association and organization, we find it pursued by isolated families, mostly without the necessary capital or credit, or the proper implements, and who only vie with each other in an ignorant and injudicious use and application of the soil. Human labor also is miserably misapplied: for, in the absence of combination between those isolated families, no appropriate adaptation of ages and sexes to functions and occupations suited to them can take place. Women, for example, are absorbed in a monotonous repetition of the trivial and degrading occupations of the kitchen and needle—degrading because they have to be so continually repeated and on so small a scale. Moreover three-fourths of the labor of children, who are naturally very active, are wasted, owing to the absence of association between neighboring households, who, if united, could organize minor branches of industry adapted to their strength and capacity, which besides being a pleasure to them, would develop their instincts and talents.

The root then of social incoherence is to be found in our system of separate households, or as many distinct houses as there are families, which is the essence of complication and waste. It absorbs the time, as we observed, of one sex or one-half of the human race, in an unproductive function, which has to be gone through with as many times as there are families. The monotony of such an operation so eternally and uselessly repeated (uselessly because in association one vast kitchen with every commodity would replace the two or three hundred little kitchens of the present system) must be fatiguing beyond conception, and its endurance must require all the patience of the female character. Let not the system be excused by saying that the character of woman is particularly adapted to it. It is not so: her destiny is not to waste her life in a kitchen, or in the petty cares of a household. Nature made her the equal of man, and equally capable of shining with him in industry and in the cultivation of the arts and sciences; not to be his inferior, to cook and sew for him, and live dependently at his board. No class could bring so many well founded complaints against the social mechanism as women, for they are truly its slaves. . . .

If we wish to find the most perfect picture of waste and disorder, we must search for it in our large cities. It is there that we will find our *cut-up* system, in which every thing is reduced to the measure and selfishness of the individual, producing an incoherence and complication, which might properly be termed a combination for the production of evil; for it would seem as if things were so organized, as to cause the greatest possible number of evils, and ensure their most rapid propagation. Each house, for example, has its sink of filth, the miasmas of which the whole population must breathe: the poverty or neglect, or both combined, of a single family, produce a contagious disease, which extends to a thousand others, among which there will be indigent ones enough, to keep it in existence.

The neglect of one person, of a child or a servant perhaps, in whom it is often necessary to confide, burns down not only the house of one family, but a hundred others with it; or the misplaced economy of a stove-pipe, causes a loss of the same kind, which would be sufficient to construct all the apparatus necessary for warming a town or the manor house of a Phalanx. Where everything is left to the ignorance, cupidity, carelessness or inability of individuals, no guarantees of a general nature can exist or be put in practice.

It is from the poverty of the mass in our large cities, that the greatest abuses take place. If a capitalist builds damp cellars, garrets without ventilation, small and confined rooms, close courtyards without light and circulation, and with hardly the conveniencies necessary to the wants of its inmates, he is sure to find droves of indigent families, who will stow themselves away in these tenements, making of them hotbeds of disease, and nurseries of demoralization. Moralists wonder that human nature can be as depraved as they find it in our societies, and they seek in the *heart* the source of all this depravity; it is only surprising that human nature should bear so much, and murmur so little, and that with its load of social evil and misery, so much good will and gaiety still remain.

If we cite examples of material waste, we should rank, next to that of fires, which we mentioned above, the loss occasioned by the tearing down of buildings, from being badly constructed, or from speculation. This waste in many of our large cities must be enormous, and is due to want of combination and foresight. What absence of order, in an architectural point of view, on the part of society, not to be able to plan its buildings, so as to answer the wants of the community for twenty years in advance! The widening, straightening and lengthening of streets form another gigantic item of waste. All these abuses arise from the fact that in planning our cities and towns, no system, no method exists. There is no adaptation of architecture to our wants and requirements; our houses are as little suited to our physical welfare, as our social laws are to our attractions and passions. It is to be observed, that this enormous waste and expenditure are *paid* by productive industry, upon which an immense indirect tax is laid, which is not perceived. The farmers, manufacturers and mechanics, must produce the means for paying in the end for every thing, cities, ships, canals, railroads, etc.

Men become, however, so accustomed to the order of things in which they live, that these facts do not strike them: not conceiving the possibility of changing the social mechanism, it appears to them natural and permanent: if, however, they could be brought to doubt its efficacy, or rather its infallibility; and examine it with scrutinizing attention, a social skepticism would take the place of their present blindness. It is a result deeply to be desired: vegetating as the world does in its present social condition, all improvements in science and industry are of no use to the great mass; their poverty does not diminish with these improvements; and the increased means of enjoyment, the refinement of luxury, to which they give rise, only excite that mass to every kind of fraud and falseness to obtain a share of and participate in them.

Riches are the leading wish of man, and in this country wealth has become the all absorbing object of desire. In this strife after wealth, in which millions are engaged, why has it not been perceived, that not one-twentieth can succeed? If but one-third of the population are producers, if production is the only source of riches, and if our system of consumption in isolated households is so complicated, that the small amount produced by the third does not go one-half as far as it would in a system of combination and association (or in other words, if one-half of the small product created by the producing third of society is wasted), how is it possible that even the common wants of the entire population, setting aside all superfluity, can be satisfied? . . .

One-third of the population produce; two-thirds are non-producers. . . . The result is that the population of all countries, except this, are removed but one degree from starvation. Those of China are so poor that they eat vermin, those of India subsist on a little rice without salt, and tens of thousands die of starvation and are thrown into the Ganges. The Pariahs, the most degraded class, are driven even to eat sometimes these starved carcasses. The agricultural classes often plant their crops in the hope only of being hired to harvest them. The Irish peasantry have scarcely salt with their potatoes, and in many parts of the country, they eat bread and meat but once a year. . . .

Judge a tree by its fruit, a society by its results; let us not be carried away by the endless praises which are lavished on our advanced state of civilization, as the present system is called. It is time some positive ameliorations were demanded at the hands of our politicians and legislators: we have party politics and legislation enough; if any good could come from the incoherent laws and arbitrary constitutions of civilization, it would have been realized long since. Experience, and the condition of mankind, prove that nothing effective is to be hoped from them, and common sense dictates that we should seek elsewhere, in agricultural association, or in a reform in industry, for social good.

But politicians scarcely dare put forth the hypothesis of a social reform and a change in the condition of mankind: the human race have so long been curbed under the yoke of misfortune, that suffering is believed to be the law of their nature. The views and belief of politicians have so adapted themselves to this doctrine, that it has become a dogmatical part of their creed; they have asserted it so often, that they must stand by their declarations. Their personal and party interests have also become so entwined with the present state of things, that they are even led to support the present social subversion; add to this the apathy of the world, its disbelief in the possibility of a great social change, and we have the explanation why *no social* principles are discussed, and why no efforts are made to ameliorate the condition of that vast mass of suffering, helpless and degraded beings who form three-fourths of the population of the globe. It is time this stupid policy, if all disbelief in a social reform can be called such, should be denounced; the mass, we trust, have become intelligent enough to demand some effective reforms at the hands of their political leaders, so active in administrative reforms, and so clamorous in their protestations of love for the people.

Nine permanent evils characterize the course of our societies; let the mass call upon those leaders to discover the principles of a society which will produce nine results directly opposed to them, will guarantee social happiness, and give us the standard of a true social organization.

NINE PERMANENT SCOURGES OF CIVILIZATION

Indigence
Fraud
Oppression
War
Derangement of climate
Diseases artificially produced, plague, yellow fever, cholera, small pox, etc.
Vicious circle, without any opening for improvement
Universal selfishness
Duplicity of social action

NINE PERMANENT BENEFITS TO BE ATTAINED

General riches
Practical truth in all relations of life
Effective liberty in the same
Constant peace
Equilibrium of temperature and climate
System of preventive medicine and extirpation of artificial diseases
Opening offered to all improvements and ameliorations
Collective and individual philanthropy
Unity of social action.

Such are the benefits association would realize; but can we look for cooperation from men whose interests, as we said, are concentrated in

personal success? The circle of our civilized politics is very narrow, but it ensures the successful individual, often without merit or great effort, applause for the day, and frequently pecuniary reward with it. Immediate and personal advantage only stimulates the great majority; the idea of a social reform which would change the destiny of mankind, although vast and sublime, is too far off, too severed from all personal advantages, to find many adherents and enthusiasts. There must be, however, some characters so constituted as to feel the want of an object, high and lasting, with which to connect their efforts, so that something may remain to show that they lived upon this earth, and that their intellectual was not as fleeting as their material existence. It is among such temperaments, that we must seek for the advocates of the great social reform, which the present age may have the glory of achieving!

6

ANARCHIST INDIVIDUALISM

Stephen Pearl Andrews
THE TRUE CONSTITUTION OF GOVERNMENT

Anarchism is in one sense the most severely perfectionist of all secular social philosophies, because its call for complete abolition of governmental institutions requires an unqualified faith in the goodness of men as individuals, in accord with the optimism of the Enlightenment. The modern tradition of anarchist thought begins with the Englishman William Godwin in 1793. In 1829 it first emerged in America, in a pronouncement by Josiah Warren, who had lived in the Owenite socialist community at New Harmony, Indiana, and had come away disillusioned. Thereafter a succession of lonely writers kept the viewpoint alive in this country until immigrants gave it a new and larger base after 1880. One of these early figures was Stephen Pearl Andrews (1812–1886). From a clerical family in Massachusetts and already an impassioned abolitionist at the age of nineteen, Andrews developed radical views of his own along essentially secular lines. After living in the south and attempting to raise funds to buy freedom for the slaves, in 1847 he moved to New York. There he played a role with Warren in the founding of Modern Times, an anarchist community on Long Island where some couples practiced free love; it lasted for about twenty years. An excellent linguist who knew thirty-two languages and an enthusiastic proponent of shorthand, Andrews also worked intermittently on a self-concocted "universology," a deductive science of the entire universe, which when finally published proved to be a turgid, eccentric volume, quite unlike his lucid if rather pompous prose in the following selection. Andrews tried to reconcile Warren's anarchism with Fourier's organicist socialism and Auguste Comte's positivism. In a long debate with Horace Greeley during 1853–1854, these complexities stood forth, along with Andrews' unusual concern for women's rights. But in this earlier essay the anarchist tendency of his argument comes through strongly. Until his death Andrews remained unshakably convinced that a social millennium was at hand.

SOURCE. Stephen Pearl Andrews, *The True Constitution of Government in the Sovereignty of the Individual as the Final Development of Protestantism, Democracy and Socialism* (Boston: Sarah E. Holmes, 1888), pp. 8–11, 13–16, 23–25, 27–29, 31, 33–35, 39–40; first published in 1851.

Hitherto the struggle between conservatism and progress has seemed doubtful. Victory has kissed the banner, alternately, of either host. At length the serried ranks of conservatism falter. Reform, so called, is becoming confessedly more potent than its antagonist. The admission is reluctantly forced from pallid lips that revolutions—political, social, and religious—constitute the program of the coming age. Reform, so called, for weal or woe, but yet reform, must rule the hour. The older constitutions of society have outlived their day. No truth commends itself more universally to the minds of men now than that thus set forth by [Thomas] Carlyle: "There must be a new world, if there is to be any world at all. . . ." Nor is this state of things confined to Europe. The agitations in America may be more peaceful, but they are not less profound. The foundations of old beliefs and habits of thought are breaking up. The old guarantees of order are fast falling away. A veritable "new era" with us, too, is alike impending and inevitable.

What remains to be done, then, for wise men, is clearly this: to attempt to penetrate the future by investigating the past and the present, to ascertain whether there be not elements of calculation capable of fixing with tolerable certainty the precise point in the sidereal heavens of human destiny toward which our whole system is confessedly verging with accelerated velocity. . . .

I affirm, then, firstly, that there is at this day a marked convergence and a prospective cooperation of principles which have hitherto resisted each other, . . . that the essential spirit, the vital and fundamental principle of . . . three great modern movements . . . namely, the Protestant Reformation, the Democratic Revolution still progressing, and, finally, the Socialist Agitation, which is spreading in multiform varieties of reproduction over the whole civilized world—is one and the same, and that this common affinity is beginning in various ways to be recognized or felt. If this assertion be true, it is one of immense significance. If Protestantism, Democracy, and Socialism are merely different expressions of the same idea, then, undoubtedly, the confluent force of these three movements will expand tremendously the sweep of their results, in the direction toward which they collectively tend.

What, then, if this be so, is this common element? . . . Protestantism, Democracy, and Socialism are identical in the assertion of the Supremacy of the Individual—a dogma essentially contumacious, revolutionary, and antagonistic to the basis principles of all the older institutions of society, which make the Individual subordinate and subject to the Church, to the State, and to Society respectively. Not only is this supremacy or sovereignty of the individual a common element of all three of these great modern movements, but I will make the still more sweeping assertion that it is substantially the whole of those movements. It is not merely a feature, as I have just denominated it, but the living soul itself, the vital energy, the integral essence of being of them all.

Protestants and Protestant churches may differ in relation to every other article of their creed, and do so differ, without ceasing to be Protestants, so long as they assert the paramount right of private or individual judgment in matters of conscience. It is that, and that only, which makes them Protestants, and distinguishes them from the Catholic world, which asserts, on the contrary, the supreme authority of the church, of the priesthood, or of some dignitary or institution other than the Individual whose judgment and whose conscience is in question. In like manner, Democrats and Democratic governments and institutions may differ from each other, and may vary infinitely at different periods of time, and still remain Democratic, so long as they maintain the one essential principle and condition of Democracy—namely, that all governmental powers reside in, are only delegated by, and can be, at any moment, resumed by the people—that is, by the *individuals,* who are first Individuals, and who then, by virtue only of the act of delegating such powers, become *a people*—that is, a combined mass of Individuals. It is this dogma, and this alone, which makes the Democrat, and which distinguishes him from the Despotist, or the defender of the divine right of kings.

Again, Socialism assumes every shade and variety of opinion respecting the modes of realizing its own aspirations, and, indeed, upon every other point, except one, which, when investigated, will be found to be the paramount rights of the Individual over social institutions, and the consequent demand that all existing social institutions shall be so modified that the Individual shall be in no manner subjected to them. This, then, is the identical principle of Protestantism and Democracy carried into its application in another sphere. The celebrated formula of Fourier that "destinies are proportioned to attractions," means, when translated into less technical phraseology, that society must be so reorganized that every Individual shall be empowered to choose and vary his own destiny or condition and pursuits in life, untrammeled by social restrictions; in other words, so that every man may be a law unto himself, paramount to all other human laws, and the sole judge for himself of the divine law and of the requisitions of his own individual nature and organization. This is equally the fundamental principle of all the social theories, except in the case of the Shakers, the Rappites, etc., which are based upon religious whims, demanding submission, as a matter of duty, to a despotic rule, and which embody, in another form, the readoption of the popish or conservative principle. . . . The forms of society proposed by Socialism are the mere shell of the doctrine—means to the end—a platform upon which to place the Individual, in order that he may be enabled freely to exercise his own Individuality, which is the end and aim of all. We have seen that the shell is one which *may* be inhabited by despotism. Possibly it is unfit for the habitation of anything else than despotism, which the Socialist hopes, by ensconcing himself therein, to escape. It is possible, even, that Socialism may have mistaken its measures altogether, and that the whole system of Association and combined interests and combined responsibilities proposed by it may be essentially antagonistic to the very ends proposed. All this, however, if it be so, is merely incidental. It belongs to the shell, and not to the substance—to the means, and not to the end. The whole program of Socialism may yet be abandoned or reversed, and yet Socialism remain in substance the same thing. What Socialism demands is the emancipation of the Individual from social bondage, by whatsoever means will effect that design, in the same manner as Protestantism demands the emancipation of the Individual from ecclesiastical bondage, and Democracy from political. Whosoever makes that demand, or labors to that end, is a Socialist. . . .

This definition of Socialism may surprise some into the discovery of the fact that they have been Socialists all along, unawares. Some, on the other hand, who have called themselves Socialists may not at once be inclined to accept the definition. They may not perceive clearly that it is the emancipation of the Individual for which they are laboring, and affirm that it is, on the other hand, the freedom and happiness of the race. They will not, however, deny that it is both; and a very little reflection will show that the freedom and happiness of each individual will *be* the freedom and happiness of the race, and that the freedom and happiness of the race cannot exist so long as there is any individual of the race who is not happy and free. . . .

The doctrine of the Sovereignty of the Individual . . . grows out of the still more fundamental principle of "Individuality," which pervades universal nature. Individuality is positively the most fundamental and universal principle which the finite mind seems capable of discovering, and the best image of the Infinite. There are no two objects in the universe which are precisely alike. Each has its own constitution and peculiarities, which distinguish it from every other. Infinite diversity is the universal law. In the multitude of human countenances, for example, there are no two alike, and in the multitude of human characters there is the same variety. . . . There have been no two occurrences which were precisely alike during all the cycling periods of time. No action, transaction, or set of circumstances whatsoever ever corresponded precisely to any other action, transaction, or set of circumstances. Had I a precise knowledge of all the occurrences which have ever taken place up to this hour, it would not suffice to enable me to make a law which would be applicable in all respects to the very next occurrence which shall take place, nor to any one of the infinite millions of events which shall hereafter occur. This diversity reigns throughout every kingdom of nature, and mocks at all human attempts to make laws, or constitutions, or regulations, or governmental institutions of any sort, which shall work justly and harmoniously amidst the unforeseen contingencies of the future. . . .

Governments have hitherto been established, and have apologized for the unseemly fact of their existence, from the necessity of establishing and maintaining order; but order has never yet been maintained, revolutions and violent outbreaks have never yet been ended, public peace and harmony have never yet been secured, for the precise reason that the organic, essential, and indestructible natures of the objects which it was attempted to reduce to order have always been constricted and infringed by every such attempt. Just in proportion as the effort is less and less made to reduce men to order, just in that proportion they become more orderly, as witness the difference in the state of society in Austria and the United States. Plant an army of one hundred thousand soldiers in New York, as at Paris, to preserve the peace, and we should have a bloody revolution in a week; and be assured that the only remedy for what little of turbulence remains among us, as compared with European societies, will be found to be more liberty. When there remain positively no external restrictions, there will be positively no disturbance, provided always certain regulating principles of justice, to which I shall advert presently, are accepted and enter into the public mind, serving as substitutes for every species of repressive laws. . . .

The monads or atoms of which human society is composed are the individual men and women in it. They must be so disposed of, as we have seen, in order that society may be harmonic, that the destiny of each shall be controlled by his or her own individualities of taste, conscience, intellect, capacities, and will. But man is a being endowed with consciousness. He, and no one else, knows the determining force of his own attractions. No one else can therefore decide for him, and hence Individuality can only become the law of human action by securing to each individual the sovereign determination of his own judgment and of his own conduct, in all things, with no right reserved either of punishment or censure on the part of anybody else whomsoever; and this is what is meant by the Sovereignty of the Individual, limited only by the ever-accompanying condition, resulting from the equal Sovereignty of all others, that the onerous consequences of his actions be assumed by himself. . . .

I assert that the law of genuine progress in human affairs is identical with the tendency to individualize. In ecclesiastical affairs it is the breaking up of the Church into sects, the breaking up of the larger sects into minor sects, the breaking up of the minor sects, by continual schism, into still minuter fragments of sects, and, finally, a complete disintegration of the whole mass into *individuals*, at which point every human being becomes his own sect and his own church. . . .

It is already the axiom of Democracy that this is the best government which governs least—that, in other words, which leaves the largest domain to the Individual sovereign. It may sound strange, and yet it is rigidly true, that nothing is more foreign to the essential nature of Democracy than the rule of majorities. Democracy asserts that all men are born free and equal—that is, that every individual is of right free from the governing control of every other and of all others. Democracy asserts, also, that this right is inalienable—that it can neither be surrendered nor forfeited to another Individual, nor to a majority of other Individuals. But the practical application of this principle has been, and will always be found to be, incompatible with our existing social order. It presupposes, as I have said, the preliminary attainment of the conditions demanded by Socialism. The rule of majorities is, therefore, a compromise enforced by temporary expediency. . . .

Genuine Democracy is identical with the no-government doctrine. . . .

Is it within the bounds of possibility, and, if so, is it within the limits of rational anticipation, that all human governments, in the sense in which government is now spoken of, shall pass away, and be reckoned among the useless number of an experimental age—that forcible government of all sorts shall, at some future day, perhaps not far distant, be looked back upon by the whole world, as we in America now look back upon the maintenance of a religious establishment, supposed in other times, and in many countries still, to be essential to the existence of religion among men; and as we look back upon the ten thousand other impertinent interferences of government, as government is practiced in those countries where it is an institution of far more validity and consistency than it has among us? Is it possible, and, if so, is it rationally probable, that the time shall ever come when every man shall be, in fine, his own nation as well as his own sect? Will this tendency to universal enfranchisement—indications of which present themselves, as we have seen, in exuberant abundance on all hands in this age—ultimate itself, by placing the Individual above all political institutions—the man above all subordination to municipal law? . . .

I assert that it is not only possible and rationally probable, but that it is rigidly consequential upon the right understanding of the constitution of man, that all government, in the sense of involuntary restraint upon the Individual, or substantially all, must finally cease, and along with it the whole complicated paraphernalia and trumpery of Kings, Emperors, Presidents, Legislatures, and Judiciary. I assert that the indicia of this result abound in existing society, and that it is the instinctive or intelligent perception of that fact by those who have not bargained for so much which gives origin and vital energy to the reaction in Church and State and social life. I assert that the distance is less today forward from the theory and practice of Government as it is in these United States, to the total abrogation of all Government above that of the Individual, than it is backward to the theory and practice of Government as Government now is in the despotic countries of the old world. . . .

The highest type of human society in the existing social order is found in the parlor. In the elegant and refined reunions of the aristocratic classes there is none of the impertinent interference of legislation. The Individuality of each is fully admitted. Intercourse, therefore, is perfectly free. Conversation is continuous, brilliant, and varied. Groups are formed according to attraction. They are continuously broken up, and re-formed through the operation of the same subtle and all-pervading influence. Mutual deference pervades all classes, and the most perfect harmony, ever yet attained, in complex human relations, prevails under precisely those circumstances which legislators and statesmen dread as the conditions of inevitable anarchy and confusion. If there are laws of etiquette at all, they are mere suggestions of principles admitted into and judged of for himself or herself, by each individual mind.

Is it conceivable that in all the future progress of humanity, with all the innumerable elements of development which the present age is unfolding, society generally, and in all its relations, will not attain as high a grade of perfection as certain portions of society, in certain special relations, have already attained? . . .

The universal extension of commerce and intercommunication, by means of steam navigation, railroads, and the magnetic telegraph, together with the general progress of enlightenment, are rapidly obliterating natural boundaries, and blending the human family into one. The cessation of war is becoming a familiar idea, and with the cessation of war armies and navies will cease of course to be required. It is probable that even the existing languages of the earth will melt, within another century or two, into one common and universal tongue, from the same causes, operating upon a more extended scale, as those which have blended the dialects of the different counties of England, of the different departments of France, and of the kingdoms of Spain into the English, the French, and the Spanish languages respectively. . . . The State Department now takes charge of the intercourse of the nation with foreign nations. But with the cessation of war there will be no foreign nations, and consequently the State or Foreign Department may in turn take itself away. Patriotism will expand into philanthropy. Nations, like sects, will dissolve into the individuals who compose them. Every man will be his own nation, and, preserving his own sovereignty and respecting the sovereignty of others, he will be a nation at peace with all others. The term, "a man of the world," reveals the fact that it is the cosmopolite in manners and sentiments whom the world already recognizes as the true gentleman—the type and leader of civilization. . . .

There is abundant evidence to the man of reflection that what we have thus performed in imagination is destined to be rapidly accomplished in fact. There is, perhaps, no one consideration which looks more directly to that consummation than the growing unpopularity of politics, in every phase of the subject. In America this fact is probably more obvious than anywhere else. The pursuit of politics is almost entirely abandoned to lawyers, and generally it is the career of those who are least successful in that profession. The general repugnance of the masses of mankind for that class of the community, by which they testify an instinctive appreciation of the outrage upon humanity committed by the attempt to reduce the impertinent interference of legislation to a science, and to practice it as a learned profession, is intensified, in the case of the politician, by the element of contempt. . . .

Negatively, it is certain that in such a state of society as that which we are now contemplating no influence will be tolerated, in the place of Government, which is maintained or exerted by force in any, even the subtlest, forms of involuntary compulsion. But there is still a sense in which men are said to exert power—a sense in which the wills of the governor and the governed concur, and blend, and harmonize with each other. It is in such a sense as this that the great orator is said to control the minds of his auditory, or that some matchless queen of song sways an irresistible influence over the hearts of men. When mankind graduate out of the period of brute force, that man will be the greatest hero and conqueror who levies the heaviest tribute of homage by excellence of achievement in any department of human performance. The avenues to distinction will not be then, as now, open only to the few. Each individual will truly govern the minds, and hearts, and conduct of others. Those who have the most power to impress themselves upon the community in which they live will govern in larger, and those who have less will govern in smaller, spheres. All will be priests and kings, serving at the innumerable altars and sitting upon the thrones of that manifold hierarchy, the foundations of which God himself has laid in the constitution of man. Genius, talent, industry, discovery, the power to please, every development of Individuality, in fine, which meets the approbation of another, will be freely recognized as the divine anointing which constitutes him a sovereign over others—a sovereign having sovereigns for his subjects. . . .

It is possible that there may be a few comparatively unimportant interests of mankind which are so essentially combined in their nature that some species of artificial organization will always be necessary for their management. I do not, for example, see how the public highways can be properly laid out and administered by the private individual. Let us resort, then, to science for the solution of this anomaly, for every subject has its science, the true social relations of mankind as well as all others. . . .

The instrumentalities necessary for hastening the adoption of these principles are . . . chiefly, two: these are, first, a more intense longing for true and harmonic relations; and, secondly, a clear intellectual conception of the principles themselves, and of the consequences which would flow from their adoption. The first is a highly religious aspiration, the second is a process of scientific induction. One is the soul and the other the sensible body, the spiritual substance and the corporeal form, of social harmony. The teachings of Christianity have inspired the one, the illumination of science must provide the other. . . .

I will conclude by warning you against one other misconception . . . that Individuality has something in common with isolation, or the severance of all personal relations with one's fellowmen. . . . It is not the disruption of relationships, but the creation of distinct and independent personalities between whom relations can exist. The more distinct the personalities, and the more cautiously they are guarded and preserved, the more intimate the relations may be, without collision or disturbance. Persons may be completely individualized in their interests who are in the most immediate personal contact, as in the case of the lodgers at a hotel, or they may have combined or amalgamated interests, and be remote from each other, as in the case of partners residing in different countries. The players at shuttlecock cooperate in friendly competition with each other, while facing and opposing each other, each fully directing his own movements, which they could not do if their arms and legs were tied together, nor even if they stood side by side. The game of life is one which demands the same freedom of movement on the part of every player, and every attempt to procure harmonious cooperation by fastening different individuals in the same position will defeat its own object. . . .

Regretting that the whole circle of the new principles of society, of which the Sovereignty of the Individual is one, can not be presented at once, I invite you, ladies and gentlemen, as occasion may offer, to inform yourselves of what they are, that you may see the subject in its entire connection of parts. In the meantime I submit to your criticism, and the criticism of the world, what I have now offered, with the undoubting conviction that it will endure the ordeal of the most searching investigation, and with the hope that, however it may shock the prejudices of earlier education, you will in the end sanction and approve it, and aid, by your devoted exertions, the inauguration of The True Constitution of Government, with its foundations laid in the Sovereignty of the Individual.

7

THE RADICAL IMPACT

Horace Greeley
LIFE—THE IDEAL AND THE ACTUAL

It is impossible to measure precisely the impact of radical ideas on the nation as a whole during the thirty years preceding the Civil War. Abolitionism succeeded, according to the usual account, in converting the north to the view that slave territory must not be allowed to expand further. But the issue was clouded by northern fears over a black influx into the free territories of the west. Meanwhile, most communitarian ventures failed rapidly, and all did eventually. The causes of temperance, women's rights, pacifism, socialism, and anarchism failed to gain general acceptance, even in the twentieth century, in most cases. Yet the ferment of those years gave America a reform tradition, centering in the belief that human society might be made more perfect, which has periodically reappeared down to the present moment. The spread of these optimistic beliefs in pre-Civil War America clearly was a matter of no little importance. The single agency most responsible for their wide penetration was The New York Tribune under the highly personal editorship of Horace Greeley (1811–1872). Greeley was a self-taught, self-made man, the son of a New Hampshire day laborer. He moved to New York in 1831 and was able to launch the Tribune ten years later. It soon became not only an important Whig political organ, but a crusading force hospitable to such causes as Fourierism, labor unions, spiritualism, free speech for abolitionists, and free soil. By the late 1850s the Tribune had gained a national influence far surpassing any rival, circulating nearly 300,000 copies daily. Its weekly edition was widely read throughout the rural north. No one selection can do justice to Greeley's views, which often changed abruptly and eccentrically. Carried away by many radical enthusiasms, he nonetheless described his intent in 1850 as that of "a mediator, an interpreter, a reconciler between conservatism and radicalism." In this lecture he weighs the evidence for pessimism and for optimism in viewing the recent history of the world.

SOURCE. Horace Greeley, "Life—The Ideal and the Actual," *Hints Toward Reforms, in Lectures, Addresses, and Other Writings* (New York: Harper & Brothers, 1850), pp. 51–52, 55–63, 66, 71–80, 82–84.

Human life—unlike what we know of the lower creation, unlike what we fairly presume of the higher—is twofold, the actual and the ideal. Our daily deeds, our daily aspirations, clash with each other—are the positive and negative poles of our being. Desire and duty are the centrifugal and centripetal forces whose counterbalancing attractions hold us firm to our appointed orbit in the grand career of existence. A lofty discontent with the actual is the main impulse to whatever is noble and heroic, as a mean dissatisfaction with physical conditions—a pining for richer food, or dress, or ampler service—is the incentive to the ignobler efforts of the million. A thoroughly contented man, could such be found, might have his uses. He would tend to moderate the fierceness of aspiration and soothe the pangs of disquiet, so prevalent in the human breast; but a thoroughly contented community would be a blank, a failure, a practical nonentity. China affords us some idea of it, by approximation; and to what purpose those three hundred millions of Chinese have lived these forty centuries, who beneath omniscience can say? The divergence of the ideal from the actual liberates the electricity of life. . . .

Rare indeed are the individuals who live exactly the life they would—whose ideal and actual exist in congenial, blended harmony. The son but seldom finds the conditions he seeks beneath the kindly, paternal roof; as manhood opens to his gaze, he quits its warm shelter, and strikes off into the bleak world without, to find or make his future sphere and home. Art, trade, adventure, professional life, present their varied attractions, and each wins some; while to others, the stormy, heaving ocean wears a winning smile, and even grim and horrid war finds votaries. A discontent with the actual is pouring Europe's surplus millions on the western shore of the Atlantic, and thence over the whole surface of our continent. It is dotting the prairies of Illinois with the cabins of the sons of New England, and year by year the smoke of the squatter's lodge rises nearer and nearer the Rocky Mountains, while hardy bands have already passed those formidable barriers, and are lining with their tents the shores of the mighty Pacific. . . .

But a revolt against the tame insipidity of common life impels to evil as well as good—hurls the warrior, the slaver, the pirate, on his fell career, and blackens earth with carnage and ruin. It is not enough that man, as he is, should act up to the standard of his aspirations, for these also need to be corrected and exalted.

Two antagonist thoughts—self and all—lie at the bottom of the many warring tendencies in the breasts of mankind. . . .

The child is born a citizen of the great commonwealth of man, but his entrance to it is through the narrow gate of the family. His practical education there, during the most impressible and important period of his life, stamps into his mind three cardinal maxims, namely:

1. To take special good care of himself in all cases, and shape everything he can control to his own enjoyment or uses.

2. To bestow whatever he does not thus need, or can not make available to his personal ends, on the narrow circle by which he is surrounded.

3. To give all beyond this—his blessing, for instance—to the general good of mankind.

Who can fail to see that the soul is distorted, shriveled, dwarfed, by this schooling?—that the boy becomes a selfish, sensual, grasping man—in fact, only a politer beast of prey? The influences most immediately surrounding him from the cradle have all tended to this. *Mine* and *thine*— the former to be prized and treasured—the latter to be acquired or left to take care of itself—are the first distinctions impressed on his unfolding intellect. All within this narrow tenement, within these encircling fences, is *ours*, to be guarded, toiled for, beautified; all without is others', to be obtained, envied, or disregarded. The stranger child who oversteps that magic ring in search of some fruit or herb, which, though enjoyed to satiety by us, would be luxury to him, is to be saluted with a stone or mastiff for his depraved temerity, and driven back to sate his gnawing hunger on the nettles of the highway. Now I am not quarreling with this as a fault of the individual, or a wanton exhibition of churlishness. On the contrary, I recognize it as a necessary feature of a system—necessary while the system shall endure. I am but regarding it in the light of its influence on the molding of human character. And in this light I do not hesitate to say that the family and social influences surrounding our youth are most unfavorable to the development of manly, generous, sympathizing natures. These influences tend to educate the human race into two classes, thieves and constables—to foster an eternal antagonism between wealth and want—and throw everyone into the attitude of a scout in an enemy's country, pressing cautiously forward with eyes piercing the thickets around him and rifle in the hollow of his arm. Here and there an individual triumphs over all these influences, by the force of rare qualities or a singularly happy training, and shows us what mankind might be, give them but fair play. But a *race* of heroes of humanity—a people elevated to love and universal blessing—such we have not and can not expect until the influences which overshadow childhood, our modes of training youth for manhood, are radically changed. . . .

Our children are steeped in selfishness from their cradles, and nine-tenths of them are practically taught to dread useful labor as odious and degrading, and to regard idleness, with sensuality and ostentation, as the *summum bonum* of life. I know that something different from this is stolidly dealt out, though never pointedly, consistently taught, from the catechisms; but I am speaking of the everyday lessons, and not those which are inculcated only on Sunday, if ever. How many children in a thousand, whether rich or poor, are taught to regard virtuous poverty in humble garb as *really* more to be honored and desired than wealth undistinguished by worth? How man are taught to heed God's appointment, "Six days shalt thou labor," as plainly directed to them, and by them to be joyfully and faithfully obeyed, irrespective of riches or station? How many are early taught that they can have no right to squander on their own appetites or pride that which the law of the land says is theirs, but for want of which another suffers? What reverend monitor now says, habitually and earnestly, and not unheededly, to the child of affluence and luxury, "Sell *all* thou hast, and give to the poor, *then* follow Him, whose only personal disciples *were* the poor?" Alas! the flower of life is cankered in the bud, and what should be beauty and fragrance is turned to deformity and death!

Next to the lessons of infancy come those of the school, with its constant bickerings and ardent, envious rivalries for advancement and honors. All is intensely individual—egotistic. The schoolboy's triumphs are won *over* and not *for* his comrades. His glory is their mortification and shame; his disasters the theme of their undisguised, unchecked exultation. Thence he passes into some sphere of active life, and finds the same law everywhere prevailing, and producing its natural results. The brilliant leader at the bar makes a rapid fortune, but the unknown hundreds of middling counselors are left to starve; and the popular physician who is supposed to cure everybody dooms his fellow practitioners to that consumption for which Falstaff could "get no remedy." Everywhere the victor in the grand battle of life advances to grasp the laurel over piles of unheeded corpses. He can not afford to calculate too nicely the moral nature of consequences of each act—he must live; and the more flagrant and palpable the guilt of the felon whom the lawyer's skill saves from justice, the more brilliant is that lawyer's triumph, the extravagant his fee—the more rapid his march to fame and fortune.

But perhaps the most imperative of the influences of practical life to narrow and distort the man is that exercised by traffic. To obtain more for less—this is the aim and the impulse of trade. The game of the counter, like that of the boxing ring, places two persons opposite each other at proper distance, and bids them shake hands and begin. That each *may* be a gainer by the bargain is of course practicable (though which of them naturally cares for this!); that both may be honest men is freely conceded. The criticism impeaches not only the men but the attitude in which they are pitted against each other. Where wealth is the object of general and eager desire, where labor is loathed and luxury coveted—it is too hard on frail human nature to place it where a slight departure from rectitude may win its thousands. The temptation *may* be resisted—it doubtless often is; for trade has furnished its full quota of the upright and more than its share of the benevolent of our race; but while these may probably have owed to commerce the *means* of being liberal, I doubt whether any have been indebted to it for their *integrity*. Of that, a man must carry all into a life of buying and selling that he expects to bring out again, and he can hardly afford to commence business on a small capital either. If a man of unsettled or weak principles ever trafficked five years without becoming a rogue, he must present a striking evidence of the sustaining, saving mercy of an overruling Providence. . . .

The position and sphere of the independent, virtuous, contented farmer has from earliest time been pointed at as one of the most fortunate and healthful, mentally as well as physically, that earth can afford. . . . And yet, on practical acquaintance, we find him quite often another person—narrow, prejudiced, and selfish; perverse, sensual, and depraved. . . . The farmer's vocation needs something more than increased efficiency and mastery of nature to reconcile it with a lofty and generous ideal. We need a change in the man himself, and in those circumstances which *vitally* affect his character. He is now too nearly an isolated being. His world is a narrow circle of material objects he calls *his own*, within which he is an autocrat, though out of it little more than a cipher. His associates are few, and these mainly rude dependents and inferiors. His daily discourse savors of beeves and swine, and the death of a sheep on his farm creates more sensation in his circle than the fall of a hero elsewhere. Of the refining, harmonizing, expanding influences of general society, he has little experience. . . .

From every country village, every rural hamlet, the better class of youth are fleeing, they care not whither, to escape the insupportable exactions of a life of toil which has ceased to bear due relations to or satisfy the wants of their enkindled souls. In vain do plodding, old-school fathers grumble at the wayward and preposterous ambition of their children—in vain do they attribute their perversity to laziness or folly, and wish "the march of mind," would keep away from honest poor men's houses, and not spoil their sons. The simple truth is, that the intellectual culture of our age has outgrown its physical and social progress, creating anarchy and confusion. Idle is all grumbling at or lamenting this advance—the shadow will not go back on the dial. What we have to do is not to draw back the van, but to bring up the rear. We must renovate and reanimate our industry, by bringing to bear upon its processes all the powers of science, all the forces of nature, all the vast economies of combination. We must call on the college, the closet, the office, to send out their ablest and wisest to lead the advance of the grand army of industrial progress, as its engineers, staff, and officers of the line. We must replace the grim knights of old war with a chivalry of industry, as honored and beloved as any knightly order, and infinitely more deserving of honor than the best. We must rearouse and redirect that enthusiasm which for centuries precipitated myriads after myriads of Christendom's best and bravest to perish by sword or famine on the rocky wastes of Palestine, battling to the last to rescue the redeemer's sepulchre from the defiling tread of the infidel, and must bring its compact, resistless phalanxes to bear upon all the physical and tangible causes of man's degradation and suffering. Guided by science, impelled by a lofty devotion to human good, sustained by the sympathies and supplies of the whole civilized world, let us hope to see the vast armament of this new chivalry advance to the draining of pestilent marshes by a single week's animated, arduous exertion—a triumph nobler than any Cannae or Waterloo—the reclamation of swamps, deserts, and sterile regions, until Sahara shall rejoice once more in verdure and fragrance, the Campagna become a garden, and stately forests belt the vast, bare plains which stretch away from either declivity of the Rocky Mountains. Of the physical improvement, whether as regards fertility or accessibility, whereof the earth is susceptible, we have begun to entertain some glimmering notion; but of the facility with which science, experience, and combined effort shall enable us to effect this improvement, no adequate idea has yet been formed. The true idea, once formed and disseminated, will but briefly precede the consummation.

Enough, for the occasion, of the definitive and the critical. Let us bestow a few moments in closing on some broader, more animating aspects of life in the nineteenth century.

Say what we will and justly may of the incurable depravity of man, as evinced in the universality of sin and crime, this world is better and more hopeful than it has been. The robber and the murderer still skulk and prowl among us, insulting the lone majesty of night with revealments of their hideous presence, but murder in the face of day and heaven—the wholesale butchery of nations, the robbery of cities and provinces—is no longer perpetrated without shame nor witnessed without indignant horror. The stifling to death of a few hundred Arabs in a cave, though shielded by the panoply of undoubted and relentless war, shocks the sensibilities of Christendom, and all apologies are instinctively rejected as adding sophistry to crime. . . .

Nor am I discouraged by the fact that kings and courts still plot against liberty and justice, or even that nations, blinded by rapacity or ambition, are led into the commission of gigantic crimes. I see also that these crimes, if not less atrocious than formerly, are less frequent, less unblushing, and require to be sugared o'er with sonorous, captivating phrases, indicating a devotion to truth and good. To steal provinces for the sake of stealing or of enjoying them would not pass uncensured now, as in the days of Xerxes, or Norman William, or Prussian Frederick. It must be styled tranquilizing a frontier, or putting an end to anarchy, or establishing justice, or extending the blessings of freedom, or something of the sort. Hypocrisy, that homage paid by vice to virtue, at least testifies the existence of that virtue without which the homage would be vain. In a former age, civilized men unceremoniously robbed savages of their possessions for God's sake and kept them for their own. Now it is deemed meet and decorous to incur the expense of making some few of the intended victims thoroughly insensible from strong drink, and thus procuring what can afterward be pronounced their signatures to a treaty of cession, surrendering lands which they had no more right to sell away from their brethren and their children than to sell the waters and the sky. And, with all this formality and seeming, the operation is often deemed imperfect unless sanctified by the presence and active participation of some Christian divine. These little attentions to the unities and proprieties, which the thoughtless would pass unheeded or with a sneer of contempt, are indeed cheering signs of human progress. They demonstrate the existence of an awakening though still drugged and drowsy national and universal conscience. They irradiate by contrast the raven darkness, unabashed ferocity and unbridled lust of man's earlier career. The light they cast on the page of history heralds the dawn of a nobler and grander era, in which nations shall realize that for them no more than for individuals is there any possible escape from the inflexibility of God's Providence, which steadily puts aside all pretences, all shams, and looks intently into the impulse and essence of every action, awarding to each the exact and inexorable recompense of its merits. In the light of that era, virtue will walk abroad unshielded by force, unindebted to opinion, winning all to obey her dictates if not from intrinsic love of her, then from love of happiness and themselves.

But this, though an effective defence against wrong-doing, can never be the true impulse to a life of active, positive goodness. That virtue which is based on a conviction of the advantage of virtue as a business investment will naturally waste too much time in calculating chances, to be of great value as a practical incitement to deeds. We need a loftier Ideal to nerve us for heroic lives. Only on forgetfulness of self, or rather on a consciousness that we are all but motes in the beam whose sun is God, drops in the rivulet whose ocean is humanity, can our souls be molded into conformity with the loftiest ideal of our race. To know and feel our nothingness without regretting it; to deem fame, riches, personal happiness, but shadows of which human good is the substance—to welcome pain, privation, ignominy, so that the sphere of human knowledge, the empire of virtue, be thereby extended—such is the soul's temper in which the heroes of the coming age shall be cast. To realize profoundly that the individual is nothing, the universal everything—to feel nothing a calamity whereby the sum of human virtue or happiness is increased, this is the truest wisdom. . . .

Say not that I thus condemn and would annihilate ambition. The love of approbation, of esteem, of true glory, is a noble incentive, and should be cherished to the end. But the ambition which points the way to fame over torn limbs and bleeding hearts—which joys in the Tartarean smoke of the battlefield and the desolating tramp of the warhorse—that ambition is worthy only of "archangel ruined." To make one conqueror's reputation, at least one hundred thousand bounding, joyous, sentient beings must be transformed into writhing and hideous fragments—must perish untimely by deaths of agony and horror, leaving half a million widows and orphans to bewail their loss in anguish and destitution. This is too mighty, too awful a price to be paid for the fame of any hero, from Nimrod to Wellington. True fame demands no such sacrifices of others; it requires us to be reckless of the outward well-being of but one. It exacts no hecatomb of victims for each triumphal pile; for the more who covet and seek it the easier and more abundant is the success of each and all. With souls of the celestial temper, each human life might be a triumph, which angels would lean from the skies delighted to witness and admire.

And, beyond doubt, the loftiest ambition possible to us finds its fruition in perfect, simple manhood. A robber may be a great warrior; a pirate an admiral; a dunce a king; a slimy intriguer a president; but to be a thorough and true man, that is an aspiration which repels all accident or seeming. And let us not fear that such are too common to be distinguished or famous. Could there appear among us a realization of the full idea of manhood—no mere general, nor statesman, nor devotee, but a complete and genuine man—he need not walk naked or in fantastic garb to gather all eyes upon him. . . . Day by day it is more and more clearly felt that the world is outgrowing the dolls and rattles of its childhood, and more and more disdains to be treated childishly. Direct, earnest speech, with useful deeds evincing lofty purpose—these are more and more insisted on, and whatever lacks them is quietly left to perish. An undeserved popularity, a sham celebrity, may still be got up by due incantations; but frailer, than the spider's gossamer, the first breath resolves them into their essential nothingness. Gas to gas, they mingle with the blue surrounding ether, and neither its serenity nor its purity is visibly affected by the infusion.

Yes, a brighter day dawns for us, sinning and suffering children of Adam. Wiser in its very follies, less cruel and wanton even in its crimes, our race visibly progresses toward a nobler and happier realization of its capacities and powers. Compared century with century, this progress is not so palpable, since what is an age to individuals, is but a moment in the lifetime of the race; but, viewed on a larger scale, the advance becomes cheeringly evident. Washington is a nobler exponent of humanity than Epaminondas or Scipio; La Fayette eclipses Phocion; and Burke has a larger nature, a more universal genius than Cicero. Wonderful as are the works of Homer, they bespeak the splendid barbarian, the thoroughly developed physical, animal man; but their range of imagination, of thought, is infinitely lower and narrower than Shakspeare's; the man they depict is infinitely poorer and more dwarfed than Goethe's, and I dare add even Byron's. Compare Achilles with Hamlet or Harold; the first is the more perfect of his kind, but of nature how infinitely grosser and less exalted! To him the stars are noteworthy but as battle-lanterns—they enable him to thrust the spear with deadlier aim to the heart of his enemy. . . . Never are we so truly human as when we most daringly transcend all the vulgar limitations of humanity; and thus Hamlet, who, viewed with disparaging coldness and skepticism, is the most erratic and improbable creation of the brain, is instinctively recognized by all awakened souls as a veritable man and a brother. His unfamiliarity at first blush accused our deficiencies, not his—was caused by his combining more of the elements of our common nature than we had been accustomed to see embodied and developed in any one man. Had we but known ourselves, Hamlet had never seemed to us a stranger.

The ages of darkness—of unconscious wandering from the path of Right and Good—of that "ignorance" which we are told "God winked at" in its earlier and more excusable manifestations—are rapidly passing away. That generation is not yet all departed which witnessed the rise, progress, and termination of the struggle regarding the rightfulness and legitimacy of the African slave-trade. Commencing in the attacks of a few obscure fanatics on the usages, maxims, gains and respectability of the commercial aristocracy and sea-faring chivalry of nearly all Christendom, it has already become a struggle between nearly all that same Christendom converted, and a few abhorred, hunted, skulking pirates. Can any man rationally doubt that the discussion of slavery itself, which had a similar beginning, is destined to run a like career, to a like termination? The fact that the latter is the more strongly entrenched in the interest, convenience, custom and seeming necessity of the superior caste, may somewhat protract the struggle; yet on the other hand the contest already past, the victory already gained in a kindred encounter, immeasurably diminish the difficulties and must abridge the duration of this. Men have learned and tested the applicability of moral laws to general and public as well as individual and private relations—to the acts of communities as well as of persons. Can any suppose that the application of this principle is to cease with the initial case which has established its efficacy and value? Far from it. We see it now operating upon rulers and nations, to restrain the most ambitious and bloodthirsty from war by a power far more dreaded than that of hostile bayonets. We see it operating at home in the temperance agitation of our time, and especially that regarding the rightfulness of the traffic in intoxicating liquors. What is this but the slave-trade question over again?—varied in form, it is true, but differing nothing in substance. The essence of either controversy regards the right of any part or member of the human family to promote or countenance for private gain any practice or business whereby others are naturally degraded, impoverished, enslaved, or made wretched. Once determine that this right does not exist in any one case, and the principle instantly and naturally confronts other cases, and insists that these also shall be tested by its standard.

Let not the sensual hope, let the good never fear, that the vitality of this principle can be exhausted while moral evil or avoidable suffering shall linger on the face of the earth. The reforms which have not yet begun to be prominent are vaster and nobler than any which have thus far been favored with the smiles, or even the frowns, of coteries and clubrooms. . . .

As yet, the great reform which shall abolish all slavery, as it only *can* be effectually really abolished by leaving none coveting the position of a master, none possessing the soul of a slave, is in its infancy, silently and slowly progressing to matured energy and vigor. *Attractive industry*, the dream of the past age, the aspiration of the present, shall be the fruition and joy of the next. The reunion of desire and duty, divorced and warring since the fall, restores man at once to the unchanging, uncloying bliss of Eden. That this is a moral renovation is indeed most true, but false is the deduction that it is wrought or endures regardless of physical conditions. Idly do the lips of the widow murmur expressions of contentment and thankfulness when her children pine for bread and have no prospect of procuring it; vainly does the forlorn wretch essay to thank that Providence whose ways he cannot fathom, but whose present results are to him famine, disease, and utter, hopeless destitution. . . . We must know what happiness is ere we can rightly appreciate the prospect of it; we must have exemption from pressing wants of the body, ere we can duly heed and be faithful to the loftiest promptings of the soul. The individual engrossed in a constant and arduous struggle for daily bread, makes slow and capricious progress on the path to heaven. Those who can not obey the divine precept, "Take no [anxious] thought for the morrow," can hardly hope to obey any precept relating to their own spiritual growth and elevation. Not till the pressing demands of our outward and bodily nature shall have been provided for, may we rationally look for a general conformity of our actual state to the ideal of sentient, intelligent being.

That the physical conditions of a calmer and nobler existence for the great mass of mankind are slowly but surely preparing, I recognize with gladness; I will not doubt that the moral elements are also commingling. In all the forms and shows of present and threatening evil, I discern the shadows of approaching good. The age now dawning shall reap in gladness the fields tearfully sown in defiance of tempests of contumely and reproach. . . . The truth must soon become apparent that riches are desirable only to widen the scope and enlarge the opportunities of well-doing—that they impart no right to live prodigally, selfishly, or ostentatiously—still less to avoid the ways of industry and benign exertion. With wealth thus possessed and employed, vanish at once the privations and the envious discontent of the poor—the dreams and the desire of agrarian equality—since the most abject must then recognize the wisdom and beneficence of the dispensation which qualifies some to be the almoners and benefactors of the less gifted or provident millions, while the more fortunate would learn to feel, in extending the amplest encouragement and aid to the lowly, some faint reflection of the rapture of creative goodness. Thus harmonized in feeling, exalted in purpose, convergent in effort, the reunited human family shall move on to greater and still greater triumphs over physical obstruction, elementary perversion, and moral dissonance, until evil and anguish shall virtually be banished, our earth be restored to its primal rank among the loyal provinces of God's empire, and man, made "a little lower than the angels," shall realize in his actual the noblest, the fairest ideal of life.

Part Three

TRANSCENDENTALISTS

1

AN EXPLANATION OF THE IMPULSE

Ralph Waldo Emerson
THE TRANSCENDENTALIST

Transcendentalism was a movement among a sector of the literary and social elite in New England that paralleled the broader religious and reform crusades of the era. If it was the product of a tiny avant–garde, the members of its circle were among the most interesting and talented people then alive in America. Strongly influenced by the Romantic movement in European litera- ture and philosophy, the Transcendentalists by no means slavishly imitated these models; instead they sought, from their highly special vantage point in Boston and Concord, to give birth to a distinctively American awakening. What made them unusual, aside from their expressive force of personality, was a world view that stood outside both the evangelical Christianity and the secular rationalism of other Americans, whether radical reformers or not. Transcendentalism was closer to the pantheistic mysticism of Asian philoso- phy in its perception of reality. At the same time, it was the first movement in America to express a mood of intellectual alienation in a modern sense, although so infused with optimism as to seem mild indeed in comparison with twentieth-century versions of this stance. It recognized a conflict between the aspirations of the inwardly sensitive individual and the demands of social custom. Whereas evangelicals and rationalists blithely created utopias with drastically unusual social arrangements, the Transcen- dentalists, perhaps because they were from elite backgrounds, often felt they had to struggle self-consciously against the tugs of convention represented by their friends and neighbors. Yet as time went on they also threw their energies into some of the standard moral causes of the day, especially antislavery. In this selection from the leading Transcendentalist organ, The Dial, Ralph Waldo Emerson (1803–1882) reveals the peculiar awareness the Transcenden- talists had of the problem of self-imposed exile from the normal flow of society. In Emerson's own case, the exile was partial and short-lived; he soon renounced extreme individualism and adopted the role of a harmless moral lecturer.

SOURCE. Ralph Waldo Emerson, "The Transcendentalist," *The Dial*, III (Janu- ary 1843), pp. 297–313.

The first thing we have to say respecting what are called *new views* here in New England, at the present time, is, that they are not new, but the very oldest of thoughts cast into the mold of these new times. The light is always identical in its composition, but it falls on a great variety of objects, and by so falling is first revealed to us, not in its own form, for it is formless, but in theirs; in like manner, thought only appears in the objects it classifies. What is popularly called Transcendentalism among us is Idealism; Idealism as it appears in 1842. As thinkers, mankind have ever divided into two sects, materialists and idealists; the first class founding on experience, the second on consciousness; the first class beginning to think from the data of the senses, the second class perceive that the senses are not final, and say, the senses give us representations of things, but what are the things themselves, they cannot tell. The materialist insists on facts, on history, on the force of circumstances, and the animal wants of man; the idealist on the power of thought and of will, on inspiration, on miracle, on individual culture. These two modes of thinking are both natural, but the idealist contends that his way of thinking is in higher nature. He concedes all that the other affirms, admits the impression of sense, admits their coherency, their use and beauty, and then asks the materialist for his grounds of assurance that things are as his senses represent them. But I, he says, affirm facts not affected by the illusions of sense, facts which are of the same nature as the faculty which reports them, and not liable to doubt; facts which in their first appearance to us assume a native superiority to material facts, degrading these into a language by which the first are to be spoken; facts which it only needs a retirement from the senses to discern. Every materialist will be an idealist; but an idealist can never go backward to be a materialist.

The idealist, in speaking of events, sees them as spirits. He does not deny the sensuous fact; by no means; but he will not see that alone. He does not deny the presence of this table, this chair, and the walls of this room, but he looks at these things as the reverse side of the tapestry, as the *other end*, each being a sequel or completion of a spiritual fact which nearly concerns him. This manner of looking at things, transfers every object in nature from an independent and anomalous position without there, into the consciousness. Even the materialist Condillac, perhaps the most logical expounder of materialism, was constrained to say, "Though we should soar into the heavens, though we should sink into the abyss, we never go out of ourselves; it is always our own thought that we perceive." What more could an idealist say?

The materialist, secure in the certainty of sensation, mocks at finespun theories, at stargazers and dreamers, and believes that his life is solid, that he at least takes nothing for granted, but knows where he stands, and what he does. Yet how easy it is to show him, that he also is a phantom walking and working amid phantoms, and that he need only ask a question or two beyond his daily questions, to find his solid universe growing dim and impalpable before his sense. The sturdy capitalist, no matter how deep and square on blocks of Quincy granite he lays the foundations of his banking house or exchange, must set it, at last, not on a cube corresponding to the angles of his structure, but on a mass of unknown materials and solidity, red-hot or white-hot, perhaps at the core, which rounds off to an almost perfect sphericity, and lies floating in soft air, and goes spinning away, dragging bank and banker with it at a rate of thousands of miles the hour, he knows not whither—a bit of bullet, now glimmering, now darkling through a small cubic space on the edge of an unimaginable pit of emptiness. And this wild balloon, in which his whole venture is embarked, is a just symbol of his whole state and faculty. One thing, at least, he says is certain, and does not give me the headache, that figures do not lie; the multiplication table has been hitherto found unimpeachable truth; and, moreover, if I put a gold eagle in my safe, I find it again tomorrow; but for these thoughts, I know not whence they are. They change and pass away. But ask him why he believes that a uniform experience will continue uniform, or on what grounds he founds his faith in his figures, and he will perceive that his mental fabric is built up on just as strange and quaking foundations as his proud edifice of stone.

In the order of thought, the materialist takes his departure from the external world, and esteems a man as one product of that. The idealist takes his departure from his consciousness, and reckons the world as an appearance. The materialist respects sensible masses, society, government, social art, and luxury, every establishment, every mass, whether majority of numbers, or extent of space, or amount of objects, every social action. The idealist has another measure, which is metaphysical, namely, the *rank* which things themselves take in his consciousness; not at all, the size or appearance. Mind is the only reality, of which men and all other natures are better or worse reflectors. Nature, literature, history, are only subjective phenomena. Although in his action overpowered by the laws of action, and so, warmly cooperating with men, even preferring them to himself, yet when he speaks scientifically, or after the order of thought, he is constrained to degrade persons into representatives of truths. He does not respect labor, or the products of labor, namely, property, otherwise than as a manifold symbol, illustrating with wonderful fidelity of details the laws of being; he does not respect government, except as far as it reiterates the law of his mind; nor the church; nor charities; nor arts, for themselves; but hears, as at a vast distance, what they say, as if his consciousness would speak to him through a pantomimic scene. His thought—that is the universe. His experience inclines him to behold the procession of facts you call the world, as flowing perpetually outward from an invisible, unsounded center in himself, center alike of him and of them, and necessitating him to regard all things as having a subjective or relative existence, relative to that aforesaid unknown Center of him.

From this transfer of the world into the consciousness, this beholding of all things in the mind, follows easily his whole ethics. It is simpler to be self-dependent. The height, the deity of man is to be self-sustained, to need no gift, no foreign force. Society is good when it does not violate me; but best when it is likest to solitude. Everything real is self-existent. Everything divine shares the self-existence of Deity. All that you call the world is the shadow of that substance which you are, the perpetual creation of the powers of thought, of those that are dependent and of those that are independent of your will. Do not cumber yourself with fruitless pains to mend and remedy remote effects; let the soul be erect, and all things will go well. You think me the child of my circumstances: I make my circumstance. Let any thought or motive of mine be different from that they are, the difference will transform my whole condition and economy. I—this thought which is called I—is the mold into which the world is poured like melted wax. The mold is invisible, but the world betrays the shape of the mold. You call it the power of circumstance, but it is the power of me. Am I in harmony with myself? My position will seem to you just and commanding. Am I vicious and insane? My fortunes will seem to you obscure and descending. As I am, so shall I associate; as I am, so shall I act; Caesar's history will paint out Caesar. Jesus acted so, because he thought so. I do not wish to overlook or to gainsay any reality; I say, I make my circumstance: but if you ask me, Whence am I? I feel like other men my relation to that fact which cannot be spoken, or defined, nor even thought, but which exists, and will exist.

The Transcendentalist adopts the whole connection of spiritual doctrine. He believes in miracle, in the perpetual openness of the human mind to new influx of light and power; he believes in inspiration and in ecstasy. He wishes that the spiritual principle should be suffered to demonstrate itself to the end, in all possible applications to the state of man, without the admission of anything unspiritual; that is, anything positive, dogmatic, personal. Thus, the spiritual measure of inspiration is the depth of the thought, and never, who said it? And so he resists all attempts to palm other rules and measures on the spirit than its own.

In action, he easily incurs the charge of antinomianism by his avowal that he, who has the lawgiver, may with safety not only neglect, but even contravene every written commandment. In the play of Othello, the expiring Desdemona absolves her husband of the murder, to her attendant Emilia. Afterwards, when Emilia charges him with the crime, Othello exclaims,

"You heard her say herself it was not I."
Emilia replies,
"The more angel she, and thou the blacker devil."

Of this fine incident, Jacobi, the Transcendental moralist, makes use, with other parallel instances, in his reply to Immanuel Kant. Jacobi, refusing all measure of right and wrong except the determinations of the private spirit, remarks that there is no crime but has sometimes been a virtue. "I," he says, "am that atheist, that godless person who, in opposition to an imaginary doctrine of calculation, would lie as the dying Desdemona lied; would lie and deceive as Pylades when he personated Orestes; would assassinate like Timoleon; would perjure myself like Epaminondas, and John de Witt; I would resolve on suicide like Cato; I would commit sacrilege with David; yea, and pluck ears of corn on the Sabbath, for no other reason than that I was fainting for lack of food. For, I have assurance in myself that in pardoning these faults according to the letter, man exerts the sovereign right which the majesty of his being confers on him; he sets the seal of his divine nature to the grace he accords."[1]

In like manner, if there is anything grand and daring in human thought or virtue, any reliance on the vast, the unknown; any presentiment; any extravagance of faith, the spiritualist adopts it as most in nature. The oriental mind has always tended to this largeness. Buddhism is an expression of it. The Buddhist who thanks no man, who says, "do not flatter your benefactors," but who in his conviction that every good deed can by no possibility escape its reward, will not deceive the benefactor by pretending that he has done more than he should, is a Transcendentalist.

[1]Coleridge's translation.

You will see by this sketch that there is no such thing as a Transcendental *party*; that there is no pure Transcendentalist; that we know of none but the prophets and heralds of such a philosophy; that all who by strong bias of nature have leaned to the spiritual side in doctrine, have stopped short of their goal. We have had many harbingers and forerunners; but of a purely spiritual life, history has yet afforded no example. I mean, we have yet no man who has leaned entirely on his character, and eaten angels' food; who, trusting to his sentiments, found life made of miracles; who, working for universal aims, found himself fed, he knew not how; clothed, sheltered, and weaponed, he knew not how, and yet it was done by his own hands. Only in the instinct of the lower animals we find the suggestion of the methods of it, and something higher than our understanding. The squirrel hoards nuts, and the bee gathers honey, without knowing what they do, and they are thus provided for without selfishness or disgrace.

Shall we say, then, that Transcendentalism is the Saturnalia or excess of faith; the presentiment of a faith proper to man in his integrity, excessive only when his imperfect obedience hinders the satisfaction of his wish. Nature is transcendental, exists primarily, necessarily, ever works and advances, yet takes no thought for the morrow. Man owns the dignity of the life which throbs around him in chemistry, and tree, and animal, and in the involuntary functions of his own body; yet he is baulked when he tries to fling himself into this enchanted circle, where all is done without degradation. Yet genius and virtue predict in man the same absence of private ends, and of condescension to circumstances, united with every trait and talent of beauty and power.

This way of thinking, falling on Roman times, made Stoic philosophers; falling on despotic times, made patriot Catos and Brutuses; falling on superstitious times, made prophets and apostles; on popish times, made Protestants and ascetic monks, preachers of faith against the preachers of works; on prelatical times, made Puritans and Quakers; and falling on Unitarian and conservative times, makes the peculiar shades of Idealism which we know.

It is well known to most of my audience, that the Idealism of the present day acquired the name of Transcendental, from the use of that term by Immanuel Kant, of Konigsberg, who replied to the skeptical philosophy of Locke, which insisted that there was nothing in the intellect which was not previously in the experience of the senses, by showing that there was a very important class of ideas, or imperative forms, which did not come by experience, but through which experience was acquired; that these were intuitions of the mind itself; and he denominated them *Transcendental* forms. The extraordinary profoundness and precision of that man's thinking have given vogue to his nomenclature, in Europe and America, to that extent, that whatever belongs to the class of intuitive thought, is popularly called at the present day *Transcendental*.

Although, as we have said, there is no pure transcendentalist, yet the tendency to respect the intuitions, and to give them, at least in our creed, all authority over our experience, has deeply colored the conversation and poetry of the present day; and the history of genius and of religion in these times, though impure, and as yet not incarnated in any powerful individual, will be the history of this tendency.

It is a sign of our times, conspicuous to the coarsest observer, that many intelligent and religious persons withdraw themselves from the common labors and competitions of the market and the caucus, and betake themselves to a certain solitary and critical way of living, from which no solid fruit has yet appeared to justify their separation. They hold themselves aloof: they feel the disproportion between their faculties and the work offered them, and they prefer to ramble in the country and perish of ennui, to the degradation of such charities and such ambitions as the city can propose to them. They are striking work and crying out for somewhat worthy to do! What they do is done only because they are overpowered by the humanities that speak on all sides; and they consent to such labor as is open to them, though to their lofty dream the writing of Iliads or Hamlets, or the building of cities or empires seems drudgery.

Now every one must do after his kind, be he asp or angel, and these must. The question, which a wise man and a student of modern history will ask is, what that kind is? And truly, as in ecclesiastical history we take so much pains to know what the Gnostics, what the Essenes, what the Manichees, and what the Reformers believed, it would not misbecome us to inquire nearer home, what these companions and contemporaries of ours think and do, at least so far as these thoughts and actions appear to be not accidental and personal, but common to many, and so the inevitable flower of the Tree of Time. Our American literature and spiritual history are, we confess, in the optative mood; but whoso knows these seething brains, these admirable radicals, these unsocial worshippers, these talkers who talk the sun and moon away, will believe that this heresy cannot pass away without leaving its mark.

They are lonely; the spirit of their writing and conversation is lonely; they shed influences; they shun general society; they incline to shut themselves in their chamber in the house, to live in the country rather than in the town, and to find their tasks and amusements in solitude. Society, to be sure, does not like this very well; it saith, Whoso goes to walk alone, accuses the whole world; he declareth all to be unfit to be his companions; it is very uncivil, nay, insulting; society will retaliate. Meantime, this retirement does not proceed from any whim on the part of these separators; but if any one will take pains to talk with them, he will find that this part is chosen both from temperament and from principle; with some unwillingness, too, and as a choice of the less of two evils; for these persons are not by nature melancholy, sour, and unsocial—they are not stockish or brute—but joyous, susceptible, affectionate; they have even more than others a great wish to be loved. Like the young Mozart, they are rather ready to cry ten times a day, "But are you sure you love me?" Nay, if they tell you their whole thought, they will own that love seems to them the last and highest gift of nature; that there are persons whom in their hearts they daily thank for existing—persons whose faces are perhaps unknown to them, but whose fame and spirit have penetrated their solitude—and for whose sake they wish to exist. To behold the beauty of another character, which inspires a new interest in our own; to behold the beauty lodged in a human being, with such vivacity of apprehension, that I am instantly forced home to inquire if I am not deformity itself; to behold in another the expression of a love so high that it assures itself—assures itself also to me against every possible casualty except my unworthiness; these are degrees on the scale of human happiness, to which they have ascended; and it is a fidelity to this sentiment which has made common association distasteful to them. They wish a just and even fellowship, or none. They cannot gossip with you, and they do not wish, as they are sincere and religious, to gratify any mere curiosity which you may entertain. Like fairies, they do not wish to be spoken of. Love me, they say, but do not ask who is my cousin and my uncle. If you do not need to hear my thought, because you can read it in my face and behavior, then I will tell it you from sunrise to sunset. If you cannot divine it, you would not understand what I say. I will not molest myself for you. I do not wish to be profaned.

And yet, when you see them near, it seems as if this loneliness, and not this love, would prevail in their circumstances, because of the extravagant demand they make on human nature. That, indeed, constitutes a new feature in their portrait, that they are the most exacting and extortionate critics. Their quarrel with every man they meet, is not with his kind, but with his degree. There is not enough of him

—that is the only fault. They prolong their privilege of childhood in this wise, of doing nothing—but making immense demands on all the gladiators in the lists of action and fame. They make us feel the strange disappointment which overcasts every human youth. So many promising youths, and never a finished man! The profound nature will have a savage rudeness; the delicate one will be shallow, or the victim of sensibility; the richly accomplished will have some capital absurdity; and so every piece has a crack. 'Tis strange, but this masterpiece is a result of such an extreme delicacy, that the most unobserved flaw in the boy will neutralize the most aspiring genius, and spoil the work. Talk with a seaman of the hazards to life in his profession, and he will ask you, "Where are the old sailors? Do you not see that all are young men?" And we, on this sea of human thought, in like manner inquire, Where are the old idealists? Where are they who represented to the last generation that extravagant hope, which a few happy aspirants suggest to ours? In looking at the class of counsel, and power, and wealth, and at the matronage of the land, amidst all the prudence and all the triviality, one asks, Where are they who represented genius, virtue, the invisible and heavenly world, to these? Are they dead—taken in early ripeness to the gods—as ancient wisdom foretold their fate? Or did the high idea die out of them, and leave their unperfumed body as its tomb and tablet, announcing to all that the celestial inhabitant, who once gave them beauty, had departed? Will it be better with the new generation? We easily predict a fair future to each new candidate who enters the lists, but we are frivolous and volatile, and by low aims and ill example do what we can to defeat this hope. Then these youths bring us a rough but effectual aid. By their unconcealed dissatisfaction, they expose our poverty, and the insignificance of man to man. A man is a poor limitary benefactor. He ought to be a shower of benefits—a great influence, which should never let his brother go, but should refresh old merits continually with new ones; so that, though absent, he should never be out of my mind, his name never far from my lips; but if the earth should open at my side, or my last hour were come, his name should be the prayer I should utter to the universe. But in our experience, man is cheap, and friendship wants its deep sense. We affect to dwell with our friends in their absence, but we do not; when deed, word, or letter comes not, they let us go. These exacting children advertise us of our wants. There is no compliment, no smooth speech with them; they pay you only this one compliment, of insatiable expectation; they aspire, they severely exact, and if they only stand fast in this watchtower, and persist in demanding unto the end, and without end, then are they terrible friends, whereof poet and priest cannot choose but stand in awe; and what if they eat clouds, and drink wind, they have not been without service to the race of man.

With this passion for what is great and extraordinary, it cannot be wondered at, that they are repelled by vulgarity and frivolity in people. They say to themselves, It is better to be alone than in bad company. And it is really a wish to be met—the wish to find society for their hope and religion—which prompts them to shun what is called society. They feel that they are never so fit for friendship, as when they have quit mankind, and taken themselves to friend. A picture, a book, a favorite spot in the hills or the woods, which they can people with the fair and worthy creation of the fancy, can give them often forms so vivid, that these for the time shall seem real, and society the illusion.

But their solitary and fastidious manners not only withdraw them from the conversation, but from the labors of the world; they are not good citizens, not good members of society; unwillingly they bear their part of the public and private burdens; they do not willingly share in the public charities, in the public religious rites, in the enterprises of education, of missions foreign or domestic, in the abolition of the slave trade, or in the temperance society. They are inactive; they do not even like to vote. The philanthropists inquire whether Transcendentalism does not mean sloth. They had as lief hear that their friend was dead as that he was a Transcendentalist; for then is he paralyzed, and can never do anything for humanity. What right, cries the good world, has the man of genius to retreat from work, and indulge himself? The popular literary creed seems to be, "I am a sublime genius; I ought not therefore to labor." But genius is the power to labor better and more availably than others. Deserve thy genius: exalt it. The good, the illuminated, sit apart from the rest, censuring their dullness and vices, as if they thought that, by sitting very grand in their chairs, the very brokers, attorneys, and congressmen would see the error of their ways, and flock to them. But the good and wise must learn to act, and carry salvation to the combatants and demagogues in the dusty arena below.

On the part of these children, it is replied, that life and their faculty seem to them gifts too rich to be squandered on such trifles as you propose to them. What you call your fundamental institutions, your great and holy causes, seem to them great abuses, and, when nearly seen, paltry matters. Each "cause," as it is called—say abolition, temperance, say Calvinism, or Unitarianism—becomes speedily a little shop, where the article, let it have been at first never so subtle and ethereal, is now made up into portable and convenient cakes, and retailed in small quantities to suit purchasers. You make very free use of these words "great and holy," but few things appear to them such. Few persons have any magnificence of nature to inspire enthusiasm, and the philanthropies and charities have a certain air of quackery. As to the general course of living, and the daily employments of men, they cannot see much virtue in these, since they are parts of this vicious circle; and, as no great ends are answered by the men, there is nothing noble in the arts by which they are maintained. Nay, they have made the experiment, and found that from the liberal professions to the coarsest manual labor, and from the courtesies of the academy and the college to the conventions of the cotillion room and the morning call, there is a spirit of cowardly compromise and seeming, which intimates a frightful skepticism, a life without love, and an activity without an aim.

Unless the action is necessary, unless it is adequate, I do not wish to perform it. I do not wish to do one thing but once. I do not love routine. Once possessed of the principle, it is equally easy to make four or forty thousand applications of it. A great man will be content to have indicated in any the slightest manner his perception of the reigning idea of his time, and will leave to those who like it the multiplication of examples. When he has hit the white, the rest may shatter the target. Everything admonishes us how needlessly long life is. Every moment of a hero so raises and cheers us, that a twelve-month is an age. All that the brave Xanthus brings home from his wars, is the recollection that, at the storming of Samos, "in the heat of the battle, Pericles smiled on me, and passed on to another detachment." It is the quality of the moment, not the number of days, of events, or of actors, that imports.

New, we confess, and by no means happy, is our condition: if you want the aid of our labor, we ourselves stand in greater want of the labor. We are miserable with inaction. We perish of rest and rust. But we do not like your work.

"Then," says the world, "show me your own."

"We have none."

"What will you do, then?" cries the world.

"We will wait."

"How long?"

"Until the universe rises up and calls us to work."

"But whilst you wait, you grow old and useless."

"Be it so: I can sit in a corner and *perish* (as you call it), but I will not move until I have the highest command. If no call should come for years, for centuries, then I know that the want of the universe is the attestation of faith by this my abstinence. Your virtuous projects, so called, do not cheer me. I know that which shall come will cheer me. If I cannot work, at least I need not lie. All that is clearly due today is not to lie. In other places, other men have encountered sharp trials, and have behaved themselves well. The martyrs were sawn asunder, or hung alive on meat hooks. Cannot we screw our courage to patience and truth, and without complaint, or even with good humor, await our turn of action in the infinite counsels?"

But, to come a little closer to the secret of these persons, we must say, that to them it seems a very easy matter to answer the objections of the man of the world, but not so easy to dispose of the doubts and objections that occur to themselves. They are exercised in their own spirit with queries, which acquaint them with all adversity, and with the trials of the bravest heroes. When I asked them concerning their private experience, they answered somewhat in this wise: It is not to be denied that there must be some wide difference between my faith and other faith; and mine is a certain brief experience, which surprised me in the highway or in the market, in some place, at some time—whether in the body or out of the body, God knoweth—and made me aware that I had played the fool with fools all this time, but that law existed for me and for all; that to me belonged trust, a child's trust and obedience, and the worship of ideas, and I should never be fool more. Well, in the space of an hour, probably, I was let down from this height; I was at my old tricks, the selfish member of a selfish society. My life is superficial, takes no root in the deep world; I ask, When shall I die, and be relieved of the responsibility of seeing a universe which I do not use? I wish to exchange this flash-of-lightning faith for continuous daylight, this fever-glow for a benign climate.

These two states of thought diverge every moment, and stand in wild contrast. To whom who looks at his life from these moments of illumination, it will seem that he skulks and plays a mean, shiftless and subaltern part in the world. That is to be done which he has not skill to do, or to be said which others can say better, and he lies by, or occupies his hands with some plaything, until his hour comes again. Much of our reading, much of our labor, seems mere waiting: it was not that we were born for. Any other could do it as well, or better. So little skill enters into these works, so little do they mix with the divine life, that it really signifies little what we do, whether we turn a grindstone, or ride, or run, or make fortunes, or govern the state. The worst feature of this double consciousness is that the two lives, of the understanding and of the soul, which we lead, really show very little relation to each other, never meet and measure each other: one prevails now, all buzz and din; and the other prevails then, all infinitude and paradise; and, with the progress of life, the two discover no greater disposition to reconcile themselves. Yet, what is my faith? What am I? What but a thought of serenity and independence, an abode in the deep blue sky? Presently the clouds shut down again; yet we retain the belief that this pretty web we weave will at last be overshot and reticulated with veins of the blue, and that the moments will characterize the days. Patience, then, is for us, is it not? Patience, and still patience. When we pass, as presently we shall, into some new infinitude, out of this Iceland of negations, it will please us to reflect that, though we had few virtues or consolations, we bore with our indigence, nor once strove to repair it with hypocrisy or false heat of any kind.

But this class are not sufficiently characterized, if we omit to add that they are lovers and worshippers of beauty. In the eternal trinity of truth, goodness, and beauty, each in its perfection including the three, they prefer to make beauty the sign and head. Something of the same taste is observable in all the moral movements of the time, in the religious and benevolent enterprises. They have a liberal, even an aesthetic spirit. A reference to Beauty in action sounds, to be sure, a little hollow and ridiculous in the ears of the old church. In politics, it has often sufficed, when they treated of justice, if they kept the bounds of selfish calculation. If they granted restitution, it was prudence which granted it. But the justice which is now claimed for the black, and the pauper, and the drunkard, is for beauty—is for a necessity to the soul of the agent, not of the beneficiary. I say this is the tendency, not yet the realization. Our virtue totters and trips, does not yet walk firmly. Its representatives are austere; they preach and denounce; their rectitude is not yet a grace. They are still liable to that slight taint of burlesque which, in our strange world, attaches to the zealot. A saint should be as dear as the apple of the eye. Yet we are tempted to smile, and we flee from the working to the speculative reformer, to escape that same slight ridicule. Alas for these days of derision and criticism! We call the beautiful the highest, because it appears to us the golden mean, escaping the dowdiness of the good, and the heartlessness of the true. They are lovers of nature also, and find an indemnity in the inviolable order of the world for the violated order and grace of man.

There is, no doubt, a great deal of well-founded objection to be spoken or felt against the sayings and doings of this class, some of whose traits we have selected; no doubt, they will lay themselves open to criticism and to lampoons, and as ridiculous stories will be told of them as of any. There will be cant and pretension; there will be subtility and moonshine. These persons are of unequal strength, and do not all prosper. They complain that everything around them must be denied; and if feeble, it takes all their strength to deny, before they can begin to lead their own life. Grave seniors insist on their respect to this institution, and that usage; to an obsolete history; to some vocation, or college, or etiquette, or beneficiary, or charity, or morning or evening call, which they resist, as what does not concern them. But it costs such sleepless nights, and alienations and misgivings, they have so many moods about it; these old guardians never changed *their* minds; they have but one mood on the subject, namely, that Antony is very perverse, that it is quite as much as Antony can do, to assert his rights, abstain from what he thinks foolish, and keep his temper. He cannot help the reaction of this injustice in his own mind. He is braced-up and stilted; all freedom and flowing genius, all sallies of wit and frolic nature are quite out of the question; it is well if he can keep from lying, injustice, and suicide. There is no time for gaiety and grace. His strength and spirits are wasted in rejection. But the strong spirits overpower those around them without effort. Their thought and emotion comes in like a flood, quite withdraws them from all notice of these carping critics; they surrender themselves with glad heart to the heavenly guide, and only by implication reject the clamorous nonsense of the hour. Grave seniors talk to the deaf —church and old book mumble and virtualize to an unheeding, preoccupied and advancing mind, and thus they by happiness of greater momentum lose no time, but take the right road at first.

But all these of whom I speak are not proficients, they are novices; they only show the road in which man should travel, when the soul has greater health and prowess. Yet let them feel the dignity of their charge, and deserve a larger power. Their heart is the ark in which the fire is concealed, which shall burn in a broader and universal flame. Let them obey the genius then most when his impulse is wildest; then most when he seems to lead to uninhabitable deserts of thought and life; for the path which the hero travels alone is the highway of health and benefit to mankind. What is the privilege and nobility of our nature, but its persistency, through its power to attach itself to what is permanent?

Society also has its duties in reference to this class, and must behold them with what charity it can. Possibly some benefit may yet accrue from them to the state. In our Mechanics' Fair, there must be not only bridges, ploughs, carpenters' planes, and baking troughs, but also some few finer instruments—raingauges, thermometers, and telescopes; and in society, besides farmers, sailors, and weavers, there must be a few persons of purer fire kept specially as gauges and meters of character; persons of a fine, detecting instinct, who betray the smallest accumulations of wit and feeling in the bystander. Perhaps too there might be room for the exciters and monitors; collectors of the heavenly spark with power to convey the electricity to others. Or, as the storm-tossed vessel at sea speaks the frigate or "line-packet" to learn its longitude, so it may not be without its advantage that we should now and then encounter rare and gifted men, to compare the points of our spiritual compass, and verify our bearings from superior chronometers.

Amidst the downward tendency and proneness of things, when every voice is raised for a new road or another statute, or a subscription of stock, for an improvement in dress, or in dentistry, for a new house or a larger business, for a political party, or the division of an estate—will you not tolerate one or two solitary voices in the land, speaking for thoughts and principles not marketable or perishable? Soon these improvements and mechanical inventions will be superseded; these modes of living lost out of memory; these cities rotted, ruined by war, by new inventions, by new seats of trade, or the geologic changes—all gone, like the shells which sprinkle the sea-beach with a white colony today, forever renewed to be forever destroyed. But the thoughts which these few hermits strove to proclaim by silence, as well as by speech, not only by what they did, but by what they forbore to do, shall abide in beauty and strength, to reorganize themselves in nature, to invest themselves anew in other, perhaps higher endowed and happier mixed clay than ours, in fuller union with the surrounding system.

2

PRIVATE VISION AS SUBSTITUTE FOR SOCIAL RESPONSIBILITY

Henry David Thoreau
LIFE WITHOUT PRINCIPLE

No one has ever put the case for internal secession from society more strongly than Henry David Thoreau (1817–1862). A Harvard graduate who burned with literary ambition, he did not choose to carve out a conventional career. Instead he remained in his neighborhood haunts at Concord, Massachusetts, for a time teaching school with his brother. He and his three brothers and sisters all remained unmarried. For two years the young Thoreau lived with Emerson as a disciple. But Thoreau's dislike of compromise hindered even this friendship, the echoes of which strongly colored the preceding selection by Emerson. Thoreau's last years were spent in rugged aloneness, made bitter by the commercial failure of Walden. Nature, viewed as the manifestation of vital divine force, became his constant companion. Out of this highly unusual life came the first self-conscious concern over life-style ever to appear in America. Business, politics, and the whole network of social institutions were attacked by him because they carried a low tone inconsistent with unfettered self-development in the direction of cosmic awareness. As the slavery controversy intensified, Thoreau partially forgot these scruples to become a passionate defender of John Brown. And earlier, by refusing to pay his taxes just before the Mexican War, Thoreau combined rejection of customary political obligations with a pointed protest against particular governmental policies widely disliked in New England. This essay was first written in 1854 and was given a number of times as a lyceum lecture. Thoreau was often genuinely admired by his contemporaries for his literary eloquence, but they also regarded him as an unfortunate extremist in the substance of his views.

At a lyceum, not long since, I felt that the lecturer had chosen a theme too foreign to himself, and so failed to interest me as much as he

SOURCE. Henry David Thoreau, *"Life Without Principle,"* The Atlantic Monthly, XII (October 1863), pp. 484–495.

might have done. He described things not in or near to his heart, but toward his extremities and superficies. There was, in this sense, no truly central or centralizing thought in the lecture. I would have had him deal with his privatest experience, as the poet does. The greatest compliment that was ever paid me was when one asked me what *I thought,* and attended to my answer. I am surprised, as well as delighted, when this happens, it is such a rare use he would make of me, as if he were acquainted with the tool. Commonly, if men want anything of me, it is only to know how many acres I make of their land—since I am a surveyor—or, at most, what trivial news I have burdened myself with. They never will go to law for my meat; they prefer the shell. A man once came a considerable distance to ask me to lecture on slavery; but on conversing with him, I found that he and his clique expected seven-eights of the lecture to be theirs, and only one-eighth mine; so I declined. I take it for granted, when I am invited to lecture anywhere—for I have had a little experience in that business—that there is a desire to hear what *I think* on some subject, though I may be the greatest fool in the country—and not that I should say pleasant things merely, or such as the audience will assent to; and I resolve, accordingly, that I will give them a strong dose of myself. They have sent for me, and engaged to pay for me, and I am determined that they shall have me, though I bore them beyond all precedent.

So now I would say something similar to you, my readers. Since you are my readers, and I have not been much of a traveler, I will not talk about people a thousand miles off, but come as near home as I can. As the time is short, I will leave out all the flattery, and retain all the criticism.

Let us consider the way in which we spend our lives.

This world is a place of business. What an infinite bustle! I am awaked almost every night by the panting of the locomotive. It interrupts my dreams. There is no sabbath. It would be glorious to see mankind at leisure for once. It is nothing but work, work, work. I cannot easily buy a blank-book to write thoughts in; they are commonly ruled for dollars and cents. An Irishman, seeing me making a minute in the fields, took it for granted that I was calculating my wages. If a man was tossed out of a window when an infant, and so made a cripple for life, or scared out of his wits by the Indians, it is regretted chiefly because he was thus incapacitated for—business! I think that there is nothing, not even crime, more opposed to poetry, to philosophy, ay, to life itself, than this incessant business.

There is a coarse and boisterous money-making fellow in the outskirts of our town, who is going to build a bank wall under the hill along the edge of his meadow. The powers have put this into his head to keep him out of mischief, and he wishes me to spend three weeks digging there with him. The result will be that he will perhaps get some more money to hoard, and leave for his heirs to spend foolishly. If I do this, most will commend me as an industrious and hard-working man; but if I choose to devote myself to certain labors which yield more real profit, though but little money, they may be inclined to look on me as an idler. Nevertheless, as I do not need the police of meaningless labor to regulate me, and do not see anything absolutely praiseworthy in this fellow's undertaking any more than in many an enterprise of our own or foreign governments, however amusing it may be to him or them, I prefer to finish my education at a different school.

If a man walk in the woods for love of them half of each day, he is in danger of being regarded as a loafer; but if he spends his whole day as a speculator, shearing off those woods and making earth bald before her time, he is esteemed an industrious and enterprising citizen. As if a town had no interest in its forests but to cut them down!

Most men would feel insulted if it were proposed to employ them in throwing stones over a wall, and then in throwing them back, merely that they might earn their wages. But many are no more worthily employed now. For instance: just after sunrise, one summer morning, I noticed one of my neighbors walking beside his team, which was slowly drawing a heavy hewn stone swung under the axle, surrounded by an atmosphere of industry—his day's work begun—his brow commenced to sweat—a reproach to all sluggards and idlers—pausing abreast the shoulders of his oxen, and half turning round with a flourish of his merciful whip, while they gained their length on him. And I thought, Such is the labor which the American Congress exists to protect—honest, manly toil—honest as the day is long—that makes his bread taste sweet, and keeps society sweet—which all men respect and have consecrated; one of the sacred band, doing the needful but irksome drudgery. Indeed, I felt a slight reproach, because I observed this from a window, and was not abroad and stirring about a similar business. The day went by, and at evening I passed the yard of another neighbor, who keeps many servants, and spends much money foolishly, while he adds nothing to the common stock, and there I saw the stone of the morning lying beside a whimsical structure intended to adorn this Lord Timothy Dexter's premises, and the dignity forthwith departed from the teamster's labor, in my eyes. In my opinion, the sun was made to light worthier toil than this. I may add that his employer has since run off, in debt to a good part of the town, and, after passing through Chancery, has settled somewhere else, there to become once more a patron of the arts.

The ways by which you may get money almost without exception lead downward. To have done anything by which you earned money *merely* is to have been truly idle or worse. If the laborer gets no more than the wages which his employer pays him, he is cheated, he cheats himself. If you would get money as a writer or lecturer, you must be popular, which is to go down perpendicularly. Those services which the community will most readily pay for, it is most disagreeable to render. You are paid for being something less than a man. The state does not commonly reward a genius any more wisely. Even the poet laureate would rather not have to celebrate the accidents of royalty. He must be bribed with a pipe of wine; and perhaps another poet is called away from his muse to gauge that very pipe. As for my own business, even that kind of surveying which I could do with most satisfaction my employers do not want. They would prefer that I should do my work coarsely and not too well, ay, not well enough. When I observe that there are different ways of surveying, my employer commonly asks which will give him the most land, not which is most correct. I once invented a rule for measuring cordwood, and tried to introduce it in Boston; but the measurer there told me that the sellers did not wish to have their wood measured correctly—that he was already too accurate for them, and therefore they commonly got their wood measured in Charlestown before crossing the bridge.

The aim of the laborer should be, not to get his living, to get "a good job," but to perform well a certain work; and, even in a pecuniary sense, it would be economy for a town to pay its laborers so well that they would not feel that they were working for low ends, as for a livelihood merely , but for scientific, or even moral ends. Do not hire a man who does your work for money, but him who does it for love of it.

It is remarkable that there are few men so well employed, so much to their minds, but that a little money or fame would commonly buy them off from their present pursuit. I see advertisements for *active* young men, as if activity were the whole of a young man's capital. Yet I have been surprised when one has with confidence proposed to me, a grown man, to embark in some enterprise of his, as if I had absolutely nothing to do, my life having been a complete failure hitherto. What a doubtful compliment this to pay me! As if he had met me halfway across the ocean beating up against the wind, but bound nowhere, and proposed to me to go along with him! If I did, what do you think the underwriters would say? No, no! I am not without employment at this stage of the voyage. To tell the truth, I saw an advertisement for able-bodied seamen, when I was a boy, sauntering in my native port, and as soon as I came of age I embarked.

The community has no bribe that will tempt a wise man. You may raise money enough to tunnel a mountain, but you cannot raise money enough to hire a man who is minding *his own* business. An efficient and valuable man does what he can, whether the community pay him for it or not. The inefficient offer their inefficiency to the highest bidder, and are forever expecting to be put into office. One would suppose that they were rarely disappointed.

Perhaps I am more than usually jealous with respect to my freedom. I feel that my connection with and obligation to society are still very slight and transient. Those slight labors which afford me a livelihood, and by which it is allowed that I am to some extent serviceable to my contemporaries, are as yet commonly a pleasure to me, and I am not often reminded that they are a necessity. So far I am successful. But I foresee that if my wants should be much increased, the labor required to supply them would become a drudgery. If I should sell both my forenoons and afternoons to society, as most appear to do, I am sure that for me there would be nothing left worth living for. I trust that I shall never thus sell my birthright for a mess of pottage. I wish to suggest that a man may be very industrious, and yet not spend his time well. There is no more fatal blunderer than he who consumes the greater part of his life getting his living. All great enterprises are self-supporting. The poet, for instance, must sustain his body by his poetry, as a steam planing-mill feeds its boilers with the shavings it makes. You must get your living by loving. But as it is said of the merchants that ninety-seven in a hundred fail, so the life of men generally, tried by this standard, is a failure, and bankruptcy may be surely prophesied.

Merely to come into the world the heir of a fortune is not to be born, but to be stillborn, rather. To be supported by the charity of friends, or a government pension—provided you continue to breathe—by whatever fine synonyms you describe these relations, is to go into the almshouse. On Sundays the poor debtor goes to church to take an account of stock, and finds, of course, that his outgoes have been greater than his income. In the Catholic church, especially, they go into chancery, make a clean confession, give up all, and think to start again. Thus men will lie on their backs, talking about the fall of man, and never make an effort to get up.

As for the comparative demand which men make on life, it is an important difference between two, that the one is satisfied with a level success, that his marks can all be hit by point-blank shots, but the other, however low and unsuccessful his life may be, constantly elevates his aim, though at a very slight angle to the horizon. I should much rather be the last man—though, as the Orientals say, "Greatness doth not approach him who is forever looking down; and all those who are looking high are growing poor."

It is remarkable that there is little or nothing to be remembered written on the subject of getting a living; how to make getting a living not merely honest and honorable, but altogether inviting and glorious; for if *getting* a living is not so, then living is not. One would think, from looking at literature, that this question had never disturbed a solitary individual's musings. Is it that men are too much disgusted with their experience to speak of it? The lesson of value which money teaches, which the Author of the universe has taken so much pains to teach us, we are inclined to skip altogether. As for the means of living, it is wonderful how indifferent men of all classes are about it, even reformers, so called—whether they inherit, or earn, or steal it. I think the society has done nothing for us in this respect, or at least has undone what she has done. Cold and hunger seem more friendly to my nature than those methods which men have adopted and advise to ward them off.

The title *wise* is, for the most part, falsely applied. How can one be a wise man, if he does not know any better how to live than other men?—if he is only more cunning and intellectually subtle? Does wisdom work in a treadmill? Or does she teach how to succeed *by her example?* Is there any such thing as wisdom not applied to life? Is she merely the miller who grinds the finest logic? It is pertinent to ask if Plato got his *living* in a better way or more successfully than his contemporaries—or did he succumb to the difficulties of life like other men? Did he seem to prevail over some of them merely by indifference, or by assuming grand airs? Or find it easier to live, because his aunt remembered him in her will? The ways in which most men get their living, that is, live, are mere makeshifts, and a shirking of the business of life—chiefly because they do not know, but partly because they do not mean, any better.

The rush to California, for instance, and the attitude, not merely of merchants, but of philosophers and prophets, so called, in relation to it, reflect the greatest disgrace on mankind. That so many are ready to live by luck, and so get the means of commanding the labor of others less lucky, without contributing any value to society! And that is called enterprise! I know of no more startling development of the immorality of trade, and all the common modes of getting a living. The philosophy and poetry and religion of such a mankind are not worth the dust of a puffball. The hog that gets his living by rooting, stirring up the soil so, would be ashamed of such company. If I could command the wealth of all the worlds by lifting my finger, I would not pay *such* a price for it. Even Mahomet knew that God did not make this world in jest. It makes God to be a moneyed gentleman who scatters a handful of pennies in order to see mankind scramble for them. The world's raffle! A subsistence in the domains of nature a thing to be raffled for! What a comment, what a satire, on our institutions! The conclusion will be, that mankind will hang itself upon a tree. And have all the precepts in all the Bibles taught men only this? And is the last and most admirable invention of the human race only an improved muckrake? Is this the ground on which Orientals and Occidentals meet? Did God direct us so to get our living, digging where we never planted—and He would, perchance, reward us with lumps of gold?

God gave the righteous man a certificate entitling him to food and raiment, but the unrighteous man found a facsimile of the same in God's coffers, and appropriated it, and obtained food and raiment like the former. It is one of the most extensive systems of counterfeiting that the world has seen. I did not know that mankind was suffering for want of gold. I have seen a little of it. I know that it is very malleable, but not so malleable as wit. A grain of gold will gild a great surface, but not so much as a grain of wisdom.

The gold digger in the ravines of the mountains is as much a gambler as his fellow in the saloons of San Francisco. What difference does it made whether you shake dirt or shake dice? If you win, society is the loser. The gold digger is the enemy of the honest laborer, whatever checks and compensations there may be. It is not enough to tell me that you worked hard to get your gold. So does the devil work hard. The way of transgressors may be hard in many respects. The humblest observer who goes to the mines sees and says that gold-digging is of the character of a lottery; the gold thus obtained is not the same thing with the wages of honest toil. But, practically, he forgets what he has seen, for he has seen only the fact, not the principle, and goes into trade there, that is, buys a ticket in what commonly proves another lottery, where the fact is not so obvious.

After reading Howitt's account of the Australian gold-diggings one evening, I had in my mind's eye, all night, the numerous valleys, with their streams, all cut up with foul pits, from ten to one hundred feet deep, and half a dozen feet across, as close as they can be dug, and partly filled with water—the locality to which men furiously rush to probe for their fortunes—uncertain where they shall break ground—

not knowing but the gold is under their camp itself—sometimes digging one hundred and sixty feet before they strike the vein, or then missing it by a foot—turned into demons, and regardless of each others' rights, in their thirst for riches—whole valleys, for thirty miles, suddenly honeycombed by the pits of the miners, so that even hundreds are drowned in them—standing in water, and covered with mud and clay, they work night and day, dying of exposure and disease. Having read this, and partly forgotten it, I was thinking, accidentally, of my own unsatisfactory life, doing as others do; and with that vision of the diggings still before me, I asked myself why I might not be washing some gold daily, though it were only the finest particles—why I might not sink a shaft down to the gold within me, and work that mine. *There* is a Ballarat, a Bendigo for you—what though it were a sulky-gully? At any rate, I might pursue some path, however solitary and narrow and crooked, in which I could walk with love and reverence. Wherever a man separates from the multitude, and goes his own way in this mood, there indeed is a fork in the road, though ordinary travelers may see only a gap in the paling. His solitary path across lots will turn out the *higher way* of the two.

Men rush to California and Australia as if the true gold were to be found in that direction; but that is to go to the very opposite extreme to where it lies. They go prospecting farther and farther away from the true lead, and are most unfortunate when they think themselves most successful. Is not our *native* soil auriferous? Does not a stream from the golden mountains flow through our native valley? And has not this for more than geologic ages been bringing down the shining particles and forming the nuggets for us? Yet, strange to tell, if a digger steal away, prospecting for this true gold, into the unexplored solitudes around us, there is no danger that any will dog his steps, and endeavor to supplant him. He may claim and undermine the whole valley even, both the cultivated and the uncultivated portions, his whole life long in peace, for no one will ever dispute his claim. They will not mind his cradles or his toms. He is not confined to a claim twelve feet square, as at Ballarat, but may mine anywhere, and wash the whole wide world in his tom.

Howitt says of the man who found the great nugget which weighed twenty-eight pounds, at the Bendigo diggings in Australia: "He soon began to drink; got a horse, and rode all about, generally at full gallop, and, when he met people, called out to inquire if they knew who he was, and then kindly informed them that he was the 'bloody wretch that had found the nugget.' At last he rode full speed against a tree, and nearly knocked his brains out." I think, however, there was no danger of that, for he had already knocked his brains out against the nugget. Howitt adds, "He is a hopelessly ruined man." But he is a type of the class. They are all fast men. Hear some of the names of the places where they dig: "Jackass Flat"—"Sheep's-Head Gully"—"Murderer's Bar," etc. Is there no satire in these names? Let them carry their ill–gotten wealth where they will, I am thinking it will still be "Jackass Flat," if not "Murderer's Bar," where they live.

The last resource of our energy has been the robbing of graveyards on the Isthmus of Darien, an enterprise which appears to be but in its infancy; for, according to late accounts, an act has passed its second reading in the legislature of New Granada, regulating this kind of mining; and a correspondent of the *Tribune* writes: "In the dry season, when the weather will permit of the country being properly prospected, no doubt other rich *guacas* [that is, graveyards] will be found." To emigrants he says: "do not come before December; take the Isthmus route in preference to the Boca del Toro one; bring no useless baggage, and do not cumber yourself with a tent; but a good pair of blankets will be necessary; a pick, shovel, and axe of good material will be almost all that is required": advice which might have been taken from the "Burker's Guide." And he concludes with this line in italics and small capitals: *"If you are doing well at home,* STAY THERE," which may fairly be interpreted to mean, "If you are getting a good living by robbing graveyards at home, stay there."

But why go to California for a text? She is the child of New England, bred at her own school and church.

It is remarkable that among all the preachers there are so few moral teachers. The prophets are employed in excusing the ways of men. Most reverend seniors, the *illuminati* of the age, tell me, with a gracious, reminiscent smile, betwixt an aspiration and a shudder, not to be too tender about these things—to lump all that, that is, make a lump of gold of it. The highest advice I have heard on these subjects was groveling. The burden of it was—It is not worth your while to undertake to reform the world in this particular. Do not ask how your bread is buttered; it will make you sick, if you do—and the like. A man had better starve at once than lose his innocence in the process of getting his bread. If within the sophisticated man there is not an unsophisticated one, then he is but one of the devil's angels. As we grow old, we live more coarsely, we relax a little in our disciplines, and, to some extent, cease to obey our finest instincts. But we should be fastidious to the extreme of sanity, disregarding the gibes of those who are more unfortunate than ourselves.

In our science and philosophy, even, there is commonly no true and absolute account of things. The spirit of sect and bigotry has planted its hoof amid the stars. You have only to discuss the problem, whether the stars are inhabited or not, in order to discover it. Why must we daub the heavens as well as the earth? It was an unfortunate discovery that Dr. [Elisha Kent] Kane was a Mason, and that Sir John Franklin was another. But it was a more cruel suggestion that possibly that was the reason why the former went in search of the latter. There is not a popular magazine in this country that would dare to print a child's thought on important subjects without comment. It must be submitted to the D.D.'s.[1] I would it were the chickadee-dees.

You come from attending the funeral of mankind to attend to a natural phenomenon. A little thought is sexton to all the world.

I hardly know an *intellectual* man, even, who is so broad and truly liberal that you can think aloud in his society. Most with whom you endeavor to talk soon come to a stand against some institution in which they appear to hold stock—that is, some particular, not universal, way of viewing things. They will continually thrust their own low roof, with its narrow skylight, between you and the sky, when it is the unobstructed heavens you would view. Get out of the way with your cobwebs; wash your windows, I say! In some lyceums they tell me that they have voted to exclude the subject of religion. But how do I know what their religion is, and when I am near to or far from it? I have walked into such an arena and done my best to make a clean breast of what religion I have experienced, and the audience never suspected what I was about. The lecture was as harmless as moonshine to them. Whereas, if I had read to them the biography of the greatest scamps in history, they might have thought that I had written the lives of the deacons of their church. Ordinarily, the inquiry is, Where did you come from? or, Where are you going? That was a more pertinent question which I overheard one of my auditors put to another one—"What does he lecture for?" It made me quake in my shoes.

To speak impartially, the best men that I know are not serene, a world in themselves. For the most part, they dwell in forms, and flatter and study effect only more finely than the rest. We select granite for the underpinning of our houses and barns; we build fences of stone; but we do not ourselves rest on an underpinning of granitic truth, the lowest primitive rock. Our sills are rotten. What stuff is the man made of who is not coexistent in our thought with the purest and subtilest truth? I often accuse my finest acquaintances of an immense

[1]Doctors of Divinity. Ed.

frivolity; for, while there are manners and compliments we do not meet, we do not teach one another the lessons of honesty and sincerity that the brutes do, or of steadiness and solidity that the rocks do. The fault is commonly mutual, however; for we do not habitually demand any more of each other.

That excitement about Kossuth, consider how characteristic, but superficial, it was!—only another kind of politics or dancing.[2] Men were making speeches to him all over the country, but each expressed only the thought, or the want of thought, of the multitude. No man stood on truth. They were merely banded together, as usual one leaning on another, and all together on nothing; as the Hindus made the world rest on an elephant, the elephant on a tortoise, and the tortoise on a serpent, and had nothing to put under the serpent. For all fruit of that stir we have the Kossuth hat.

Just so hollow and ineffectual, for the most part, is our ordinary conversation. Surface meets surface. When our life ceases to be inward and private, conversation degenerates into mere gossip. We rarely meet a man who can tell us any news which he has not read in a newspaper, or been told by his neighbor; and, for the most part, the only difference between us and our fellow is that he has seen the newspaper, or been out to tea, and we have not. In proportion as our inward life fails, we go more constantly and desperately to the post office. You may depend on it, that the poor fellow who walks away with the greatest number of letters, proud of his extensive correspondence, has not heard from himself this long while.

I do not know but it is too much to read one newspaper a week. I have tried it recently, and for so long it seems to me that I have not dwelt in my native region. The sun, the clouds, the snow, the trees say not so much to me. You cannot serve two masters. It requires more than a day's devotion to know and to possess the wealth of a day.

We may well be ashamed to tell what things we have read or heard in our day. I did not know why my news should be so trivial—considering what one's dreams and expectations are, why the developments should be so paltry. The news we hear, for the most part, is not news to our genius. It is the stalest repetition. You are often tempted to ask why such stress is laid on a particular experience which you have had—that, after twenty-five years, you should meet Hobbins, Registrar of Deeds, again on the sidewalk. Have you not budged an inch, then? Such is the daily news. Its facts appear to float in the

[2]The reference is to the visit to America of Louis Kossuth, the Hungarian patriot and revolutionary. Ed.

atmosphere, insignificant as the sporules of fungi, and impinge on some neglected *thallus*, or surface of our minds, which affords a basis for them, and hence a parasitic growth. We should wash ourselves clean of such news. Of what consequence, though our planet explode, if there is no character involved in the explosion? In health we have not the least curiosity about such events. We do not live for idle amusement. I would not run round a corner to see the world blow up.

All and far into the autumn, perchance, you unconsciously went by the newspapers and the news, and now you find it was because the morning and the evening were full of news to you. Your walks were full of incidents. You attended, not to the affairs of Europe, but to your own affairs in Massachusetts fields. If you chance to live and move and have your being in that thin stratum in which the events that make the news transpire—thinner than the paper on which it is printed—then these things will fill the world for you; but if you soar above or dive below that plane, you cannot remember nor be reminded of them. Really to see the sun rise or go down every day, so to relate ourselves to a universal fact, would preserve us sane forever. Nations! What are nations? Tartars, and Huns, and Chinamen! Like insects, they swarm. The historian strives in vain to make them memorable. It is for want of a man that there are so many men. It is individuals that populate the world. Any man thinking may say with the Spirit of Lodin—

> *"I look down from my height on nations,*
> *And they become ashes before me;—*
> *Calm is my dwelling in the clouds;*
> *Pleasant are the great fields of my rest."*

Pray, let us live without being drawn by dogs, Esquimaux-fashion, tearing over hill and dale, and biting each other's ears.

Not without a slight shudder at the danger, I often perceive how near I had come to admitting into my mind the details of some trivial affair—the news of the street; and I am astonished to observe how willing men are to lumber their minds with such rubbish—to permit idle rumors and incidents of the most insignificant kind to intrude on ground which should be sacred to thought. Shall the mind be a public arena, where the affairs of the street and the gossip of the tea table chiefly are discussed? Or shall it be a quarter of heaven itself—an hypaethral temple, consecrated to the service of the gods? I find it so difficult to dispose of the few facts which to me are significant, that I hesitate to burden my attention with those which are insignificant, which only a divine mind could illustrate. Such is, for the most part, the news in newspapers and conversation. It is important to preserve the mind's chastity in this respect. Think of admitting the details of a single case of the criminal court into our thoughts, to stalk profanely through their very *sanctum sanctorum* for an hour, ay, for many hours! to make a very barroom of the mind's inmost apartment, as if for so long the dust of the street had occupied us—the very street itself, with all its travel, its bustle, and filth, had passed through our thoughts' shrine! Would it not be an intellectual and moral suicide? When I have been compelled to sit spectator and auditor in a courtroom for some hours, and have seen my neighbors, who were not compelled, stealing in from time to time, and tiptoeing about with washed hands and faces, it has appeared to my mind's eye, that, when they took off their hats, their ears suddenly expanded into vast hoppers for sound, between which even their narrow heads were crowded. Like the vanes of windmills, they caught the broad but shallow stream of sound, which, after a few titillating gyrations in their coggy brains, passed out the other side. I wondered if, when they got home, they were as careful to wash their ears as before their hands and faces. It has seemed to me, at such a time, that the auditors and the witnesses, the jury and the counsel, the judge and the criminal at the bar—if I may presume him guilty before he is convicted—were all equally criminal, and a thunderbolt might be expected to descend and consume them all together.

By all kinds of traps and signboards, threatening the extreme penalty of the divine law, exclude such trespassers from the only ground which can be sacred to you. It is so hard to forget what it is worse than useless to remember! If I am to be a thoroughfare, I prefer that it be of the mountain brooks, the Parnassian streams, and not the town sewers. There is inspiration, that gossip which comes to the ear of the attentive mind from the courts of heaven. There is the profane and stale revelation of the barroom and the police court. The same ear is fitted to receive both communications. Only the character of the hearer determines to which it shall be open, and to which closed. I believe that the mind can be permanently profaned by the habit of attending to trivial things, so that all our thoughts shall be tinged with triviality. Our very intellect shall be macadamized, as it were—its foundation broken into fragments for the wheels of travel to roll over; and if you would know what will make the most durable pavement, surpassing rolled stones, spruce blocks, and asphaltum, you have only to look into some of our minds which have been subjected to this treatment so long.

If we have thus desecrated ourselves—as who has not?—the remedy will be by wariness and devotion to reconsecrate ourselves, and make once more a fane of the mind. We should treat our minds, that is, ourselves, as innocent and ingenuous children, whose guardians we are and be careful what objects and what subjects we thrust on their attention. Read not the Times. Read the Eternities. Conventionalities are at length as bad as impurities. Even the facts of science may dust the mind by their dryness, unless they are in a sense effaced each morning, or rather rendered fertile by the dews of fresh and living truth. Knowledge does not come to us by details, but in flashes of light from heaven. Yes, every thought that passes through the mind helps to wear and tear it, and to deepen the ruts, which, as in the streets of Pompeii, evince how much it has been used. How many things there are concerning which we might well deliberate whether we had better know them—had better let their peddling carts be driven, even at the slowest trot or walk, over that bridge of glorious span by which we trust to pass at last from the farthest brink of time to the nearest shore of eternity! Have we no culture, no refinement—but skill only to live coarsely and serve the devil?—to acquire a little worldly wealth, or fame, or liberty, and make a false show with it, as if we were all husk and shell, with no tender and living kernel to us? Shall our institutions be like those chestnut burs which contain abortive nuts, perfect only to prick the fingers?

America is said to be the arena on which the battle of freedom is to be fought; but surely it cannot be freedom in a merely political sense that is meant. Even if we grant that the American has freed himself from a political tyrant, he is still the slave of an economical and moral tyrant. Now that the republic—the *res-publica*—has been settled, it is time to look after the *res-privata*—the private state—to see, as the Roman senate charged its consuls, *"ne quid res-*PRIVATA *detrimenti caperet,"* that the *private* state receive no detriment.

Do we call this the land of the free? What is it to be free from King George and continue the slaves of King Prejudice? What is it to be born free and not to live free? What is the value of any political freedom, but as a means to moral freedom? Is it a freedom to be slaves, or a freedom to be free, of which we boast? We are a nation of politicians, concerned about the outmost defenses only of freedom. It is our children's children who may perchance be really free. We tax ourselves unjustly. There is a part of us which is not represented. It is taxation without representation. We quarter troops, we quarter fools and cattle of all sorts upon ourselves. We quarter our gross bodies on our poor souls, till the former eat up all the latter's substance.

With respect to a true culture and manhood, we are essentially provincial still, not metropolitan—mere Jonathans. We are provincial, because we do not find at home our standards; because we do not worship truth, but the reflection of truth; because we are warped and narrowed by an exclusive devotion to trade and commerce and manufactures and agriculture and the like, which are but means, and not the end.

So is the English Parliament provincial. Mere country bumpkins, they betray themselves, when any more important question arises for them to settle, the Irish question, for instance—the English question why did I not say? Their natures are subdued to what they work in. Their "good breeding" respects only secondary objects. The finest manners in the world are awkwardness and fatuity when contrasted with a finer intelligence. They appear but as the fashions of past days—mere courtliness, knee-buckles and small-clothes, out of date. It is the vice, but not the excellence of manners, that they are continually being deserted by the character; they are cast-off-clothes or shells, claiming the respect which belonged to the living creature. You are presented with the shells instead of the meat, and it is no excuse generally, that, in the case of some fishes, the shells are of more worth than the meat. The man who thrusts his manners upon me does as if he were to insist on introducing me to his cabinet of curiosities, when I wished to see himself. It was not in this sense that the poet Decker called Christ "the first true gentleman that ever breathed." I repeat that in this sense the most splendid court in Christendom is provincial, having authority to consult about Transalpine interests only, and not the affairs of Rome. A praetor or proconsul would suffice to settle the questions which absorb the attention of the English Parliament and the American Congress.

Government and legislation! these I thought were respectable professions. We have heard of heavenborn Numas, Lycurguses, and Solons, in the history of the world, whose *names* at least may stand for ideal legislators; but think of legislating to *regulate* the breeding of slaves, or the exportation of tobacco! What have divine legislators to do with the exportation or the importation of tobacco? what humane ones with the breeding of slaves? Suppose you were to submit the question to any son of God—and has He no children in the nineteenth century? is it a family which is extinct?—in what condition would you get it again? What shall a state like Virginia say for itself at the last day, in which these have been the principal, the staple productions? What ground is there for patriotism in such a state? I derive my facts from statistical tables which the states themselves have published.

A commerce that whitens every sea in quest of nuts and raisins, and makes slaves of its sailors for this purpose! I saw, the other day, a vessel which had been wrecked, and many lives lost, and her cargo of rags, juniper berries, and bitter almonds were strewn along the shore. It seemed hardly worth the while to tempt the dangers of the sea between Leghorn and New York for the sake of a cargo of juniper berries and bitter almonds. America sending to the Old World for her bitters! Is not the sea brine, is not shipwreck, bitter enough to make the cup of life go down here? Yet such, to a great extent, is our boasted commerce; and there are those who style themselves statesmen and philosophers who are so blind as to think that progress and civilization depend on precisely this kind of interchange and activity—the activity of flies about a molasses hogshead. Very well, observes one, if men were oysters. And very well, answer I, if men were mosquitoes.

Lieutenant Herndon, whom our government sent to explore the Amazon, and, it is said, to extend the area of slavery, observed that there was wanting there "an industrious and active population, who know what the comforts of life are, and who have artificial wants to draw out the great resources of the country." But what are the "artificial wants" to be encouraged? Not the love of luxuries, like the tobacco and slaves of, I believe, his native Virginia, nor the ice and granite and other material wealth of our native New England; nor are "the great resources of a country" that fertility or barrenness of soil which produces these. The chief want, in every state that I have been into, was a high and earnest purpose in its inhabitants. This alone draws out "the great resources" of Nature, and at last taxes her beyond her resources; for man naturally dies out of her. When we want culture more than potatoes, and illumination more than sugarplums, then the great resources of a world are taxed and drawn out, and the result, or staple production, is, not slaves, nor operatives, but men—those rare fruits called heroes, saints, poets, philosophers, and redeemers.

In short, as a snowdrift is formed where there is a lull in the wind, so, one would say, where there is a lull of truth, an institution springs up. But the truth blows right on over it, nevertheless, and at length blows it down.

What is called politics is comparatively something so superficial and inhuman, that practically I have never fairly recognized that it concerns me at all. The newspapers, I perceive, devote some of their columns specially to politics or government without charge; and this, one would say, is all that saves it; but as I love literature and to some extent the truth also, I never read those columns at any rate. I do not wish to blunt my sense of right so much. I have not got to answer for having read a single president's Message. A strange age of the world this, when empires, kingdoms, and republics come a-begging to a private man's door, and utter their complaints at his elbow! I cannot take up a newspaper but I find that some wretched government or other, hard pushed and on its last legs, is interceding with me, the reader, to vote for it—more importunate than an Italian beggar; and if I have a mind to look at its certificate, made, perchance, by some benevolent merchant's clerk, or the skipper that brought it over, for it cannot speak a word of English itself, I shall probably read of the eruption of some Vesuvius, or the overflowing of some Po, true or forged, which brought it into this condition. I do not hesitate, in such a case, to suggest work, or the almshouse; or why not keep its castle in silence, as I do commonly? The poor president, what with preserving his popularity and doing his duty, is completely bewildered. The newspapers are the ruling power. Any other government is reduced to a few marines at Fort Independence. If a man neglects to read the *Daily Times*, government will go down on its knees to him, for this is the only treason in these days.

Those things which now most engage the attention of men, as politics and the daily routine, are, it is true, vital functions of human society, but should be unconsciously performed, like the corresponding functions of the physical body. They are *infra*-human, a kind of vegetation. I sometimes awake to a half-consciousness of them going on about me, as a man may become conscious of some of the processes of digestion in a morbid state, and so have the dyspepsia, as it is called. It is as if a thinker submitted himself to be rasped by the great gizzard of creation. Politics is, as it were, the gizzard of society, full of grit and gravel, and the two political parties are its two opposite halves—sometimes split into quarters, it may be, which grind on each other. Not only individuals, but states, have thus a confirmed dyspepsia, which expresses itself, you can imagine by what sort of eloquence. Thus our life is not altogether a forgetting, but also, alas! to a great extent, a remembering, of that which we should never have been conscious of, certainly not in our waking hours. Why should we not meet, not always as dyspeptics, to tell our bad dreams, but sometimes as *eu*peptics, to congratulate each other on the ever-glorious morning? I do not make an exorbitant demand, surely.

3

WOMANHOOD AND INDIVIDUALITY

Margaret Fuller
THE GREAT LAWSUIT: MAN VERSUS MEN; WOMAN VERSUS WOMEN

The Transcendentalists were probably the only circle in America unconventional enough to freely admit a woman on terms of intellectual equality. The daughter of a Harvard graduate, Margaret Fuller (1810–1850) had been pushed toward literary pursuits by her father when she showed signs of precocity in childhood. As a result, until near the end of her life she betrayed all the signs of an overly intense preoccupation with ideas. From 1839 to 1844 she held formal "conversations" with classes of young ladies who paid her for the instruction; during the same period she edited The Dial. *For two more years she worked for Horace Greeley's New York Tribune as literary critic. She then lived for some time in Europe, where she married a penniless Italian count. Later, while returning to America with him and their child, she was killed in a shipwreck. Margaret Fuller was an important pioneer figure in the cause of women's rights, though her writings were on a philosophical plane that did not connect easily with the struggle for suffrage. Trying to advance both the cause of womanhood and the Transcendental view of purely individual capacities, she was the first to wrestle with the dilemma over the special and the universal aspects of woman's plight. Much of her argument strikingly anticipates the tone of the recent movement for women's liberation.*

[Man] is still kept out of his inheritance, still a pleader, still a pilgrim. But his reinstatement is sure. And now, no mere glimmering consciousness, but a certainty, is felt and spoken, that the highest ideal man can form of his own capabilities is that which he is destined to attain. Whatever the soul knows how to seek, it must attain. Knock, and it shall be opened; seek, and ye shall find. It is demonstrat-

SOURCE. Margaret Fuller, "The Great Lawsuit: Man *versus* Men; Woman *versus* Women," *The Dial*, IV (July 1843), pp. 4–5, 7–19, 23–24, 28, 32–33, 35, 38, 43–47.

ed, it is a maxim. He no longer paints his proper nature in some peculiar form and says, "Prometheus had it," but "Man must have it." However disputed by many, however ignorantly used, or falsified, by those who do receive it, the fact of an universal, unceasing revelation, has been too clearly stated in words, to be lost sight of in thought, and sermons preached from the text, "Be ye perfect," are the only sermons of a pervasive and deep-searching influence.

But among those who meditate upon this text, there is great difference of view, as to the way in which perfection shall be sought.

Through the intellect, say some; gather from every growth of life its seed of thought; look behind every symbol for its law. If thou canst *see* clearly, the rest will follow.

Through the life, say others; do the best thou knowest today. Shrink not from incessant error, in this gradual, fragmentary state. Follow thy light for as much as it will show thee, be faithful as far as thou canst, in hope that faith presently will lead to sight. Help others, without blame that they need thy help. Love much, and be forgiven.

It needs not intellect, needs not experience, says a third. If you took the true way, these would be evolved in purity. You would not learn through them, but express through them a higher knowledge. In quietness, yield thy soul to the casual soul. Do not disturb its teachings by methods of thine own. Be still, seek not, but wait in obedience. Thy commission will be given.

Could we, indeed, say what we want, could we give a description of the child that is lost, he would be found. As soon as the soul can say clearly, that a certain demonstration is wanted, it is at hand. When the Jewish prophet described the Lamb, as the expression of what was required by the coming era, the time drew nigh. But we say not, see not, as yet, clearly, what we would. Those who call for a more triumphant expression of love, a love that cannot be crucified, show not a perfect sense of what has already been expressed. Love has already been expressed, that made all things new, that gave the worm its ministry as well as the eagle; a love, to which it was alike to descend into the depths of hell, or to sit at the right hand of the Father.

Yet, no doubt, a new manifestation is at hand, a new hour in the day of man. We cannot expect to see him a completed being, when the mass of men lie so entangled in the sod, or use the freedom of their limbs only with wolfish energy. The tree cannot come to flower till its root be freed from the cankering worm, and its whole growth open to air and light. Yet something new shall presently be shown of the life of man, for hearts crave it now, if minds do not know how to ask it. . . .

Meanwhile, not a few believe, and men themselves have expressed the opinion, that the time is come when Euridice is to call for an Orpheus, rather than Orpheus for Euridice; that the idea of man, however imperfectly brought out, has been far more so than that of woman, and that an improvement in the daughters will best aid the reformation of the sons of this age.

It is worthy of remark, that, as the principle of liberty is better understood and more nobly interpreted, a broader protest is made in behalf of woman. As men become aware that all men have not had their fair chance, they are inclined to say that no women have had a fair chance. The French revolution, that strangely disguised angel, bore witness in favor of woman, but interpreted her claims no less ignorantly than those of man. Its idea of happiness did not rise beyond outward enjoyment, unobstructed by the tyranny of others. The title it gave was Citoyen, Citoyenne, and it is not unimportant to woman that even this species of equality was awarded her. Before, she could be condemned to perish on the scaffold for treason, but not as a citizen, but a subject. The right, with which this title then invested a human being, was that of bloodshed and license. The Goddess of Liberty was impure. Yet truth was prophesied in the ravings of that hideous fever induced by long ignorance and abuse. Europe is conning a valued lesson from the bloodstained page. The same tendencies, farther unfolded, will bear good fruit in this country.

Yet, in this country, as by the Jews, when Moses was leading them to the promised land, everything has been done that inherited depravity could, to hinder the promise of heaven from its fulfillment. The cross, here as elsewhere, has been planted only to be blasphemed by cruelty and fraud. The name of the Prince of Peace has been profaned by all kinds of injustice towards the Gentile whom he said he came to save. But I need not speak of what has been done towards the red man, the black man. These deeds are the scoff of the world; and they have been accompanied by such pious words, that the gentlest would not dare to intercede with, "Father forgive them, for they know not what they do."

Here, as elsewhere, the gain of creation consists always in the growth of individual minds, which live and aspire, as flowers bloom and birds sing, in the midst of morasses; and in the continual development of that thought, the thought of human destiny, which is given to eternity to fulfill, and which ages of failure only seemingly impede. Only seemingly, and whatever seems to the contrary, this country is as surely destined to elucidate a great moral law, as Europe was to promote the mental culture of man.

Though the national independence be blurred by the servility of individuals; though freedom and equality have been proclaimed only to leave room for a monstrous display of slave dealing and slave keeping; though the free American so often feels himself free, like the Roman, only to pamper his appetites and his indolence through the misery of his fellow beings, still it is not in vain, that the verbal statement has been made, "All men are born free and equal." There it stands, a golden certainty, wherewith to encourage the good, to shame the bad. The new world may be called clearly to perceive that it incurs the utmost penalty, if it reject the sorrowful brother. And if men are deaf, the angels hear. But men cannot be deaf. It is inevitable that an external freedom, such as has been achieved for the nation, should be so also for every member of it. That, which has once been clearly conceived in the intelligence, must be acted out. . . .

We sicken no less at the pomp than at the strife of words. We feel that never were lungs so puffed with the wind of declamation, on moral and religious subjects, as now. We are tempted to implore these "word-heroes," these word-Catos, word-Christs, to beware of cant above all things; to remember that hypocrisy is the most hopeless as well as the meanest of crimes, and that those must surely be polluted by it, who do not keep a little of all this morality and religion for private use. We feel that the mind may "grow black and rancid in the smoke" even of altars. We start up from the harangue to go into our closet and shut the door. But, when it has been shut long enough, we remember that where there is so much smoke, there must be some fire; with so much talk about virtue and freedom must be mingled some desire for them; that it cannot be in vain that such have become the common topics of conversation among men; that the very newspapers should proclaim themselves Pilgrims, Puritans, Heralds of Holiness. The king that maintains so costly a retinue cannot be a mere Count of Carabbas fiction. We have waited here long in the dust; we are tired and hungry, but the triumphal procession must appear at last.

Of all its banners, none has been more steadily upheld, and under none has more valor and willingness for real sacrifices been shown, than that of the champions of the enslaved African. And this band it is, which, partly in consequence of a natural following out of principles, partly because many women have been prominent in that cause, makes, just now, the warmest appeal in behalf of woman.

Though there has been a growing liberality on this point, yet society at large is not so prepared for the demands of this party, but that they are, and will be for some time, coldly regarded as the Jacobins of their day.

"Is it not enough," cries the sorrowful trader, "that you have done all you could to break up the national Union, and thus destroy the prosperity of our country, but now you must be trying to break up family union, to take my wife away from the cradle, and the kitchen hearth, to vote at polls, and preach from a pulpit? Of course, if she does such things, she cannot attend to those of her own sphere. She is happy enough as she is. She has more leisure than I have, every means of improvement, every indulgence."

"Have you asked her whether she was satisfied with these indulgences?"

"No, but I know she is. She is too amiable to wish what would make me unhappy, and too judicious to wish to step beyond the sphere of her sex. I will never consent to have our peace disturbed by any such discussions."

" 'Consent'—you? it is not consent from you that is in question, it is assent from your wife."

"Am I not the head of my house?"

"You are not the head of your wife. God has given her a mind of her own."

"I am the head and she the heart."

"God grant you play true to one another then. If the head represses no natural pulse of the heart, there can be no question as to your giving your consent. Both will be of one accord, and there needs but to present any question to get a full and true answer. There is no need of precaution, of indulgence, or consent. But our doubt is whether the heart consents with the head, or only acquiesces in its decree; and it is to ascertain the truth on this point, that we propose some liberating measures."

Thus vaguely are these questions proposed and discussed at present. But their being proposed at all implies much thought, and suggests more. Many women are considering within themselves what they need that they have not, and what they can have, if they find they need it. Many men are considering whether women are capable of being and having more than they are and have, and whether, if they are, it will be best to consent to improvement in their condition.

The numerous party, whose opinions are already labeled and adjusted too much to their mind to admit of any new light, strive, by lectures on some model woman of bridallike beauty and gentleness, by writing or lending little treatises, to mark out with due precision the limits of woman's sphere, and woman's mission, and to prevent other than the rightful shepherd from climbing the wall, or the flock from using any chance gap to run astray.

Without enrolling ourselves at once on either side, let us look upon the subject from that point of view which today offers. No better, it is to be feared, than a high housetop. A high hilltop, or at least a cathedral spire, would be desirable.

It is not surprising that it should be the Antislavery party that pleads for woman, when we consider merely that she does not hold property on equal terms with men; so that, if a husband dies without a will, the wife, instead of stepping at once into his place as head of the family, inherits only a part of his fortune, as if she were a child, or ward only, not an equal partner.

We will not speak of the innumerable instances, in which profligate or idle men live upon the earnings of industrious wives; or if the wives leave them and take with them the children, to perform the double duty of mother and father, follow from place to place, and threaten to rob them of the children, if deprived of the rights of a husband, as they call them, planting themselves in their poor lodgings, frightening them into paying tribute by taking from them the children, running into debt at the expense of these otherwise so overtasked helots. Though such instances abound, the public opinion of his own sex is against the man, and when cases of extreme tyranny are made known, there is private action in the wife's favor. But if woman be, indeed, the weaker party, she ought to have legal protection, which would make such oppression impossible.

And knowing that there exists, in the world of men, a tone of feeling towards women as towards slaves, such as is expressed in the common phrase, "Tell that to women and children"; that the infinite soul can only work through them in already ascertained limits; that the prerogative of reason, man's highest portion, is allotted to them in a much lower degree; that it is better for them to be engaged in active labor, which is to be furnished and directed by those better able to think, etc. etc.; we need not go further, for who can review the experience of last week, without recalling words which imply, whether in jest or earnest, these views, and views like these? Knowing this, can we wonder that many reformers think that measures are not likely to be taken in behalf of women, unless their wishes could be publicly represented by women?

That can never be necessary, cry the other side. All men are privately influenced by women; each has his wife, sister, or female friends, and is too much biased by these relations to fail of representing their interests. And if this is not enough, let them propose and enforce their wishes with the pen. The beauty of home would be destroyed, the delicacy of the sex be violated, the dignity of halls of legislation destroyed, by an attempt to introduce them there. Such duties are inconsistent with those of a mother; and then we have ludicrous pictures of ladies in hysterics at the polls, and senate chambers filled with cradles.

But if, in reply, we admit as truth that woman seems destined by nature rather to the inner cicle, we must add that the arrangements of civilized life have not been as yet such as to secure it to her. Her circle, if the duller, is not the quieter. If kept from excitement, she is not from drudgery. Not only the Indian carries the burdens of the camp, but the favorites of Louis the Fourteenth accompany him in his journeys, and the washerwoman stands at her tub and carries home her work at all seasons, and in all states of health.

As to the use of the pen, there was quite as much opposition to woman's possessing herself of that help to free-agency as there is now to her seizing on the rostrum or the desk; and she is likely to draw, from a permission to plead her cause that way, opposite inferences to what might be wished by those who now grant it.

As to the possibility of her filling, with grace and dignity, any such position, we should think those who had seen the great actresses, and heard the Quaker preachers of modern times, would not doubt, that woman can express publicly the fullness of thought and emotion, without losing any of the peculiar beauty of her sex.

As to her home, she is not likely to leave it more than she now does for balls, theaters, meetings for promoting missions, revival meetings, and others to which she flies, in hope of an animation for her existence, commensurate with what she sees enjoyed by men. . . . The female Greek, of our day, is as much in the street as the male, to cry, What news? We doubt not it was the same in Athens of old. The women, shut out from the marketplace, made up for it at the religious festivals. For human beings are not so constituted, that they can live without expansion; and if they do not get it one way, must another, or perish.

And, as to men's representing women fairly, at present, while we hear from men who owe to their wives not only all that is comfortable and graceful, but all that is wise in the arrangement of their lives, the frequent remark, "You cannot reason with a woman," when from those of delicacy, nobleness, and poetic culture, the contemptuous phrase, "Women and children," and that in no light sally of the hour, but in works intended to give a permanent statement of the best experiences, when not one man in the million, shall I say, no, not in the hundred million, can rise above the view that woman was made *for man*, when such traits as these are daily forced upon the attention, can we feel that man will always do justice to the interests of woman? Can we think that he takes a sufficiently discerning and religious view of her office and destiny, ever to do her justice, except when prompted by sentiment; accidentally or transiently, that is, for his sentiment will vary according to the relations in which he is placed. The lover, the poet, the artist, are likely to view her nobly. The father and the philosopher have some chance of liberality; the man of the world, the legislator for expediency, none.

Under these circumstances, without attaching importance in themselves to the changes demanded by the champions of woman, we hail them as signs of the times. We would have every arbitrary barrier thrown down. We would have every path laid open to woman as freely as to man. Were this done, and a slight temporary fermentation allowed to subside, we believe that the Divine would ascend into nature to a height unknown in the history of past ages, and nature, thus instructed, would regulate the spheres not only so as to avoid collision, but to bring forth ravishing harmony.

Yet then, and only then, will human beings be ripe for this, when inward and outward freedom for woman, as much as for man, shall be acknowledged as a right, not yielded as a concession. As the friend of the Negro assumes that one man cannot, by right, hold another in bondage, should the friend of woman assume that man cannot, by right, lay even well-meant restrictions on woman. If the Negro be a soul, if the woman be a soul, appareled in flesh, to one master only are they accountable. There is but one law for all souls, and, if there is to be an interpreter of it, he comes not as man, or son of man, but as Son of God.

Were thought and feeling once so far elevated that man should esteem himself the brother and friend, but nowise the lord and tutor of woman, were he really bound with her in equal worship, arrangements as to function and employment would be of no consequence. What woman needs is not as a woman to act or rule, but as a nature to grow, as an intellect to discern, as a soul to live freely, and unimpeded to unfold such powers as were given her when we left our common home. If fewer talents were given her, yet, if allowed the free and full employment of these, so that she may render back to the giver his own with usury, she will not complain, nay, I dare to say she will bless and rejoice in her earthly birthplace, her earthly lot.

Let us consider what obstructions impede this good era, and what signs give reason to hope that it draws near.

I was talking on this subject with Miranda, a woman, who, if any in the world, might speak without heat or bitterness of the position of her sex. Her father was a man who cherished no sentimental reverence for woman, but a firm belief in the equality of the sexes. She was his eldest child, and came to him at an age when he needed a companion. From the time she could speak and go alone, he addressed her not as a plaything, but as a living mind. Among the few verses he ever wrote were a copy addressed to this child, when the first locks were cut from her head, and the reverence expressed on this occasion for that cherished head he never belied. It was to him the temple of immortal intellect. He respected his child, however, too much to be an indulgent parent. He called on her for clear judgment, for courage, for honor and fidelity, in short for such virtues as he knew. In so far as he possessed the keys to the wonders of this universe, he allowed free use of them to her, and by the incentive of a high expectation he forbade, as far as possible, that she should let the privilege lie idle.

Thus this child was early led to feel herself a child of the spirit. She took her place easily, not only in the world of organized being, but in the world of mind. A dignified sense of self-dependence was given as all her portion, and she found it a sure anchor. Herself securely anchored, her relations with others were established with equal security. She was fortunate, in a total absence of those charms which might have drawn to her bewildering flatteries, and of a strong electric nature, which repelled those who did not belong to her, and attracted those who did. With men and women her relations were noble; affectionate without passion, intellectual without coldness. The world was free to her, and she lived freely in it. Outward adversity came, and inward conflict, but that faith and self-respect had early been awakened, which must always lead at last to an outward serenity, and an inward peace.

Of Miranda I had always thought as an example, that the restraints upon the sex were insuperable only to those who think them so, or who noisily strive to break them. She had taken a course of her own, and no man stood in her way. Many of her acts had been unusual, but excited no uproar. Few helped, but none checked her; and the many men, who knew her mind and her life, showed to her confidence as to a brother, gentleness as to a sister. And not only refined, but very coarse men approved one in whom they saw resolution and clearness of design. Her mind was often the leading one, always effective.

When I talked with her upon these matters, and had said very much what I have written, she smilingly replied, And yet we must admit that I have been fortunate, and this should not be. My good father's early trust gave the first bias, and the rest followed of course. It is true that I have had less outward aid, in after years, than most women, but that is of little consequence. Religion was early awakened in my soul, a sense that what the soul is capable to ask it must attain, and that, though I might be aided by others, I must depend on myself as the only constant friend. This self-dependence, which was honored in me, is deprecated as a fault in most women. They are taught to learn their rule from without, not to unfold it from within.

This is the fault of man, who is still vain, and wishes to be more important to woman than by right he should be.

Men have not shown this disposition towards you, I said.

No, because the position I early was enabled to take, was one of self-reliance. And were all women as sure of their wants as I was, the result would be the same. The difficulty is to get them to the point where they shall naturally develop self-respect, the question how it is to be done.

Once I thought that men would help on this state of things more than I do now. I saw so many of them wretched in the connections they had formed in weakness and vanity. They seemed so glad to esteem women whenever they could!

But early I perceived that men never, in any extreme of despair, wished to be women. Where they admired any woman they were inclined to speak of her as above her sex. Silently I observed this, and feared it argued a rooted skepticism, which for ages had been fastening on the heart, and which only an age of miracles could eradicate.

Ever I have been treated with great sincerity; and I look upon it as a most signal instance of this, that an intimate friend of the other sex said in a fervent moment, that I deserved in some star to be a man. Another used as highest praise, in speaking of a character in literature, the words "a manly woman."

It is well known that of every strong woman they say she has a masculine mind.

This by no means argues a willing want of generosity towards woman. Man is as generous towards her, as he knows how to be.

Wherever she has herself arisen in national or private history, and nobly shone forth in any ideal of excellence, men have received her, not only willingly, but with triumph. Their encomiums indeed are always in some sense mortifying, they show too much surprise. . . .

The sexes should not only correspond to and appreciate one another, but prophesy to one another. In individual instances this happens. Two persons love in one another the future good which they aid one another to unfold. This is very imperfectly done as yet in the general life. Man has gone but little way, now he is waiting to see whether woman can keep step with him, but instead of calling out like a good brother: You can do it if you only think so; or impersonally; Any one can do what he tries to do, he often discourages with schoolboy brag; Girls can't do that, girls can't play ball. But let any one defy their taunts, break through, and be brave and secure, they rend the air with shouts. . . .

We will not speak of the enthusiasm excited by actresses, improvisatrici, female singers, for here mingles the charm of beauty and grace, but female authors, even learned women, if not insufferably ugly and slovenly, from the Italian professor's daughter, who taught behind the curtain, down to Mrs. Carter and Madame Dacier, are sure of an admiring audience, if they can once get a platform on which to stand.

But how to get this platform, or how to make it of reasonably easy access is the difficulty. Plants of great vigor will almost always struggle into blossom, despite impediments. But there should be encouragement, and a free, genial atmosphere for those of more timid sort, fair play for each in its own kind. Some are like the little, delicate flowers, which love to hide in the dripping mosses by the sides of mountain torrents, or in the shade of tall trees. But others require an open field, a rich and loosened soil, or they never show their proper hues.

It may be said man does not have his fair play either; his energies are repressed and distorted by the interposition of artificial obstacles. Aye, but he himself has put them there; they have grown out of his own imperfections. If there *is* a misfortune in woman's lot, it is in obstacles being interposed by men, which do *not* mark her state, and if they express her past ignorance, do not her present needs. As every man is of woman born, she has slow but sure means of redress, yet the sooner a general justness of thought makes smooth the path, the better.

Man is of woman born, and her face bends over him in infancy with an expression he can never quite forget. Eminent men have delighted to pay tribute to this image, and it is a hacknied observation, that most men of genius boast some remarkable development in the mother. The rudest tar brushes off a tear with his coat sleeve at the hallowed name. The other day I met a decrepit old man of seventy, on a journey, who challenged the stage company to guess where he was going. They guessed aright, "To see your mother." "Yes," said he, "she is ninety-two, but has good eyesight still, they say. I've not seen her these forty years, and I thought I could not die in peace without." . . .

It is not the transient breath of poetic incense, that women want; each can receive that from a lover. It is not lifelong sway; it needs but to become a coquette, a shrew, or a good cook to be sure of that. It is not money, nor notoriety, nor the badges of authority, that men have appropriated to themselves. If demands made in their behalf lay stress on any of these particulars, those who make them have not searched deeply into the need. It is for that which at once includes all these and precludes them; which would not be forbidden power, lest there be temptation to steal and misuse it; which would not have the mind perverted by flattery from a worthiness of esteem. It is for that which is the birthright of every being capable to receive it—the freedom, the religious, the intelligent freedom of the universe, to use its means, to learn its secret as far as nature has enabled them, with God alone for their guide and their judge.

Ye cannot believe it, men; but the only reason why women ever assume what is more appropriate to you, is because you prevent them from finding out what is fit for themselves. Were they free, were they wise fully to develop the strength and beauty of woman, they would never wish to be men, or manlike. The well-instructed moon flies not from her orbit to seize on the glories of her partner. No; for she knows that one law rules, one heaven contains, one universe replies to them alike. . . .

In slavery, acknowledged slavery, women are on a par with men. Each is a work tool, an article of property—no more! In perfect freedom, such as is painted in Olympus, in Swedenborg's angelic state, in the heaven where there is no marrying nor giving in marriage, each is a purified intelligence, an enfranchised soul—no less! . . .

Where the thought of equality has become pervasive, it shows itself in four kinds.

The household partnership. In our country the woman looks for a "smart but kind" husband, the man for a "capable, sweet-tempered" wife.

The man furnishes the house, the woman regulates it. Their relation is one of mutual esteem, mutual dependence. Their talk is of business, their affection shows itself by practical kindness. They know that life goes more smoothly and cheerfully to each for the other's aid; they are grateful and content. The wife praises her husband as a "good provider," the husband in return compliments her as a "capital housekeeper." This relation is good as far as it goes.

Next comes a closer tie which takes the two forms, either of intellectual companionship, or mutual idolatry. The last, we suppose, is to no one a pleasing subject of contemplation. The parties weaken and narrow one another; they lock the gate against all the glories of the universe that they may live in a cell together. To themselves they seem the only wise, to all others steeped in infatuation, the gods smile as they look forward to the crisis of cure, to men the woman seems an unlovely siren, to women the man an effeminate boy.

The other form, of intellectual companionship, has become more and more frequent. Men engaged in public life, literary men, and artists have often found in their wives companions and confidants in thought no less than in feeling. And, as in the course of things the intellectual development of woman has spread wider and risen higher, they have, not unfrequently, shared the same employment. As in the case of Roland and his wife, who were friends in the household and the nation's councils, read together, regulated home affairs, or prepared public documents together indifferently. . . .

I have not spoken of the higher grade of marriage union, the religious, which may be expressed as pilgrimage towards a common shrine. This includes the others; home sympathies, and household wisdom, for these pilgrims must know how to assist one another to carry their burdens along the dusty way; intellectual communion, for how sad it would be on such a journey to have a companion to whom you could not communicate thoughts and aspirations, as they sprang to life, who would have no feeling for the more and more glorious prospects that open as we advance, who would never see the flowers that may be gathered by the most industrious traveler. It must include all these. . . .

We cannot wonder at the aversion with which old bachelors and old maids have been regarded. Marriage is the natural means of forming a sphere, of taking root on the earth: it requires more strength to do this without such an opening, very many have failed of this, and their imperfections have been in everyone's way. They have been more partial, more harsh, more officious and impertinent than others. Those, who have a complete experience of the human instincts, have a distrust as to whether they can be thoroughly human and humane, such as is hinted at in the saying, "Old maids' and bachelors' children are well cared for," which derides at once their ignorance and their presumption. . . .

Women are indeed the easy victims of priestcraft, or self-delusion, but this might not be, if the intellect was developed in proportion to the other powers. They would then have a regulator and be in better equipoise, yet must retain the same nervous susceptibility, while their physical structure is such as it is.

It is with just that hope, that we welcome everything that tends to strengthen the fibre and develop the nature on more sides. When the intellect and affections are in harmony, when intellectual conscious-ness is calm and deep, inspiration will not be confounded with fancy.

The electrical, the magnetic element in woman has not been fairly developed at any period. Everything might be expected from it; she has far more of it than man. This is commonly expressed by saying, that her intuitions are more rapid and more correct. . . .

The especial genius of woman I believe to be electrical in move-ment, intuitive in function, spiritual in tendency. She is great not so easily in classification, or re-creation, as in an instinctive seizure of causes, and a simple breathing out of what she receives that has the singleness of life, rather than the selecting or energizing of art.

More native to her is it to be the living model of the artist, than to set apart from herself any one form in objective reality; more native to inspire and receive the poem than to create it. In so far as soul is in her completely developed, all soul is the same; but as far as it is modified in her as woman, it flows, it breathes, it sings, rather than deposits soil, or finishes work, and that which is especially feminine flushes in blossom the face of earth, and pervades like air and water all this seeming solid globe, daily renewing and purifying its life. Such may be the especially feminine element, spoken of as *femality*. But it is no more the order of nature that it should be incarnated pure in any form, than that the masculine energy should exist unmingled with it in any form.

Male and female represent the two sides of the great radical dualism. But, in fact, they are perpetually passing into one another. Fluid hardens to solid, solid rushes to fluid. There is no wholly masculine man, no purely feminine woman.

History jeers at the attempts of physiologists to bind great original laws by the forms which flow from them. They make a rule; they say from observation what can and cannot be. In vain! Nature provides exceptions to every rule. She sends women to battle, and sets Hercules spinning; she enables women to bear immense burdens, cold, and frost; she enables the man, who feels maternal love, to nourish his infant like a mother. Of late she plays still gayer pranks. Not only she deprives organizations, but organs, of a necessary end. She enables people to read with the top of the head, and see with the pit of the stomach. Presently she will make a female Newton, and a male Siren.

Man partakes of the feminine in the Apollo, woman of the mascu-line as Minerva.

Let us be wise and not impede the soul. Let her work as she will. Let us have one creative energy, one incessant revelation. Let it take what form it will, and let us not bind it by the past to man or woman, black or white. Jove sprang from Rhea, Pallas from Jove. So let it be.

If it has been the tendency of the past remarks to call woman rather to the Minerva side—if I, unlike the more generous writer, have spoken from society no less than the soul—let it be pardoned. It is love that has caused this, love for many incarcerated souls, that might be freed could the idea of religious self-dependence be established in them, could the weakening habit of dependence on others be broken up.

Every relation, every gradation of nature, is incalculably precious, but only to the soul which is poised upon itself, and to whom no loss, no change, can bring dull discord, for it is in harmony with the central soul.

If any individual live too much in relations, so that he becomes a stranger to the resources of his own nature, he falls after a while into a distraction, or imbecility, from which he can only be cured by a time of isolation, which gives the renovating fountains time to rise up. With a society it is the same. Many minds, deprived of the tradition-ary or instinctive means of passing a cheerful existence, must find help in self-impulse or perish. It is therefore that while any elevation, in the view of union, is to be hailed with joy, we shall not decline celibacy as the great fact of the time. It is one from which no vow, no arrangement, can at present save a thinking mind. For now the rowers are pausing on their oars, they wait a change before they can pull together. All tends to illustrate the thought of a wise contemporary. Union is only possible to those who are units. To be fit for relations in time, souls, whether of man or woman, must be able to do without them in the spirit.

It is therefore that I would have woman lay aside all thought, such as she habitually cherishes, of being taught and led by men. I would have her, like the Indian girl, dedicate herself to the Sun, the Sun of Truth, and go no where if his beams did not make clear the path. I would have her free from compromise, from complaisance, from help-lessness, because I would have her good enough and strong enough to love one and all beings, from the fullness, not the poverty of being.

Men, as at present instructed, will not help this work, because they also are under the slavery of habit. I have seen with delight their poetic impulses. A sister is the fairest ideal, and how nobly Words-worth, and even Byron, have written of a sister.

There is no sweeter sight than to see a father with his little daugh-ter. Very vulgar men become refined to the eye when leading a little girl by the hand. At that moment the right relation between the sexes seems established, and you feel as if the man would aid in the noblest purpose, if you ask him in behalf of his little daughter. Once two fine figures stood before me, thus. The father of very intellectual aspect, his falcon eye softened by affection as he looked down on his fair child, she the image of himself, only more graceful and brilliant in expression. I was reminded of Southey's Kehama, when lo, the dream was rudely broken. They were talking of education, and he said:

"I shall not have Maria brought too forward. If she knows too much, she will never find a husband; superior women hardly ever can."

"Surely," said his wife, with a blush, "you wish Maria to be as good and wise as she can, whether it will help her to marriage or not."

"No," he persisted, "I want her to have a sphere and a home, and someone to protect her when I am gone."

It was a trifling incident, but made a deep impression. I felt that the holiest relations fail to instruct the unprepared and perverted mind. If this man, indeed, would have looked at it on the other side, he was the last that would have been willing to have been taken himself for the home and protection he could give, but would have been much more likely to repeat the tale of Alcibiades with his phials.

But men do not look at both sides, and women must leave off asking them and being influenced by them, but retire within themselves, and explore the groundwork of being till they find their peculiar secret. Then when they come forth again, renovated and baptized, they will know how to turn all dross to gold, and will be rich and free though they live in a hut, tranquil, if in a crowd. Then their sweet singing shall not be from passionate impulse, but the lyrical overflow of a divine rapture, and a new music shall be elucidated from this many-chorded world.

Grant her then for a while the armor and the javelin. Let her put from her the press of other minds and meditate in virgin loneliness. The same idea shall reappear in due time as Muse, or Ceres, the all-kindly, patient Earth-Spirit.

I tire everyone with my Goethean illustrations. But it cannot be helped.

Goethe, the great mind which gave itself absolutely to the leadings of truth, and let rise through him the waves which are still advancing through the century, was its intellectual prophet. Those who know him, see, daily, his thought fulfilled more and more, and they must speak of it, till his name weary and even nauseate, as all great names have in their time. And I cannot spare the reader, if such there be, his wonderful sight as to the prospects and wants of women.

As his Wilhelm grows in life and advances in wisdom, he becomes acquainted with women of more and more character, rising from Mariana to Macaria.

Macaria, bound with the heavenly bodies in fixed revolutions, the center of all relations, herself unrelated, expresses the Minerva side.

Mignon, the electrical, inspired lyrical nature.

All these women, though we see them in relations, we can think of as unrelated. They all are very individual, yet seem nowhere restrained. They satisfy for the present, yet arouse an infinite expectation.

The economist Theresa, the benevolent Natalia, the Fair Saint, have chosen a path, but their thoughts are not narrowed to it. The functions of life to them are not ends, but suggestions.

Thus to them all things are important, because none is necessary. Their different characters have fair play, and each is beautiful in its minute indications, for nothing is enforced or conventional, but everything, however slight, grows from the essential life of the being.

Mignon and Theresa wear male attire when they like, and it is graceful for them to do so, while Macaria is confined to her armchair behind the green curtain, and the Fair Saint could not bear a speck of dust on her robe.

All things are in their places in this little world because all is natural and free, just as "there is room for everything out of doors." Yet all is rounded in by natural harmony which will always arise where truth and love are sought in the light of freedom.

Goethe's book bodes an era of freedom like its own, of "extraordinary generous seeking," and new revelations. New individualities shall be developed in the actual world, which shall advance upon it as gently as the figures come out upon his canvas.

A profound thinker has said "no married woman can represent the female world, for she belongs to her husband. The idea of woman must be represented by a virgin."

But that is the very fault of marriage, and of the present relation between the sexes, that the woman does belong to the man, instead of forming a whole with him. Were it otherwise there would be no such limitation to the thought.

Woman, self-centered, would never be absorbed by any relation; it would be only an experience to her as to man. It is a vulgar error that love, a love to woman is her whole existence; she also is born for truth and love in their universal energy. Would she but assume her inheritance, Mary would not be the only Virgin Mother. Not Manzoni alone would celebrate in his wife the virgin mind with the maternal wisdom and conjugal affections. The soul is ever young, ever virgin.

And will not she soon appear? The woman who shall vindicate their birthright for all women; who shall teach them what to claim, and how to use what they obtain? Shall not her name be for her era Victoria, for her country and her life Virginia? Yet predictions are rash; she herself must teach us to give her the fitting name.

Part Four

THE EVE OF CIVIL WAR

1

MORAL LAW HIGHER THAN THE CONSTITUTION

William Lloyd Garrison
THE UNITED STATES CONSTITUTION
and
SPEECH ON JOHN BROWN

As the Civil War approached, all other reform causes tended to be swallowed up in the urgency of the crusade against the blatant evil of slavery, which threatened after 1845 to extend itself onto an ever wider geographical base in the United States. It is not surprising that slavery drew out the most uncompromising arguments and the most uncontrolled emotions from those who believed in the possibility of perfecting society. Other evils, such as the dramshop, were spread more or less evenly across the nation. But slavery clearly divided the country into two parts. Its aggressive partisans were deeply entrenched in Congress and the Supreme Court, defending human bondage from officially sanctioned platforms. The cause of abolitionism had been gathering steam in New England since 1830. Some abolitionists, intensely convinced of the rightness of their cause, yet faced with a federal government largely on the other side, came to doubt that the federal Constitution could any longer be supported. Their leading figure was William Lloyd Garrison (1805–1879). Garrison spent his fatherless youth as a printer's apprentice in Newburyport, Massachusetts. He came to Boston as a young man, and in 1829 he began speaking out publicly against slavery. In 1831 he started his famous journal The Liberator. *Unrestrained in language, humorless, and untiringly zealous, Garrison eventually crossed many of his friends as well as his declared foes. He supported the whole range of radical causes, including women's rights, though never slackening his main outcry against slavery. Garrison rejected political action (voting only once in his lifetime) in favor of a direct appeal to individual moral conscience. His religious views grew unorthodox; a meeting with John Humphrey Noyes in 1837 converted him to Christian Perfectionism. Later he rejected biblical authority and*

SOURCE. William Lloyd Garrison, "The United States Constitution," *Selections from the Writings and Speeches of William Lloyd Garrison* (Boston: R.F. Wallcut, 1852), pp. 302–303, 307–315; William Lloyd Garrison, speech on the evening of John Brown's execution, *The Liberator* (Boston), December 16, 1859.

flirted with spiritualism. Thus, though Garrison's spurning of the Constitution was boldly unusual in an age of Constitution-worship, it is not clear exactly where he located the ultimate source of authority to replace it. What did become apparent was that his growing militancy against the white south conflicted with his long-time pacifism. How he faced this major dilemma is revealed in the short closing excerpt, reflecting a new pitch of emotionalism in the wake of John Brown's raid.

THE UNITED STATES CONSTITUTION

There are some very worthy men, who are gravely trying to convince this slaveholding and slavetrading nation, that it has an Antislavery Constitution, if it did but know it—always has had it since it was a nation—and so designed it to be from the beginning! Hence, all slaveholding under it is illegal, and ought in virtue of it to be forthwith abolished by act of Congress. As rationally attempt to convince the American people that they inhabit the moon, and "run upon all fours," as that they have not intelligently, deliberately and purposely entered into a covenant, by which three millions of slaves are now held securely in bondage! They are not to be let off so easily, either by indignant Heaven or outraged Earth! To tell them that, for three score years, they have misunderstood and misinterpreted their own Constitution, in a manner gross and distorted beyond any thing known in human history; that Washington, Jefferson, Adams, all who framed that Constitution—the Supreme Court of the United States, and all its branches, and all other Courts—the national Congress and all state legislatures—have utterly perverted its scope and meaning—is the coolest and absurdest thing ever heard of beneath the stars! No, not thus are they to be allowed to escape hot censure and unsparing condemnation. They have committed no blunder; they have not erred through stupidity; they have not been misled by any legal sophistry. They are verily guilty of the most atrocious crimes, and have sinned against the clearest light ever vouchsafed to any people. They have designedly "framed mischief by a law," and consigned to chains and infamy an inoffensive and helpless race. Hence, it is not an error in legal interpretation that they are to correct, but they are to be arraigned as criminals of the deepest dye, warned of the wrath to come, and urged to the immediate confession and abandonment of this great "besetting sin." "Now, therefore, go to, speak to the men of

Judah, and to the inhabitants of Jerusalem, saying, Thus saith the Lord, Behold, I frame evil against you, and devise a device against you; return ye now every one from his evil way, and make your ways and your doings good."

Some are unwilling to admit the possibility of legalizing slavery, because of its foul and monstrous character. But what iniquity may not men commit by agreement? and what obligations so diabolical, that men may not promise to perform them to the letter? To say that men have no right to do wrong is a truism; to intimate that they have not the power to do so is an absurdity. If they have the power, it is possible for them to use it; and no where do they use it with more alacrity, or on a more gigantic scale, than in the United States. . . .

Away with all verbal casuistry, all legal quibbling, the idle parade of Lord Mansfield's decision in the case of Somerset, the useless appeals to Blackstone's Commentaries, and the like, to prove that the United States Constitution is an Antislavery instrument! It is worse than labor lost, and, as a false issue, cannot advance, but must rather retard, the Antislavery movement. Let there be no dodging, no shuffling, no evasion. Let us confess the sin of our fathers, and our own sin as a people, in conspiring for the degradation and enslavement of the colored race among us. Let us be honest with the facts of history, and acknowledge the compromises that were made to secure the adoption of the Constitution, and the consequent establishment of the Union. Let us, who profess to abhor slavery, and who claim to be freemen indeed, dissolve the bands that connect us with the slave power, religiously and politically; not doubting that a faithful adherence to principle will be the wisest policy, the highest expediency, for ourselves and our posterity, for the miserable victims of southern oppression, and for the cause of liberty throughout the world.

We regard this as indeed a solemn crisis, which requires of every man sobriety of thought, prophetic forecast, independent judgment, invincible determination, and a sound heart. A revolutionary step is one that should not be taken hastily, nor followed under the influence of impulsive imitation. To know what spirits they are of—whether they have counted the cost of the warfare—what are the principles they advocate—and how they are to achieve their object—is the first duty of revolutionists.

But, while circumspection and prudence are excellent qualities in every great emergency, they become the allies of tyranny whenever they restrain prompt, bold and decisive action against it.

We charge upon the present national compact, that it was formed at the expense of human liberty, by a profligate surrender of principle, and to this hour is cemented with human blood.

We charge upon the American Constitution, that it contains provisions, and enjoins duties, which make it unlawful for freemen to take the oath of allegiance to it, because they are expressly designed to favor a slaveholding oligarchy, and, consequently, to make one portion of the people a prey to another.

It was pleaded at the time of its adoption, it is pleaded now, that, without such a compromise, there could have been no union; that, without union, the colonies would have become an easy prey to the mother country; and, hence, that it was an act of necessity, deplorable indeed when viewed alone, but absolutely indispensable to the safety of the republic.

To this we reply: the plea is as profligate as the act was tyrannical. It is the jesuitical doctrine, that the end sanctifies the means. It is a confession of sin, but the denial of any guilt in its perpetration. This plea is sufficiently broad to cover all the oppression and villainy that the sun has witnessed in his circuit, since God said, "Let there be light." It assumes that to be practicable, which is impossible, namely, that there can be freedom with slavery, union with injustice, and safety with bloodguiltiness. A union of virtue with pollution is the triumph of licentiousness. A partnership between right and wrong is wholly wrong. A compromise of the principles of justice is the deification of crime.

Better that the American Union had never been formed, than that it should have been obtained at such a frightful cost! If they were guilty who fashioned it, but who could not foresee all its frightful consequences, how much more guilty are they, who, in full view of all that has resulted from it, clamor for its perpetuity! If it was sinful at the commencement to adopt it, on the ground of escaping a greater evil, is it not equally sinful to swear to support it for the same reason, or until, in process of time, it be purged from its corruption?

The fact is, the compromise alluded to, instead of effecting a union, rendered it impracticable; unless by the term union we are to understand the absolute reign of the slaveholding power over the whole country, to the prostration of northern rights. It is not certain, it is not even probable, that if the present Constitution had not been adopted, the mother country would have reconquered the colonies. The spirit that would have chosen danger in preference to crime, to perish with justice rather than live with dishonor, to dare and suffer whatever might betide, rather than sacrifice the rights of one human being, could never have been subjugated by any mortal power. Surely, it is paying a poor tribute to the valor and devotion of our revolutionary fathers in the cause of liberty, to say that, if they had sternly refused to sacrifice their principles, they would have fallen an easy prey to the despotic power of England.

To the argument, that the words "slaves" and "slavery" are not to be found in the Constitution, and therefore that it was never intended to give any protection or countenance to the slave system, it is sufficient to reply, that though no such words are contained in the instrument, other words were used, intelligently and specifically, to meet the necessities of slavery; and that these were adopted in good faith, to be observed until a constitutional change could be effected. On this point, as to the design of certain provisions, no intelligent man can honestly entertain a doubt. . . .

Again, if it be said, that those clauses, being immoral, are null and void—we reply, it is true they are not to be observed; but it is also true, that they are portions of an instrument, the support of which, as a whole, is required by oath or affirmation; and, therefore, because they are immoral, and because of this obligation to enforce immorality, no one can innocently swear to support the Constitution.

Again, if it be objected, that the Constitution was formed by the people of the United States, in order to establish justice, to promote the general welfare, and secure the blessings of liberty to themselves and their posterity; and, therefore, it is to be so construed as to harmonize with these objects; we reply . . . that its language is not to be interpreted in a sense which neither of the contracting parties understood, and which would frustrate every design of their alliance —to wit, union at the expense of the colored population of the country. Moreover, nothing is more certain than that the preamble alluded to never included, in the minds of those who framed it, those who were then pining in bondage—for, in that case, a general emancipation of the slaves would have instantly been proclaimed throughout the United States. The words, "secure the blessings of liberty to ourselves and our posterity," assuredly did not mean to include the slave population. "To promote the general welfare," referred to their own welfare exclusively. "To establish justice," was understood to be for their sole benefit as slaveholders, and the guilty abettors of slavery. This is demonstrated by other parts of the same instrument, and by their own practice under it.

We would not detract aught from what is justly their due; but it is as reprehensible to give them credit for what they did not possess, as it is to rob them of what is theirs. It is absurd, it is false, it is an insult to the common sense of mankind, to pretend that the Constitution was intended to embrace the entire population of the country under its sheltering wings; or that the parties to it were actuated by a sense of justice and the spirit of impartial liberty; or that it needs no alteration, but only a new interpretation, to make it harmonize with the object aimed at by its adoption. As truly might it be argued, that because it is asserted in the Declaration of Independence, that all men are created equal, and endowed with an inalienable right to liberty, therefore none of its signers were slaveholders, and since its adoption slavery has been banished from the American soil! The truth is, our fathers were intent on securing liberty to themselves, without being very scrupulous as to the means they used to accomplish their purpose. They were not actuated by the spirit of universal philanthropy; and though in words they recognized occasionally the brotherhood of the human race, in practice they continually denied it. They did not blush to enslave a portion of their fellowmen, and to buy and sell them as cattle in the market, while they were fighting against the oppression of the mother country, and boasting of their regard for the rights of man. Why, then, concede to them virtues which they did not possess? Why cling to the falsehood, that they were no respecters of persons in the formation of the government?

Alas! that they had no more fear of God, no more regard for man, in their hearts! "The iniquity of the house of Israel and Judah (the North and South) is exceeding great, and the land is full of blood, and the city full of perverseness; for they say, the Lord hath forsaken the earth, and the Lord seeth not."

If, in utter disregard of all historical facts, it is still asserted, that the Constitution needs no amendment to make it a free instrument, adapted to all the exigencies of a free people, and was never intended to give any strength or countenance to the slave system—the indignant spirit of insulted Liberty replies: "What though the assertion be true? Of what avail is a mere piece of parchment? In itself, though it be written all over with words of truth and freedom—though its provisions be as impartial and just as words can express, or the imagination paint—though it be as pure as the gospel, and breathe only the spirit of Heaven—it is powerless; it has no executive vitality; it is a lifeless corpse, even though beautiful in death. I am famishing for lack of bread! How is my appetite relieved by holding up to my gaze a painted loaf? I am manacled, wounded, bleeding, dying! What consolation is it to know, that they who are seeking to destroy my life, profess in words to be my friends? If the liberties of the people have been betrayed—if judgment has been turned away backward, and justice standeth afar off, and truth has fallen in the streets, and equity cannot enter—if the princes of the land are roaring lions, the judges evening wolves, the people light and treacherous persons, the priests covered with pollution—if we are living under a frightful despotism, which scoffs at all constitutional restraints, and wields the resources of the nation to promote its own bloody purposes—tell us not that the forms of freedom are still left to us! Would such tameness and submission have freighted the Mayflower for Plymouth Rock? Would it have resisted the Stamp Act, the Tea Tax, or any of those entering wedges of tyranny with which the British government sought to rive the liberties of America? The wheel of the Revolution would have rusted on its axle, if a spirit so weak had been the only power to give it motion. Did our fathers say, when their rights and liberties were infringed—'Why, what is done cannot be undone! That is the first thought!' No, it was the last thing they thought of: or, rather, it never entered their minds at all. They sprang to the conclusion at once— 'What is done shall be undone! That is our first and only thought!' "

"Is water running in our veins? Do we remember still
Old Plymouth Rock, and Lexington, and famous Bunker Hill?
The debt we owe our fathers' graves? and to the yet unborn;
Whose heritage ourselves must make a thing of pride or scorn?

Gray Plymouth Rock hath yet a tongue, and Concord is not dumb;
And voices from our fathers' graves and from the future come:
They call on us to stand our ground—they charge us still to be
Not only free from chains ourselves, but foremost to make free!"

It is of little consequence who is on the throne, if there be behind it a power mightier than the throne. It matters not what is the theory of the government, if the practice of the government be unjust and tyrannical. We rise in rebellion against a despotism incomparably more dreadful than that which induced the colonists to take up arms against the mother country; not on account of a three-penny tax on tea, but because fetters of living iron are fastened on the limbs of millions of our countrymen, and our most sacred rights are trampled in the dust. As citizens of the state, we appeal to the state in vain for protection and redress. As citizens of the United States, we are treated as outlaws in one half of the country, and the national government consents to our destruction. We are denied the right of locomotion, freedom of speech, the right of petition, the liberty of the press, the right peaceably to assemble together to protest against oppression and plead for liberty—at least, in fifteen states of the Union. If we venture, as avowed and unflinching abolitionists, to travel south of Mason and Dixon's line, we do so at the peril of our lives. If we would escape torture and death, on visiting any of the slave states, we must stifle our conscientious convictions, bear no testimony against cruelty and tyranny, suppress the struggling emotions of humanity, divest ourselves of all letters and papers of an antislavery character, and do homage to the slaveholding power—or run the risk of a cruel martyrdom! These are appalling and undeniable facts.

Three millions of the American people are crushed under the American Union! They are held as slaves, trafficked as merchandise, registered as goods and chattels! The government gives them no protection—the government is their enemy, the government keeps them in chains! Where they lie bleeding, we are prostrate by their side—in their sorrows and sufferings we participate—their stripes are inflicted on our bodies, their shackles are fastened on our limbs, their cause is ours! The Union which grinds them to the dust rests upon us, and with them we will struggle to overthrow it! The Constitution which subjects them to hopeless bondage is one that we cannot swear to support. Our motto is, "No Union with Slaveholders," either religious or political. They are the fiercest enemies of mankind, and the bitterest foes of God! We separate from them, not in anger, not in malice, not for a selfish purpose, not to do them an injury, not to cease warning, exhorting, reproving them for their crimes, not to leave the perishing bondman to his fate—O no! But to clear our skirts of innocent blood—to give the oppressor no countenance—and to hasten the downfall of slavery in America, and throughout the world!

Do you ask what can be done if you abandon the ballot box? What did the crucified Nazarene do without the elective franchise? What did the apostles do? What did the glorious army of martyrs and confessors do? What did Luther and his intrepid associates do?

"If thou must stand alone, what then? The honor shall be more!
But thou canst never stand alone while Heaven still arches o'er—
While there's a God to worship, a devil to be denied—
The good and true of every age stand with thee, side by side!"

The form of government that shall succeed the present government of the United States, let time determine. It would be a waste of time to argue that question, until the people are regenerated and turned from their iniquity. Ours is no anarchical movement, but one of order and obedience. In ceasing from oppression, we establish liberty. What is now fragmentary shall in due time be crystalized, and shine like a gem set in the heavens, for a light to all coming ages.

JOHN BROWN

A word upon the subject of peace. I am a nonresistant—a believer in the inviolability of human life, under all circumstances; I, therefore, in the name of God, disarm John Brown, and every slave at the south. But I do not stop there; if I did, I should be a monster. I also disarm, in the name of God, every slaveholder and tyrant in the world. (Loud applause.) For wherever that principle is adopted, all fetters must instantly melt, and there can be no oppressed, and no oppressor, in the nature of things. How many agree with me in regard to the doctrine of the inviolability of human life? How many nonresistants are there here tonight? (A single voice—"I.") There is *one!* (Laughter.) Well, then, you who are otherwise are not the men to point the finger at John Brown, and cry "traitor"—judging you by your own standard. (Applause.) Nevertheless, I am a nonresistant and I not only desire, but have labored unremittingly to effect, the peaceful abolition of slavery, by an appeal to the reason and conscience of the slaveholder; yet, as a peace man—an "ultra" peace man—I am prepared to say, "Success to every slave insurrection at the south, and in every slave country." (Enthusiastic applause.) And I do not see how I compromise or stain my peace profession in making that declaration. Whenever there is a contest between the oppressed and the oppressor—the weapons being equal between the parties—God knows my heart must be with the oppressed, and always against the oppressor. Therefore, whenever commenced, I cannot but wish success to all slave insurrections. (Loud applause.) I thank God when men who believe in the right and duty of wielding carnal weapons are so far advanced that they will take those weapons out of the scale of despotism, and throw them into the scale of freedom. It is an indication of progress, and a positive moral growth; it is one way to get up to the sublime platform of nonresistance; and it is God's method of dealing retribution upon the head of the tyrant. Rather than see men wear their chains in a cowardly and servile spirit, I would, as an advocate of peace, much rather see them breaking the head of the tyrant with their chains. Give me, as a nonresistant, Bunker Hill, and Lexington, and Concord, rather than the cowardice and servility of a southern slave plantation.

2

THE ODOR OF POLITICS IN THE 1850S

Walt Whitman
THE EIGHTEENTH PRESIDENCY

A clearer indication of the impact of unusual times on the man is found in an essay written by the poet Walt Whitman (1819–1892) during the election campaign of 1856. It was out of character for Whitman to be carried away by a mood of extremism. He usually felt at home striking the lyrically inclusive note. Yet here he joins the outcry of the most militant radicals against the basic results of the political process, though his intention was also to support John C. Fremont. Perhaps an awareness of these conflicting impulses caused Whitman to put the essay away in a desk drawer without publishing it. (It has never been printed before, except in one limited edition.) The language Whitman uses to attack the proslavery politicians who dominated the federal government in this period is more pungent than anything from the pen of Garrison. Calling for a grassroots moral regeneration of the country, Whitman strikes a different note from the abolitionists with religious backgrounds. The tone is lustily populistic, to the point where one suspects that some of Whitman's sexual dreams intrude. He also sounds the call for a generational and social class revolt not unlike some of the New Left rhetoric of the 1960s. And yet he also faithfully reproduces the free soil position of the day, with its special concern for the rights of white labor in the west. In his stridently negative appraisal of the contemporary power structure, Whitman registers the pull of the unusual forces that were tearing the Union apart.

VOICE OF WALT WHITMAN TO EACH YOUNG MAN IN THE NATION,
NORTH, SOUTH, EAST, AND WEST

Before the American era, the program of the classes of a nation read thus, first the king, second the noblemen and gentry, third the great

SOURCE. Walt Whitman, "The Eighteenth Presidency," in Clifton Joseph Furness, ed., *Walt Whitman's Workshop* (Cambridge, Mass.: Harvard University Press, 1928), pp. 92–106, 112–113; written in 1856 but not published until 1928. Reprinted with permission of Harvard University Press.

mass of mechanics, farmers, men following the water, and all laboring persons. The first and second classes are unknown to the theory of the government of these states; the likes of the class rated third on the old program were intended to be, and are in fact, to all intents and purposes, the American nation, the people.

Mechanics, farmers, sailors, etc., constitute some six millions of the inhabitants of these states; merchants, lawyers, doctors, teachers and priests, count up as high as five hundred thousand; the owners of slaves number three hundred and fifty thousand; the population of the states bring altogether about thirty millions, seven tenths of whom are women and children. At present, the personnel of the government of these thirty millions, in executives and elsewhere, is drawn from limber-tongued lawyers, very fluent but empty feeble old men, professional politicians, dandies, dyspeptics, and so forth, and rarely drawn from the solid body of the people; the effects now seen, and more to come. Of course the fault, if it be a fault, is for reasons, and is of the people themselves, and will mend when it should mend. . . .

I expect to see the day when the like of the present personnel of the governments, federal, state, municipal, military, and naval, will be looked upon with derision, and when qualified mechanics and young men will reach Congress and other official stations, sent in their working costumes, fresh from their benches and tools, and returning to them again with dignity. The young fellows must prepare to do credit to this destiny, for the stuff is in them. Nothing gives place, recollect, and never ought to give place except to its clean superiors. There is more rude and undeveloped bravery, friendship, conscientiousness, clear-sightedness, and practical genius for any scope of action, even the broadest and highest, now among the American mechanics and young men, than in all the official persons in these states, legislative, executive, judicial, military, and naval, and more than among all the literary persons. I would be much pleased to see some heroic, shrewd, fully informed, healthy-bodied, middle-aged, beard-faced American blacksmith or boatman come down from the west across the Alleghenies, and walk into the presidency, dressed in a clean suit of working attire, and with the tan all over his face, breast, and arms; I would certainly vote for that sort of man, possessing the due requirements, before any other candidate. . . .

At present, we are environed with nonsense under the name of respectability. Everywhere lowers that stifling atmosphere that makes all the millions of farmers and mechanics of these states the helpless supple-jacks of a comparatively few politicians. Somebody must make a bold push. The people, credulous, generous, deferential, allow the American government to be managed in many respects as is only proper under the personnel of a king and hereditary lords; or, more truly, not proper under any decent men anywhere. If this were to go on, we ought to change the title of the president, and issue patents of nobility. Of course it is not to go on. We Americans are no fools. I perceive meanwhile that nothing less than marked inconsistencies and usurpations will arouse a nation, and make ready for better things afterwards.

But what ails the present way of filling the offices of the states? Is it not good enough? I should say it was not. Today, of all the persons in public office in these states, not one in a thousand has been chosen by any spontaneous movement of the people, nor is attending to the interests of the people; all have been nominated and put through by great or small caucuses of the politicians, or appointed as rewards for electioneering; and all consign themselves to personal and party interests. Neither in the presidency, nor in Congress, nor in foreign ambassadorships, nor in the governorships of the states, nor in legislatures, nor in the mayoralties of cities, nor the aldermanships, nor among the police, nor on the benches of judges, do I observe a single bold muscular, young, well-informed, well-beloved, resolute American man, bound to do a man's duty, aloof from all parties, and with a manly scorn of all parties. Instead of that, every trustee of the people is a traitor, looking only to his own gain, and to boost up his party. The berths, the presidency included, are bought, sold, electioneered for, prostituted, and filled with prostitutes. In the north and east, swarms of doughfaces, office-vermin, kept-editors, clerks, attaches of the ten thousand officers and their parties, aware of nothing further than the drip and spoil of politics—ignorant of principles, the true glory of a man. In the south, no end of blusterers, braggarts, windy, melodramatic, continually screaming in falsetto, a nuisance to these states, their own just as much as any; altogether the most impudent persons that have yet appeared in the history of lands, once with the most incredible successes, having pistoled, bludgeoned, yelled and threatened America, the past twenty years into one long train of cowardly concessions, and still not through, but rather at the commencement. Their cherished secret scheme is to dissolve the union of these states.

Well, what more? Is nothing but breed upon breed like these to be represented in the presidency? Are parties to forever usurp the government? Are lawyers, doughfaces, and the three hundred and fifty thousand owners of slaves, to sponge the mastership of thirty millions?

Where is the real America? Where are the laboring persons, plough-men, men with axes, spades, scythes, flails? Where are the carpenters, masons, machinists, drivers of horses, workmen in factories? Where is the spirit of the manliness and common sense of these states? It does not appear in the government. It does not appear at all in the presidency.

The sixteenth and seventeenth terms of the American presidency[1] have shown that the villainy and shallowness of great rulers are just as eligible to these states as to any foreign despotism, kingdom, or empire—there is not a bit of difference. History is to record these two presidencies as so far our topmost warning and shame. Never were publicly displayed more deformed, mediocre, sniveling, unreliable, falsehearted men! Never were these states so insulted, and attempted to be betrayed! All the main purposes for which government was established are openly denied. The perfect equality of slavery with freedom is flauntingly preached in the north—nay, the superiority of slavery. The slave trade is proposed to be renewed. Everywhere frowns and misunderstandings—everywhere exasperations and humiliations. The president eats dirt and excrement for his daily meals, likes it, and tries to force it on the states. The cushions of the presidency are nothing but filth and blood. The pavements of Congress are also bloody. The land that flushed amazed at the basest outrage of our times, grows pale with a far different feeling to see the outrage unanimously commended back again to those who only half rejected it. The national tendency toward populating the territories full of free work-peoples, established by the organic compacts of these states, promulged by the fathers, the presidents, the old warriors, and the earlier Congresses, a tendency vital to the life and thrift of the masses of the citizens, is violently put back under the feet of slavery, and against the free people the masters of slaves are everywhere held up by the president by the red hand. In fifteen of the states the three hundred and fifty thousand masters keep down the true people, the millions of white citizens, mechanics, farmers, boatmen, manufacturers, and the like, excluding them from politics and from office, and punishing by the lash, by tar and feathers, binding fast to rafts on the river or trees in the woods, and sometimes by death, all attempts to discuss the evils of slavery in its relations to the whites. The people of the territories are denied the power to form state governments unless they

[1]The sixteenth term was that of Zachary Taylor and, when he died in office, his successor Millard Fillmore. The seventeenth term was that of Franklin Pierce. Ed.

consent to fasten upon them the slave-hopple, the iron wristlet, and the neck-spike. For refusing such consent, the governor and part of the legislature of the state of Kansas are chased, seized, chained, by the creatures of the president, and are today in chains. Over the vast continental tracts of unorganized American territory, equal in extent to all the present organized states, and in future to give the law to all, the whole executive, judicial, military, and naval power of these states is forsworn to the people, the rightful owners, and sworn to the help of the three hundred and fifty thousand masters of slaves, to put them through this continent, with their successors, at their pleasure, and to maintain by force their mastership over their slave men and women, slave farmers, slave miners, slave cartmen, slave sailors, and the like. Slavery is adopted as an American institution, superior, national, constitutional, right in itself, and under no circumstances to take any less than freedom takes. Nor is that all; today, tonight, the constables and commissioners of the president can by law step into any part of these states and pick out whom they please, deciding which man or woman they will allow to be free, and which shall be a slave, no jury to intervene, but the commissioner's mandate to be enforced by the federal troops and cannon, and has been actually so enforced.

Are the states retarded then? No; while all is drowned and desperate that the government has had to do with, all the outside influence of government (forever the largest part), thrives and smiles. The sun shines, corn grows, men go merrily about their affairs, houses are built, ships arrive and depart. Through evil and through good, the republic stands, and is for centuries yet to stand immovable from its foundations. No, no; out at dastards and disgraces, fortunate are the wrongs that call forth stout and angry men; then is shown what stuff there is in a nation.

The young genius of America is not going to be emasculated and strangled just as it arrives toward manly age. It shall live, and yet baffle the politicians and the three hundred and fifty thousand masters of slaves.

Now the term of the seventeenth presidency passing hooted and spurned to its close, the delegates of the politicians have nominated for the eighteenth term, Buchanan of Pennsylvania, and Fillmore of New York, separate tickets, but men both patterned to follow and match the seventeenth term, both disunionists, both old politicians, both sworn down to the theories of special parties, and of all others the theories that balk and reverse the main purposes of the founders of these states. Such are the nominees that have arisen out of the power of the politicians, but another power has also arisen. A new race copiously appears, with resolute tread, soon to confront presidents, congresses and parties, to look them sternly in the face, to stand no nonsense, American young men, the offspring and proof of these states, the west the same as the east, and the south alike with the north.

America sends these young men in good time, for they were needed. Much waits to be done. First, people need to realize who are poisoning the politics of these states.

Whence the delegates of the politicians? Whence the Buchanan and Fillmore conventions? Not from sturdy American freemen; not from industrious homes; not from thrifty farms; not from the ranks of fresh-bodied young men; not from among teachers, poets, savants, learned persons, beloved persons, temperate persons; not from among shipbuilders, engineers, agriculturists, scythe swingers, corn hoers; not from the race of mechanics; not from that great strong stock of southerners that supplied the land in old times; not from the real west, the log hut, the clearing, the woods, the prairie, the hillside; not from the sensible, generous, rude Californian miners; not from the best specimens of Massachusetts, Maine, New Jersey, Pennsylvania, Ohio, Illinois, Wisconsin, Indiana, nor from the untainted unpolitical citizens of the cities.

Whence then do these nominating dictators of America year after year start out? From lawyers' offices, secret lodges, backyards, bed houses, and barrooms; from out of the custom houses, marshals' offices, post offices, and gambling hells; from the president's house, the jail, the venereal hospital, the station house; from unnamed by-places where devilish disunion is hatched at midnight; from political hearses, and from the coffins inside, and from the shrouds inside of the coffins; from the tumors and abcesses of the land; from the skeletons and skulls in the vaults of the federal almshouses; from the running sores of the great cities; thence to the national, state, city, and district nominating conventions of these states, come the most numerous and controlling delegates.

Who are they personally? Officeholders, office seekers, robbers, pimps, exclusives, malignants, conspirators, murderers, fancy-men, portmasters, custom-house clerks, contractors, kept-editors, Spaniels well trained to carry and fetch, jobbers, infidels, disunionists, terrorists, mail riflers, slave catchers, pushers of slavery, creatures of the president, creatures of would-be presidents, spies, blowers, electioneers, body snatchers, bawlers, bribers, compromisers, runaways, lobbyers, sponges, ruined sports, expelled gamblers, policy backers, monte-dealers, duelists, carriers of concealed weapons, blind men, deaf men, pimpled men, scarred inside with the vile disorder, gaudy outside with gold chains made from the people's money and harlot's money twisted together; crawling, serpentine men, the lousy combings and born freedom sellers of the earth.

Stripped of padding and paint, who are Buchanan and Fillmore? What has this age to do with them? Two galvanized old men, close on the summons to depart this life, their early contemporaries long since gone, only they two left, relics and proofs of the little political bargains, chances, combinations, resentments of a past age, having nothing in common with this age, standing for the first crop of political graves and gravestones planted in these states, but in no sort standing for the lusty young growth of the modern times of the states. It is clear from all these two men say and do, that their hearts have not been touched in the least by the flowing fire of the humanitarianism of the new world, its best glory yet, and a moral control stronger than all its governments. It is clear that neither of these nominees of the politicians has thus far reached an inkling of the real scope and character of the contest of the day, probably now only well begun, to stretch through years, with varied temporary successes and reverses. Still the two old men live in respectable little spots, with respectable little wants. Still their eyes stop at the edges of the tables of committees and cabinets, beholding not the great round world beyond. What has this age to do with them? . . .

To butchers, sailors, stevedores, and drivers of horses—to ploughmen, woodcutters, marketmen, carpenters, masons, and laborers—to workmen in factories—and to all in these states who live by their daily toil—mechanics! A parcel of windy northern liars are bawling in your ears the easily spoken words democracy and the Democratic party. Others are making a great ado with the word Americanism, a solemn and great word.[2] What the so-called democracy is now sworn to perform would eat the faces off the succeeding generations of common people worse than the most horrible disease. . . .

As the broad fat states of the west, the largest and best parts of the inheritance of the American farmers and mechanics, were ordained to common people and workmen long in advance by Jefferson, Washington, and the earlier Congresses, now a far ampler west is to be ordained. Is it to be ordained to workmen, or to the masters of workmen? Shall the future mechanics of America be serfs? Shall labor be degraded, and women be whipped in the fields for not performing their tasks? If slaves are not prohibited from all national territory by law, as prohibited in the beginning, as the organic compacts authorize

[2]Fillmore was running as the candidate of the American party, otherwise called the Know-Nothings. Ed.

and require, and if, on the contrary, the entrance and establishment of slave labor through the continent is secured, there will steadily wheel into the Union, for centuries to come, slave state after slave state, the entire surface of the land owned by great proprietors, in plantations of thousands of acres, showing no more sight for free races of farmers and work-people than there is now in any European despotism or aristocracy; and the existence of our present free states put in jeopardy, because out of the vast territory are to come states enough to overbalance all.

Workmen! Workwomen! Those universe national American tracts belong to you; they are in trust with you; they are latent with the populous cities, numberless farms, herds, granaries, groves, golden gardens, and inalienable homesteads, of your successors. The base political blowers and kept-editors of the north are raising a fog of prevarications around you. . . .

Are not political parties about played out? I say they are, all round. America has outgrown parties; henceforth it is too large, and they too small. They habitually make common cause just as soon in advocacy of the worst deeds and men as the best, or probably a little sooner for the worst. I place no reliance upon any old party, nor upon any new party. Suppose one to be formed under the noblest auspices, and getting into power with the noblest intentions, how long would it remain so? How many years? Would it remain so one year? As soon as it becomes successful, and there are offices to be bestowed, the politicians leave the unsuccessful parties, and rush toward it, and it ripens and rots with the rest.

What right has any one political party, no matter which, to wield the American government? No right at all. Not the so-called democratic, not abolition, opposition to foreigners, nor any other party, should be permitted the exclusive use of the presidency; and every American young man must have sense enough to comprehend this. I have said the old parties are defunct; but there remains of them empty flesh, putrid mouths, mumbling and squeaking the tones of these conventions, the politicians standing back in shadow, telling lies, trying to delude and frighten the people; and nominating such candidates as Fillmore and Buchanan . . . .

Much babble will always be heard in the land about the federal Constitution, this, that, and the other concerning it. The federal Constitution is a perfect and entire thing, an edifice put together, not for the accommodation of a few persons, but for the whole human race; not for a day or a year, but for many years, perhaps a thousand, perhaps many thousand. Its architecture is not a single brick, a beam, an apartment, but only the whole. It is the grandest piece of moral building ever constructed; I believe its architects were some mighty prophets and gods. Few appreciate it, Americans just as few as any. Like all perfect works or persons, time only is great enough to give its area. Five or six centuries hence, it will be better understood from results, growths. . . .

The times are full of great portents in these states and in the whole world. Freedom against slavery is not issuing here alone, but is issuing everywhere. The horizon rises, it divides I perceive, for a more august drama than any of the past. Old men have played their parts, the act suitable to them is closed, and if they will not withdraw voluntarily, must be bid to do so with unmistakable voice. Landmarks of masters, slaves, kings, aristocracies, are moth-eaten, and the peoples of the earth are planting new vast landmarks for themselves. Frontiers and boundaries are less and less able to divide men. The modern inventions, the wholesale engines of war, the world-spreading instruments of peace, the steamship, the locomotive, the electric telegraph, the common newspaper, the cheap book, the ocean mail, are interlinking the inhabitants of the earth together as groups of one family—America standing, and for ages to stand, as the host and champion of the same, the most welcome spectacle ever presented among nations. Everything indicates unparalleled reforms. Races are marching and countermarching by swift millions and tens of millions. Never was justice so mighty amid injustice; never did the idea of equality erect itself so haughty and uncompromising amid inequality, as today. Never were such sharp questions asked as today. Never was there more eagerness to know. Never was the representative man more energetic, more like a god, than today. He urges on the myriads before him, he crowds them aside, his daring step approaches the arctic and antarctic poles, he colonizes the shores of the Pacific, the Asiatic Indias, the birthplace of languages and of races, the Archipelagoes, Australia; he explores Africa, he unearths Assyria and Egypt, he restates history, he enlarges morality, he speculates anew upon the soul, upon original premises; nothing is left quiet, nothing but he will settle by demonstrations for himself. What whispers are these running through the eastern continents, and crossing the Atlantic and Pacific? What historic denouements are these we are approaching? On all sides tyrants tremble, crowns are unsteady, the human race restive, on the watch for some better era, some divine war. No man knows what will happen next, but all know that some such things are to happen as mark the greatest moral convulsions of the earth. Who shall play the hand for America in these tremendous games?

3

REASON HIGHER THAN THE BIBLE

Gerrit Smith
BIBLE CIVIL GOVERNMENT

A few days after the election of 1860, the wealthy philanthropist and abolitionist Gerrit Smith gave the following address to an audience assembled at his estate in Madison County, New York. He explained why he could not vote for any party candidate, including Lincoln, and disclosed the spirit in which he faced the prospect of the southern states' secession from the Union. Altogether it is a remarkable revelation of the perfectionist state of mind on the very brink of Civil War. Given a fortune of $400,000 by his father, who had made shrewd investments in real estate, Smith chose to spend it on a lifetime of good works. He poured his money into a variety of churches, theological schools, and colleges, and into an unsuccessful colonization scheme for freed blacks in the Adirondacks. Smith promoted Sabbath observance, vegetarianism, pacifism, women's suffrage, and prison reform; he fought against tobacco, alcohol, and capital punishment. A friend of Garrison's, Smith was not as extreme, but despite his own later denials, it is probable that he gave practical aid to John Brown in organizing his slave insurrection. Unlike Garrison, Smith did not usually abstain from politics, through until now he had worked outside the major parties. A backer of the Liberty party in 1840, he had served briefly in Congress as an independent. Thus his abstention from the election of 1860 was uncharacteristic, another symptom of the extremity of the times. As the Civil War went on, Smith was gradually won over to the Republican party, supporting Lincoln in 1864 and Grant in 1868, and by the time of Reconstruction, he had become a moderate. Earlier, his religious beliefs also changed. Originally a Presbyterian in the style of Finney, he deserted Christianity to advocate a religion based on nature and reason. Some explanations for this shift appear in the address below. Facing the problem of ultimate authority more boldly than Garrison, Smith announces his willingness to abandon the Bible itself if it condones slavery. Reason is his sole remaining standard. Here, the Enlightenment has won out against evangelicalism. The supreme irony of the selection is that Smith's rationalism, which in one sense looks ahead to the postwar age of Darwinian skepticism,

SOURCE. Gerrit Smith, "Bible Civil Government: Peterboro, New York, November 18, 1860," *Sermons and Speches* (New York: Ross & Tousey, 1861), pp. 103–120.

here marches hand in hand with an awesome vision of divine judgment to be visited on the south by force of arms. The paradox is somehow central to that entire reform generation.

Another election has come and gone. Much of good, in both its near and remote results, do we look for. Nevertheless, we are not to overlook its many baleful influences, and its wide havoc of virtue and happiness. We have again passed through the great quadrennial demoralization, which sinks into a lower deep tens of thousands of drunkards; which turns into drunkards tens of thousands of the sober; which makes tens of thousands of new liars, and makes worse tens of thousands of old ones; which cheapens sincerity and simplicity, by putting high prices upon intrigue and dishonesty; which puts falsehood for truth and darkness for light, and makes ten appeals to passion and prejudice where it makes one to reason.

While, however, we affirm that this is the general character of a presidential election, we are free to admit that some of the actors in it are candid, and some of the influences in it enlightening and elevating. But with all this, and every other conceivable alleviation, still who does not see that a presidential election frightfully lowers the standard of morality, pours tides of wickedness through all ranks and classes, and preys fatally with its rampant vices on numberless bodies and numberless souls? Many and mighty are the influences needed to redeem great popular elections from the coarseness and corruption which characterize them. Preeminent among these influences is the presence and the part of woman. The conduct and character of men as voters will become far better after the advancing stages of civilization shall have brought up women to vote by their side.

And where were our church people in the late election? They were voting for slave-catching and dramshop candidates. Nay, some of them were themselves such candidates. Our church people were mixed up with the abominations of the election, and not a few of them were drenched in its corruptions.

I turn for a moment from the church people to notice the fact that even the rescuers of slaves did, with very few exceptions, vote for these candidates. In their measureless inconsistency and infatuation, they voted power into hands ready to use it both for reseizing the slave and punishing his rescuers. Doubtless these inconsistent and infatuated men will still wonder that we should refuse to join them in celebrations of slave rescues.

To return to the church people. It must be confessed that thousands of them honestly believed that their candidate would be found faithful to all the claims of freedom and righteousness, and it must also be confessed that, but for this belief, they would not have voted for him. Admit, too, will we that thousands of them voted as they did because they believed the Constitution to be for slavery, and thousands because they believed the Bible sustains it. I believe both to be against it. But what if both are for it? Why, only that both are so far void of obligation. The Bible and the Constitution are the work of men; but freedom is the great gift of the Great God. Hence, believing, as I do, with "Peter and the other Apostles that we ought to obey God rather than man," I must insist that all shall go for freedom, however the Constitution and the Bible may go. "The law of his God," or, in other words, the law of justice, was Daniel's law, and it should be every man's law, the Constitution and even the Bible to the contrary notwithstanding.

Will the church people never believe in the religion of the Bible? They believe in its theologies and its philosophies, or in what are interpreted to be such. Why will they not believe in its religion also? One answer is that they are sectaries; that their sects are organized to uphold, some this part and some that of these theologies and philosophies; and that in this wise religion is in general greatly undervalued, and often quite ignored or lost sight of. Indeed, the mistake becomes almost universal among them, that these theologies or philosophies are themselves religion, or at least a part of it, and that their zeal and contention for them have all the merit of zeal and contention for religion itself. Another explanation is, that whilst the good man alone is willing to be religious, these theologies or philosophies are a substitute for religion so cheap and easy that the wickedest man finds no cross in adopting them. And still another explanation of the refusal of these church people to receive the religion of the Bible is, that whilst this true religion enters a man's heart through his heaven-enlightened and heaven-sanctified reason, they are educated to distrust reason in the province of religion, and to receive upon authority what passes with them for religion. Much, too, might be said to show that religions imposed by authority are not only like to differ very widely from the religion which a sound understanding and a sound heart make their own, but are also peculiarly effective in shutting it out.

I have spoken of the religion of the Bible as one with the true religion. It manifestly is; and nowhere else is that true religion presented so simply, so sublimely, or so perfectly. Foolish skepticism rejects the Bible; credulous and unquestioning superstition gulps it down. But reason—the reason blest with divine illumination—the reason coupled with a renewed heart—though sitting, as it is bound to do, in stern and unsparing, whilst yet in meek and humble judgment, on the Bible, and deciding for itself on the popular interpretations of it, and on the theological and philosophical structures built upon it, comes at last to acknowledge the preeminence of its inspirations and the truth of its religion.

What is the religion of the Bible? The churches hold that it is largely contained in their speculations and theories respecting Trinity, Atonement, Heaven, Hell, etc. But the Bible resolves it into love, especially love to the destitute and afflicted. It says that, "God is love," and that man should be also. It says that, "Love is the fulfilling of the law," and that, "All the law is fulfilled in one word, even in this, Thou shalt love thy neighbor as thyself." It says that to do justice to the poor and needy is to know God (Jeremiah 22:16). It says that, "Pure religion and undefiled before God and the Father, is this: to visit the fatherless and widows in their affliction, and to keep himself unspotted from the world." It says: "Remember them that are in bonds as bound with them, and them which suffer adversity as being yourselves also in the body." It says: "Who is weak, and I am not weak? Who is offended, and I burn not?" It says, in short, that the whole of religion consists in doing as you would be done by. The churches make religion to consist mainly in creeds, but the Bible wholly in deeds, and in the spirit of which they are the necessary outflow. Church religion dreams, but Bible religion bids us do.

Nothing in all the Bible, save the life of Jesus, which was given to reflect before men the life of the Father, and in which the character of God shines out in the character of the God-filled Man, is so rich in tenderness and beauty and so powerful in appeals to love and admiration as its portrayal of righteous civil government. Nothing, with that exception, so clearly and attractively reveals the genius of the religion of the Bible. How little the church people appreciate this religion is manifest from their indifference to the Bible view of civil government. Altogether welcome to them would be this view, and altogether corresponding with it their political action, did they but love this religion.

Civil government is, in the eye of reason, the collective people caring for each of the people—the combination of all for the protection of each one. Such is it also in spirit and scope on the pages of the Bible. We there see it to be, next to God himself, the great protector; and, as is reasonable, the special protector of the innocent and helpless poor. The Bible requires for civil rulers "able men, such as fear God, men of truth, hating covetousness"; men who "shall judge the people with just judgment, shall not respect persons, neither take a gift"; "shall judge [do justice to] the poor of the people, save the children of the needy, and break in pieces the oppressor." Of this true and Bible type of civil rulers was Job, who says: "I delivered the poor that cried; and the fatherless and him that had none to help him. The blessing of him that was ready to perish came upon me, and I caused the widow's heart to leap for joy. I put on righteousness, and it clothed me; my judgment was as a robe and a diadem. I was eyes to the blind, and feet was I to the lame. I was a father to the poor, and the cause which I knew not I searched out. And I brake the jaws of the wicked, and plucked the spoil out of his teeth."

I am always pained when I hear Christians praise certain persons as great statesmen. Great statesmen they are—not because they care for the poor, for they uphold statutes and execute decrees for enslaving and crushing the poor—but because they have talents and learning, and talk ingeniously and eloquently about banks and tariffs and internal improvements, and prate cunningly and winningly of human rights. Were these Christians more Christian, they would see more statesmanship in that noble ruler who "was a father to the poor," than in the sum total of those sham statesmen who are so unwisely and guiltily lauded.

For the reason that it looks upon the civil ruler as the protector of the needy, the Bible says to him: "Open thy mouth for the dumb in the cause of all such as are appointed to destruction. Open thy mouth, judge righteously, and plead the cause of the poor and needy." "Seek judgment, relieve the oppressed." "Let the oppressed go free: break every yoke." It is for this reason that it pronounces "Woe unto them that decree unrighteous decrees and that write grievousness which they have prescribed; to turn aside the needy from judgment and to take away the right from the poor of my people"; and says: "Execute judgment in the morning, and deliver him that is spoiled out of the hand of the oppressor."

We can not mistake the Bible apprehension of civil government, when it tells us that "rulers are not a terror to good works but to the evil"; nor when it says that the ruler is "the minister of God," or in other words, acts on and acts out the principles of God. And who can mistake it, or fail to be touched and melted by it, when he reads the injunction upon civil government: "Take counsel, execute judgment, make thy shadow as the night in the midst of the noon day; hide the outcasts, betray not him that wandereth. Let mine outcasts dwell with thee; be thou a covert to them from the face of the spoiler." Or who can misapprehend it, or not be moved by it, when he reads: "Thou shalt not deliver unto his master the servant which is escaped from his master unto thee. He shall dwell with thee, even among you, in that place which he shall choose, in one of thy gates where it liketh him best: thou shalt not oppress him."

I need quote no further from the Bible to prove that the civil government it commends is the protector of the innocent and helpless poor; nor to prove how widely it contrasts with the civil governments of the whole earth, and especially with the oppressive and murderous rule which, in our own nation, usurps the name of civil government—a rule so sanctioned by the priesthood and upheld by the people, as forcibly to recall the prophet's description of a similar conspiracy. "There is a conspiracy of her prophets in the midst thereof, like a roaring lion ravening the prey; they have devoured souls; they have taken the treasure and precious things; they have made her many widows in the midst thereof. Her priests have violated my law, and have profaned my holy things: they have put no difference between the holy and profane, neither have they showed difference between the unclean and the clean, and have hid their eyes from my Sabbaths, and I am profaned among them. Her princes in the midst thereof are like wolves ravening the prey, to shed blood, and to destroy souls, to get dishonest gain. And her prophets have daubed them with untempered mortar, seeing vanity, and divining lies unto them, saying, Thus saith the Lord God, when the Lord hath not spoken. The people of the land have used oppression and exercised robbery, and have vexed the poor and needy: yea, they have oppressed the stranger wrongfully." Need I add that the civil government of this land is the devourer, instead of the protector, of the poor? and that, while continuing to devour them with land monopoly, and rum, and slavery, the protection it boastingly and lyingly professes and promises is no better than that which the prophet here describes—the protection which wolves give to lambs.

I have said enough to warrant me in asserting—

First. That of all the institutions of earth, civil government is unspeakably the most important.

Second. That religious men only are fit to bear civil rule, and that therefore none other should be chosen for it. This says reason, and this says the Bible, whose religion is the religion of reason. In what sublimely eloquent and commanding language is it said by the psalmist, when, having reserved it for his last, because most important utterance and admonition, he exclaims: "The Spirit of the Lord spake by me, and his word was in my tongue. The God of Israel said, The Rock of Israel spake to me: He that ruleth over men must be just, ruling in the fear of God. And he shall be as the light of the morning when the sun riseth, even a morning without clouds; as the tender grass springing out of the earth by clear shining after rain."

Surely none but a religious man can answer to the psalmist's description of the civil ruler. Surely none but a religious man can have the broad, undeviating justice, the honest, comprehensive care for others, the quick, tender, and thorough sympathy with the poor, helpless, and trodden down, which should ever characterize the civil ruler.

Are not religious better than irreligious men? None can doubt it. Why, then, should they not be chosen to fill the most important and responsible places in human affairs? That they are not, dishonors religion and sets reason at naught. If religious men are needed anywhere, it is in the capacity of civil rulers.

My hearers know what I mean by a religious man, and they will not go away saying that I refuse to vote for persons unless they belong to the church. I vote for those who do and for those who do not belong to it. But I aim to vote for religious persons only. Believing in the Bible, and accepting its religion with my whole head and heart, I am shut up to such voting. Other men, and immeasurably better than myself, can vote otherwise. But I cannot. I cannot without severing my connection with this Book of books, dishonoring and disowning my God-given and God-present reason, debauching my conscience, and sinking myself into atheism.

With me a religious man is simply a just man. Show me a just man, and you show me a religious one. The more just he is the more religious he is. And when, under the new-creating influences of Heaven, he has reached the sublime height of doing in all things as he would be done by, then has he fulfilled the claims of justice and religion, of the Bible and reason, of earth and heaven. Beliefs in regard to the Trinity, Atonement, Election, etc., etc., have their value. They may favor or hinder religion; but they are no part of it.

Say not that my stress on doing ignores faith. Say not that I forget the Bible words: "The just shall live by faith." Readily do I admit that our moral and spiritual nature cannot live unless it be fed by faith. But in what must this faith be? Must it be, as is generally held, in ecclesiastical dogmas and formulas? No; but in justice and goodness. Must it not be in Christ? Not necessarily in the historic Christ; but it must be in the spirit he breathed, the principles he taught, and the aims he pursued. In the high and essential sense every man has faith in Christ just as far as this spirit, these principles, and these aims become his own, and no farther; or, in other words, to the precise extent that he is like Christ.

And say not that I have omitted from my definition of a religious man love to God. No one, destitute of this element, can love his brother as he should do. No one can do this without loving God for having made him capable of it. I add that everyone's love to God is proved and measured by his love to man.

The little handful of uncompromising abolitionists are blamed for refusing to vote at the late election for this, that, or the other party ticket. But there were irreligious men upon each—men whose principles and practices proved their disposition to wield government for the destruction instead of the protection of the people. Men there were upon all these tickets, who would license the dramshop, that great manufactory of paupers and madmen, that great slaughterhouse of bodies and souls, that great source of peril to the persons and property of the sober, as well as of suffering to the families of drunkards, that great multiplier of our taxes, but for which we should pay only shillings to the tax gatherers where we now pay them dollars, and but for which there would be comparatively little occasion for courts and prisons, and probably none at all for poorhouses. Men there were upon all these tickets, who would replunge into the deep pit of slavery the poor trembling ones who have escaped from it; and who would degrade and dishearten millions of their countrymen by excluding them from citizenship and the ballot box.

How, then, could we vote for any one of these tickets? How could we do so, and still honor the Bible view of religion and civil government? What! vote for men who would worse than murder their innocent brothers and sisters by enslaving them? Impossible, without most deeply dishonoring that view. I said worse than murder—for who would not rather have his child murdered than enslaved? What! vote for men who would use the power we give them to punish complexion with civil and political disabilities! Surely, we could not do so without outraging all our convictions of what the Bible teaches of religion and civil government. All the varieties of the human family are equally dear to Him who "hath made of one blood all nations of men"; and if the religion of the Bible is both his and ours, then are they equally dear to us also. The recent refusal of the majority of the voters of this state to restore suffrage to the black man proves that majority to be atheists. The contempt which that refusal pours upon human nature is wholly incompatible with true religion. A man may love himself, and this or that branch of the human family; but unless he love all its branches, he is the guilty enemy of human nature, and of the God in whose image it is made.

Some of these abolitionists are blamed for entertaining, as did their sainted brother, James G. Birney, so small a hope that the voters of our country will bring slavery to a peaceful end through the ballot box. Their little faith in these voters is construed into evidence of their want of faith in God. But more properly might little faith in such of these voters as love to cast proslavery and dramshop votes be construed into want of faith in the devil. Our speeches and writings for a quarter of a century show that we look for a speedy termination of American slavery. But our growing fear, in the light of our growing knowledge of American voters, is, that the termination will be violent instead of peaceful. It will come in some way in God's providence, and it will come soon. But to say that because we doubt its coming in the bloodless and desired way, we doubt His providence, and have a reduced faith in Himself, is to do us a groundless and a great wrong.

It is very true that our hope of seeing slavery voted to death is small. This is as true as that the facts in the case forbid it to be large. And if I may be allowed to speak for some of these abolitionists, I will add that not only do they apprehend that a people who receive their religion upon authority, instead of understandingly, will be found inadequate to the task of putting away peaceably a system of slavery so inwoven as is ours with political, ecclesiastical, commercial, [and] social interests, but inadequate also to the maintenance of democratic institutions. The religions of the world, being authority religions, harmonize with monarchies and despotisms. If peoples who are swayed by them call for democratic forms of government, then do they call for what is far above them—for what they are not yet educated to meet the cost of. Were the Italians now to put away their authority religion, and now to assert their right to judge for themselves as freely of every page in the Bible as of every page in any other book, and as freely of every proceeding in the Church as of every proceeding in any other association, it would not be strange if, fifty years hence, that happily delivered people should look out from the midst of their flourishing democratic institutions upon the ruin of ours.

Some of these abolitionists hold that the north is *particeps criminis* in American slavery, and should therefore consent to share with the south in the present loss of emancipation. They hold that here is a case for applying the motto: "Honor among thieves." Now, to charge them, therefore, with recognizing the right of property in man is as unjust as to deduce from their lack of faith in American voters their lack of faith in God. But these abolitionists would *buy* the slaves!—*all* the slaves! Well, let it pass for *buying*. And, pray, do not their accusers sometimes help *buy* a slave? Oh, yes!—but they have never undertaken to buy *all* the slaves! Nevertheless, does not what they themselves do estop them from complaining of the morality of this undertaking? Moreover, would not *all* their accusers consent to be bought out of slavery were they to fall under its heavy yoke? If they would, then let them first become so self-crucifying as to be able to reduce to practice in their own case that sublime morality by which they presume to try and condemn others. . . .

Nor less is the injustice of classing with "disunionists" those Abolitionists, who, opposing by all moral and political influences the secession of states from the Union, would nevertheless not have the seceders pursued with armies. Those abolitionists believe in love rather than in hatred; and, hence, they would be more disposed to bless than to curse the seceders; to protect them rather than to shed their blood. For my own part, I still feel on this subject as I felt half a dozen years ago, when I said on the floor of Congress: "If they will go, let them go, and we, though loving the Union, and every part of it, and willing to lose no part, will let them go in peace, and follow them with our blessing, and with our warm prayer that they may return to us, and with our firm belief that they will return to us after they shall have spent a few miserable years, or perhaps no more than a few miserable months in their miserable experiment of separating themselves from their brethren. Of course I can not forget that many—alas, that they are so many—would prefer following the seceders with curses and guns. Oh! how slow are men to emerge from the brutehood into which their passions and their false education have sunk them. I say brutehood, for rage and violence and war belong to it, while love and gentleness and peace, are the adornments of true manhood."

What will be the spirit of the north toward the seceding states, bids fair to be soon proved. It is even probable that the slave states will secede—a part now and nearly all the remainder soon. This will not be because of the election of Lincoln. That is at the most an occasion or pretext for secession. Nor will this be because it has long been resolved on. There is something, but not so much, in that. It will be because their "iniquity—is full," and the time for their destruction at hand. During the last few years the south has been busy in leaving nothing to add to her iniquity. I speak not so much of her reopening the African slave trade, nor of her increasingly tenacious grasp of her slaves as of her purpose to banish what she can of her long-tortured free colored people, and reenslave the rest. This crowning iniquity ripens her for ruin. It ripens her for secession, which is ruin. Maryland, having refused to be guilty of this crowning iniquity, will, we trust, be saved from the fate of secession. Missouri means to be a free state, and Delaware is already substantially one. Hence they will not secede.

The south would know herself to be hurrying on to destruction were she not blind to the lessons of history and deaf to the voice of Providence. She ought to know it if but from the fate of the oppressors of Haiti. They were not slaughtered until they undertook to reenslave the free—and then they were.

Divine Providence has its course in the southern states as well as elsewhere; and there as well as elsewhere, both the wickedness and righteousness of men contribute to shape that course. In the words of a precious Moravian hymn:

> "He every where hath rule,
> And all things serve his might." . . .

I spoke of the secession as ruin. It will be only a present ruin, however. It will result in a glorious renovation. The seceding states will return to us, not to be slave states again, but to be free states; not again to oppress the poor, but cordially and practically to acknowledge the equal rights of all; not again to disgrace America, and hinder the spread of democracy over the earth, but to honor the one and extend the other; not again to be a heavy curse, but to be a rich blessing to mankind.

But we pass on, to speak of another injustice. It is that of denouncing as enemies of the Bible those of us who believe there are a few errors in it, and of denouncing, as guilty of setting their reason above the word of God, those of us who would let their reason inquire what is and what is not the word of God.

There is a child who deeply loves and honors his mother; but he confesses that the few pimples or moles upon her face are blemishes, slight indeed, but still blemishes upon her beauty. Is it to the shame and discredit of his filial piety that he makes this confession? Even if it is, it does not become such of her children to say so, as disgrace her, and break her heart by their flagrant disobedience, and make no other atonement than their hollow ascription of entire perfection to her.

It is argued that reason, having once decided that the whole Bible, and nothing else, is the word of God, is bound to rest there. This is sound argument. But is it bound to rest there always? By no means. Reason must ever be left free to revise and repeal its own decisions, and to deny to a verse today the inspiration is admitted yesterday.

When I was young, my reason (if reason it was) accepted the statement that God ordered the Jews to plunge into bloody wars, and to torture innocent women and children. But now it does not, and does not because it has, as I believe, become more enlightened. It now refuses to regard the loving Father as an arbitrary, revengeful, bloody, pagan deity.

Good and wise men (and I admit that both this age and former ages are on their side) call on us to abandon our claim for the ceaseless free play of reason upon the pages of the Bible. So, too, did the ages call on Galileo to abandon his belief that the world moves. But Galileo has come to be justified; and so also will they who, in opposition to the world—both the present and the past world—claim that even the Bible itself does never, at any period of his life, fall without the jurisdiction of any man's reason. There is great astonishment that the Church so dreaded the influence of astronomy upon the Bible; but there will be greater that it so dreaded the influence of reason upon it. The dread in both cases is explained by its foolishly regarding a book instead of nature as absolute authority, and the Divine inspiration of every page in it as a fact no more to be questioned than the existence of the sun.

We admit that we cannot honestly deny that we make our reason final arbiter in all our investigations—even our investigations of the Bible. We dare not hold it in abeyance, nor disclaim its supremacy even there. At all times and in all places we must let it decide what is the word of God. If Dr. Cheever makes it turn supremely and finally upon the Bible whether immortal man can be rightfully enslaved; or, in other words, rightfully reduced to brutehood and merchandise, we cannot go with him in that. We must there diverge from this dear and noble man of God. We cannot leave it to the interpretation of any words whether a hog is a hog, a horse a horse, or a man a man. Whatever words may say to the contrary, we must, in all circumstances, treat each according to its nature. So should everything be treated, and what is its nature should be learned (because there it can be more surely learned) from itself rather than from any, even the best account of itself. The world admits that Shakspeare is a wonderfully deep and accurate reader of human nature. But it admits this because Shakspeare agrees with its own observations of human nature. Does it test man by Shakspeare's knowledge of him? Far more does it test Shakspeare by its own knowledge of man. And so, likewise, instead of making the Bible either the exclusive or the conclusive expounder of man, the Bible reading of him is also to be judged of by our own observations of him.

This leaving it to words whether slavery is right or wrong accounts for the sad fact that the church people south are all proslavery, and that a large share of them north are also. Dr. Cheever found the like in his recent travels in Switzerland—the church people in favor of slavery, because they read the Bible to be in favor of it. Lamentable effect, we admit, of their misinterpretation of this precious book! but far more lamentable effect of the ecclesiastical requirement to turn from man to a book in order to learn what he is and what are his rights! Possibly Dr. Cheever himself may yet become proslavery. Should he wake up some morning with the conviction that there are words in the Bible on the side of slavery, he would either have to renounce the authority of the Bible, or have to become proslavery. I do not doubt that he would renounce it, even though he should see that he would thereby make himself as odious as I, by doing so, have made myself.

Jesus saw that men were enslaved to authority, and that their own experience of truth could alone set them free. He took up men out of their bondage to superstitions, and out of their debasing and blinding submission to authority, and threw them back upon their own consciences and convictions, and demanded that they should judge for themselves, yes, and of themselves, what is right. Thus to individualize and insulate each man was his first step towards getting each man right.

The question which Jesus puts to the slaveholder is not, "What does the Church or the Bible think of slavery?" but it is: "What think *you* of it—*you yourself?*" "What think you of it in the light of human nature?—of that high nature it tramples under foot—whose holy affections it outrages—whose sweet hopes and loves it mocks—whose sublime aspirations it chokes and kills—and of all whose rich and glorious relations to earth and heaven, to time and eternity, it makes no account?" "What think you of it in the light of the golden rule, to do as you would be done by?" "What think you of slavery as a condition for yourself—as a yoke upon your own neck, by however solemn enactments imposed, or however poor and helpless you were at the time of the imposition?" "What think you of it for your children—for even the dullest of them, and for those least able to take care of themselves?" In a word, "What think you of slavery, when you try it by that self-application mode of reasoning which Jesus taught?" Could you pin the slaveholder to such questions; could you prevent his escape from the tribunal of his own conscience, he would soon cease to be a slaveholder. But, unhappily, the Church has taught him how to evade the pressure of your questions, and of his conscience. He finds shelter in an authoritative religion, and is relieved of the necessity of self-arraignment.

This self-application mode of reasoning, when faithfully wielded, makes the problems simple and the duties plain. The presidential candidates in the late election would send other people's children into slavery. But would they send their own, even if pressed to it by ten thousand Constitutions and ten thousand statutes, and ten thousand judicial decrees, ay, and ten thousand Bibles also? My neighbors voted for them. But would they have done so, had it been my neighbors' children, whom these candidates proposed to send into slavery?

The sincere and self-sacrificing John Brown was adjudged worthy of death because he would put weapons into the hands of slaves wherewith to defend themselves in their flight from slavery. But would not his judges, ay, and the famous Harper's Ferry Committee also, were they in slavery, welcome such a service? Such are my own ethics and education that I had rather live and die in slavery than shed blood to escape from it. But had they?

The work Dr. Cheever has chosen for himself is to persuade the Swiss, the Americans, and the world, that the Bible is against slavery. But far more important, far more hopeful, and far shorter would be his work, were it to convince them that, say what the Bible may, slavery is wrong; and to convince them of it by carrying them straight to man, and demanding their solution of the problem amid the influences shed upon them by that august and godlike presence. It is when pervaded by these influences—the solemn influences of the most holy and glorious of all earthly temples—the temple of man—that we feel how exceedingly poor, compared with its real authority—the authority of God in man—is that which is so falsely claimed for traditions, books, and churches.

Dr. Cheever sees no hope for freedom, if the Bible shall be given to the side of slavery. But I see no hope for the Bible if it shall be proved to be for slavery. Slavery is not to be tried by the Bible, but the Bible by freedom. All this talk that the Bible is the charter of man's rights is nonsense. His nature is that charter; and his rights are the rights of his nature—no more nor less—every book to the contrary notwithstanding. The nature of a monkey determines its rights. The nature of a man his.

Nothing can be more degrading to the high nature God has given us than to argue that its rights stand in a book, and that we need run to it to learn whether we may or may not get drunk, commit theft, murder, or enslave men. No book points out men's crimes so clearly, or protests against them so strongly as their own nature; and if they turn away from the best teacher, under the plea of hearing a better, they will, in the end, be apt to hear neither. There is no safety for us any further than we respond to the utterances of our being. We may, and we should, study that being in the light of the Bible and of all other lights at our command. Nevertheless, it is that which we are to study. We may, and we should, have respect to the wise judgments which abound both within and without the Bible. Nevertheless, the final and decisive judgment is that which we are ourselves to form. We are never, nor in the least, to doubt our capacity to judge rightly in regard to everything which enters into the essence of religion—every such thing being entirely plain and simple. Were it not so, Jesus would not have said to the people: "And why judge ye not even of yourselves what is right?"

But it will be long, very long, ere the people are weaned from depending on book interpreters for their religion, and are brought to study it for themselves in nature. The education of the age has served to enslave men to authority; and an authority religion is therefore just what their education calls for. They must not presume to go to the plain volume of nature for their religion. But, with blind faith in others, and boundless submission to authority, they must receive for religion what the churches, who quarrel among themselves as to the meanings of a book, tell them is the religion of that book. . . .

Although the mass of the voters at the late election were for slave-catching and dramshop candidates; and although they who sternly refused to vote for men in favor of licensing the dramshop, or for men who know as law any form of piracy, and least of all the superlative piracy of slavery, were but a very little handful, nevertheless we are not to be discouraged. This very little handful, even though it shall never increase, will not fail to exert a growing influence for freedom, truth, and righteousness. But it may increase rapidly—ay, under the Divine blessing, even triumphantly. Like the "handful of corn on the top of the mountains, the fruit thereof may yet shake like Lebanon."

SUGGESTIONS FOR FURTHER READING

The classic comprehensive account of all phases of the pre-Civil War radical movement is Alice Felt Tyler, *Freedom's Ferment* (Minneapolis: University of Minnesota Press, 1944), which is friendly to the reform spirit. A briefer, sweeping interpretation, mainly negative but attempting balance, is John L. Thomas, "Reform in America, 1815–1865," *American Quarterly*, XVII (Winter 1965), 656–681. George W. Frederickson, *The Inner Civil War* (New York: Harper and Row, 1965), thoughtfully analyzes the movement, especially its decline. For a basic statement of the conservative argument that America and the reformers were dangerously "anti-institutional," see Stanley Elkins, *Slavery* (Chicago: University of Chicago Press, 1959), Part IV; Rowland Berthoff, *An Unsettled People* (New York: Harper and Row, 1971), Part Two, tries to argue that the reformers were really conservatives in a changing society.

Works that emphasize the importance of the evangelical Christian strand in producing social reform include Timothy L. Smith, *Revivalism and Social Reform* (New York: Abingdon Press, 1957); Gilbert H. Barnes, *The Anti-Slavery Impulse, 1830–1844* (Washington, D.C.: American Historical Association, 1933); Charles C. Cole, Jr., *The Social Ideas of the Northern Evangelists, 1826–1860* (New York: Columbia University Press, 1954); Perry Miller, *The Life of the Mind in America* (New York: Harcourt, Brace, and World, 1965); and Whitney R. Cross, *The Burned-Over District* (Ithaca, N.Y.: Cornell University Press, 1950), which combines careful sociology with a deep appreciation for the millennialist character of the outburst. A useful corrective to an overemphasis on the evangelicals is Bertram Wyatt-Brown, *Lewis Tappan and the Evangelical War Against Slavery* (Cleveland: Press of Case Western Reserve University, 1969), probably the single most illuminating book yet to appear on the abolitionists.

Several major studies stress the secular rationalist strand: Arthur M. Schlesinger, Jr., *The Age of Jackson* (Boston: Little, Brown, 1945), which must be used with caution; Arthur A. Ekirch, Jr., *The Idea of*

Progress in America, 1815–1860 (New York: Columbia University Press, 1944); and Edward Pessen, *Most Uncommon Jacksonians* (Albany: State University of New York Press, 1967), which is definitive on Skidmore and the labor radicals. Daniel W. Howe, *The Unitarian Conscience* (Cambridge: Harvard University Press, 1970), shows how rationalism could be synthesized with religious humanism. Two analyses of the philosophy of perfectionism are Donald H. Meyer, *The Instructed Conscience* (Philadelphia: University of Pennsylvania Press, 1972), Chapter 9; Edward H. Madden, *Civil Disobedience and the Moral Law in Nineteenth-Century America* (Seattle: University of Washington Press, 1968). For the early socialists, see Donald Drew Egbert and Stow Persons, eds., *Socialism and American Life* (Princeton, N.J.: Princeton University Press, 1952), Chapter 5. John Humphrey Noyes, *A History of American Socialisms* (Philadelphia: Lippincott, 1870), is still very useful.

General interpretations of Transcendentalism include Octavius B. Frothingham, *Transcendentalism in New England* (New York: G. P. Putnam's Sons, 1876); Van Wyck Brooks, *The Flowering of New England, 1815–1865* (New York: Dutton, 1936); and, in skeletal form, Perry Miller, ed., *The Transcendentalists* (Cambridge, Mass.: Harvard University Press, 1950). The topic suffers from the lack of a modern, balanced treatment on a full scale.

Other useful books are devoted to specific causes and movements. See Merle Curti, *The American Peace Crusade, 1815–1860* (Durham, N.C.: Duke University Press, 1929); Constance Noyes Robertson, ed., *The Oneida Community* (Syracuse, N.Y.: Syracuse University Press, 1970); Thomas F. O'Dea, *The Mormons* (Chicago: University of Chicago Press, 1957); James J. Martin, *Men Against the State* (DeKalb, Ill.: Adrian Allen Associates, 1953), a fine study of the anarchists; Arthur E. Bestor, *Backwoods Utopias* (Philadelphia: University of Pennsylvania Press, 1950); Lindsay Swift, *Brook Farm* (New York: Macmillan, 1900); and Alma Lutz, *Crusade for Freedom* (Boston: Beacon Press, 1968), on the special problems of women reformers.

Abolitionism has inspired unusual controversy. The negative case is presented in David Donald, *Lincoln Reconsidered* (New York: Knopf, 1956), Chapter II; in David Donald, *Charles Sumner and the Coming of the Civil War* (New York: Knopf, 1960); and in John L. Thomas, *The Liberator* (Boston: Little, Brown, 1963), a hostile treatment of the life of Garrison. Powerful arguments on the abolitionists' behalf are mustered by the many talented essayists in Martin Duberman, ed., *The Antislavery Vanguard* (Princeton, N.J.: Princeton University Press, 1965); and by Aileen S. Kraditor, *Means and Ends in American Abolitionism* (New York: Pantheon Books, 1969); though the most convincing defense of Garrison is in Wyatt-Brown, cited above. For general histories of the antislavery movement, see Louis Filler, *The Crusade Against Slavery* (New York: Harper, 1960), and Dwight L. Dumond, *Antislavery* (Ann Arbor, Mich.: University of Michigan Press, 1961).

Reasonably satisfactory biographies of most of the writers in this anthology can be readily found in the card catalog of any major library, and all of them except Thomas Skidmore are in the *Dictionary of American Biography*.